Early Medical Abortion, Equality of Access, and the Telemedical Imperative

Early Medical Abortion, Equality of Access, and the Telemedical Imperative

JORDAN A. PARSONS

PhD Candidate, University of Bristol, UK

&

ELIZABETH CHLOE ROMANIS

Assistant Professor in Biolaw, Durham University, UK

OXFORD

UNIVERSITY PRESS

OXFORD
UNIVERSITY PRESS

Great Clarendon Street, Oxford, OX2 6DP,
United Kingdom

Oxford University Press is a department of the University of Oxford.
It furthers the University's objective of excellence in research, scholarship,
and education by publishing worldwide. Oxford is a registered trade mark of
Oxford University Press in the UK and in certain other countries

© Oxford University Press 2021

First Edition published in 2021
Impression: 1

Published in the United States of America by Oxford University Press
198 Madison Avenue, New York, NY 10016, United States of America

British Library Cataloguing in Publication Data
Data available

Library of Congress Control Number: 2021940435

ISBN 978-0-19-289615-5

DOI: 10.1093/oso/9780192896155.001.0001

Printed and bound by
CPI Group (UK) Ltd, Croydon, CR0 4YY

We dedicate this book to abortion providers globally who have worked tirelessly to continue to provide care during the COVID-19 pandemic, including entirely redesigning care pathways in a matter of days.

Foreword

This timely book addresses how medical service lockdowns designed to reduce the spread of COVID-19 infection caused by human face-to-face interactions have affected access to abortion services in two technologically comparable Western economies—the UK and US. Middle-income populations in both have relatively easy access to personal internet-enabled electronic devices as a means of accessing medical information and advice. Both also have disadvantaged rural and resource-poor populations whose access to healthcare services faces obstacles. In the UK, the National Health Service is primarily responsible for equitable provision of accessible abortion services, whereas in the US the mixed private-sector/public-sector provision of services is constrained by federal and state laws that exclude abortion from public funding and might bar abortion coverage under private health insurance plans.

The book is justifiably ahistorical, its chronology beginning for modern purposes with the criminal punishment of unlawful abortion in England, Wales, and Northern Ireland under the Offences Against the Person Act 1861, and the substantial pre–fetal-viability decriminalisation of abortion in 1973 by the US Supreme Court decision in *Roe v. Wade*. We may gauge where the UK and US might be moving in approaches to abortion by considering where they have been and, as explained in this book, where they are now.

Evidence shows that the practice of abortion reaches back through history into anthropology, from when humans first came to understand the causes and symptoms of pregnancy. Unwanted pregnancies might be terminated by crude interventions, some violent and others by consumption of abortifacient substances (notably grown products such as plants endorsed for this purpose by folklore). More experienced early service providers, usually women, were herbalists applying plant extracts that by tradition and pragmatism they believed were effective. Some interventions in pregnancy were physically dangerous or toxic, however, and in Greek antiquity, the physician Hippocrates forbad health care providers to assist women to employ them. Women herbalists possessed the power of knowledge that in medieval Europe threatened the authority of male religious and community leaders, who suppressed such women under claims of witchcraft.

With the emergence of scientific medicine, reputable interest arose in the healing properties of plants, and after the mid-sixteenth century herbal gardens, often called botanic or physic gardens, became popular. The Medical School at the University of Edinburgh traces its origins to the city's barber-surgeons of the early sixteenth century. In 1670, Dr Robert Sibbald, who later became the University's first Professor of Medicine, founded what today continues to serve research at the Medical School as the Royal Botanic Garden. The garden's identification of medicinal plants included abortifacients, which might lawfully be applied as such because England's first abortion legislation, the Offences Against the Person Act 1803, which displaced the historical common law condemning abortion only of a woman shown to be 'quick with child' (taken to be in the second trimester) was not applicable to Scotland. The Act's goals were to protect the exclusively male medical profession's monopoly on therapeutic interventions, and women against unskilled induced termination of pregnancy, but its status as 'right- to life' legislation was compromised by reliance on the death penalty.

When settlers in the British North American colony broke away in 1776 to found the US, they retained much of English law, but saw it in the context of their circumstances. Social leaders measured wealth by ownership of property, which included enslaved people. Such people's children, born into slavery, added to their owners' wealth, but abortion denied owners increased wealth. As Christians, they eschewed the deadly sins of material greed and pride, but invoked biblical precepts, such as to be fruitful and multiply, to condemn what was contrary to their material prosperity, and to translate perceived sin into crime. In the US today, the devout Christian evangelical movement seeks to maintain family-building momentum, without supporting enslavement, in the strident and politically influential urging of legal prohibition of contraception and abortion.

In both the UK and US, a high percentage of abortions occur in the first trimester. Being minimally invasive, such as by vacuum aspiration, they do not require the surgical interventions necessary for safe mid- and late-term procedures. With the development of early medical abortion by the drugs mifepristone and misoprostol, trained health service providers with prescribing privileges can meet abortion patients' requests, having first screened their eligibility in discussions by telephone, e-mail, and similar electronic communications that obviate the need for face-to-face interactions. The onset of social lockdowns compelled by the COVID-19 pandemic created an opportunity to advance access to abortion services by telemedical strategies. These could benefit communities often underserved due, for instance, to geographical remoteness and/or dependence on public transport. This book explains how early medical abortion is facilitated, resisted, inadvertently or deliberately obstructed, and prevented in the UK and US, and might be similarly approached elsewhere.

The discomfort that conservatively disposed persons and institutions, including within governmental administrations, feel with accommodation of abortion, for instance for religious, cultural, or pragmatic reasons, makes abortion unlike other comparably (non)invasive and sensitive medical procedures. This book's authors recognise the reality of 'abortion exceptionalism' seen in the laws and regulations that relate to counselling for and provision of services attract, such as state-level TRAP (targeted regulation of abortion providers) laws in the US.

Some claim that, outside instances of risk of imminent death or severely impairing chronic disability or pain from continuation of pregnancy, abortion procedures are elective and not medically necessary. With advances in medical care, such instances are fortunately rare in economically developed settings, justifying exclusion of abortion, for instance in the US, from public funding of medically necessary services. Funding and accommodation are justified, however, on recognition that abortion is a necessary health service, the Constitution of the World Health Organization describing 'health' as a state of 'physical, mental and social well-being and not merely the absence of disease or infirmity'. Convenient access to timely abortion care, including postabortion care, serves the physical, mental, and social well-being—that is, the health—of patients seeking such care, and of potential patients.

Commentators might see the introduction of nonsurgical early abortion by drug prescription as heralding women's enhanced autonomy of abortion choice, guided if preferred by trained nurses or midwives rather than doctors. This would place abortion regulation under predominantly women's control, a modern scientific variant of the early history of women herbalists helping their neighbours. However, soon after hesitant governments responded to medical abortion by requiring health service providers, often doctors, to administer the drugs by in-person supervision, the onset of COVID-19 lockdowns rendered in-person interactions contraindicated and often impossible. The pandemic caused medical office closures, made access to any open facilities by public transportation difficult and hazardous, and, for instance, impaired securing childcare services whilst mothers travelled by unavailability of caregivers, or their unaffordability due to COVID-induced economic downturns and parental unemployment. Abortion counselling and prescription at distance would afford access to care.

History shows that, despite antiabortion initiatives, abortion will remain accessible as long as plants are cultivated and pharmacists and chemists are resourceful. The COVID-19 pandemic exemplifies technological responses that reduce risks of viral spread caused by in-person contact through resort to telemedicine. This well-conceived book urges the imperative to facilitate early medical abortion remotely by telemedical strategies, and explains how services are legally and otherwise accommodated and developed, but might be obstructed and frustrated. The example of telemedical abortion elaborated in this study gives impetus to the equitable provision of medical services beyond early abortion to many other forms of healthcare after the COVID-19 pandemic passes.

Bernard Dickens & Rebecca Cook
Faculty of Law, University of Toronto
May 2021

Preface

The nature of writing a book about a current policy issue is that publication timescales prevent work from being entirely up to date. In the weeks following submission of the final draft of this book to the publisher, there were policy changes and the publication of empirical findings from continuing research on telemedical abortion services. As such, we have included this preface with a dual purpose; to highlight some more recent developments, but also as a disclaimer that, upon publication, some of the issues discussed may have developed.

Abortion access in the United States

Shortly after the Biden administration took office, the US Food and Drug Administration (FDA) U-turned on its position on the in-person dispensing requirement for mifepristone (detail of the REMS restrictions on mifepristone are discussed in Chapter 9). In April 2021, after receiving a request to do so from President Biden and Vice President Harris, a letter to the American College of Obstetricians and Gynecologists detailed the FDA's intention to 'exercise enforcement discretion' during the COVID-19 pandemic with respect to the in-person dispensing requirement due to the additional risks presented to both patients and healthcare professionals (Woodcock 2021).

This has been heralded as a victory for abortion access in the US (American College of Obstetricians and Gynecologists 2021). However, whilst this move should be welcomed, there are limitations to what it will achieve. First, it is temporary, and the in-person dispensing requirement will seemingly resume when the pandemic ends. Since the REMS have also not been changed—they are merely not being enforced—this could happen with little notice for providers. Though in May 2021, the FDA announced that it would commit to a comprehensive review of the REMS protocol, which is a 'critical step towards ensuring that patient access to mifepristone is dictated by evidence, in accordance with statutory requirements and the Constitution' (Kaye et al. 2021). Second, whilst the FDA's decision means that there is now no *federal* restriction preventing telemedical provision of early medical abortion (TEMA) in the US, there are still a significant number of *state* laws that either explicitly ban TEMA or impose a mandatory in-person dispensing requirement (see Chapter 9). In these states, little has changed in terms of access. Finally, this move comes far too late, with pregnant people having suffered the burden of this requirement through the peak of the crisis. TEMA still improves access outside of the pandemic context, but only 're-sponding to the crisis' at this late stage is a significant failure.

There is/was substantial public support for a change in the FDA restrictions. LaRoche and colleagues (2021) surveyed US adults, finding that 43.8% support

TEMA during the pandemic, with a further 21.3% of respondents unsure. With 39.6% of respondents identifying as pro-life, these data suggest a (temporary) suspension of such a commitment in the extreme circumstances. Indeed, the authors note that it was more common for pro-life respondents to depart from that position than for pro-choice respondents to depart from theirs. Taking the evidence of how necessary and safe this change was, in combination with significant public support, highlights the FDA's failure to respond appropriately in a timely manner.

An additional concern is the looming Supreme Court decision in *Dobbs v. Jackson Women's Health Organization*, which is specifically a challenge to the right to abortion. It is expressly considering '[w]hether all pre-viability prohibitions on elective abortions are unconstitutional',[i] despite the long-standing and settled precedent that answers this question in the affirmative. In Chapter 2, we discuss concerns about the future of abortion access in the US because of the conservative make-up of the Supreme Court—a challenge of this nature could end the abortion right as currently construed in US law.

Abortion provision in Northern Ireland

We criticise the Health Minister in Northern Ireland throughout this book for failing to commission abortion services in Northern Ireland. The impact of his not doing so was that, despite the legality of abortion in Northern Ireland following partial de-criminalisation in 2019 and new regulations in 2020, people needing abortions are still having to travel to Great Britain to access care. Robin Walker, the Minister for Northern Ireland, spoke of this impact in April 2020:

> I have learned of the distress and the unacceptable circumstances that [pregnant people] continue to face at a time when local access should be readily available, given that the law was changed by this [Westminster] Parliament over a year ago.[ii]

Given this unacceptable continued failure to commission services (see Chapters 3 and 8), the Minister explained that action was necessary to perform his statutory duties.[iii] The Abortion (Northern Ireland) Regulations 2021 thus came into force on 31 March 2021. Regulation 2 affords the Secretary of State the power to direct action by the Northern Ireland Minister or other suitable persons to ensure necessary steps are taken to implement recommendations made by the Convention on the Elimination of All Forms of Discrimination against Women—which includes access to safe abortion (see Chapter 4). This is a big step and will hopefully ensure better abortion access in Northern Ireland. However, there is some degree to which this action may be perceived as constitutionally uncomfortable because it interferes in an area—health—over

---

[i] *Dobbs v. Jackson Women's Health Organization*, U.S. _ (2021). The Supreme Court granted certiorari to the petition filed by Dobbs and others in June 2020 on 17 May 2021.
[ii] Abortion (Northern Ireland) Regulations Deb 26 April 2021, col 4.
[iii] Ibid.

which the Northern Ireland Assembly, rather than Westminster, has had legislative competence since devolution in 1998.[iv]

A growing evidence base

There have been several recent additions to the ever-growing body of literature appraising TEMA services from the perspectives of patients and providers alike. Data explored in later chapters are sufficient to highlight TEMA as something of a no-brainer policy (see Chapter 5), and more recent research strengthens this further.

Two TEMA services we explore in this book are among those evaluated in recent publications—Pills by Post in the UK and TelAbortion in the US (see Chapter 6). Analysing patient satisfaction with the Pills by Post service, Meurice and colleagues (2021) report that 96.9% of patients were either very satisfied or satisfied overall, with 75.8% finding home use of abortion medications straightforward and 79.5% satisfied with pain control options. Only 15.7% of patients had difficulty determining the abortion outcome. Incidentally, this study also provides self-reported data on when patients took the abortion medications—50.1% took them the day they arrived, with a further 47.4% taking them within a week. One concern raised about TEMA is the risk of patients taking the medications later in pregnancy than intended and/or permitted by law. These recent data indicate that such a concern may be misplaced.

TelAbortion has similarly reported high satisfaction, with 99.1% of those whose abortion outcome is known being very satisfied or satisfied with the service, and 99.4% being very satisfied or satisfied with speaking to the provider remotely (Chong et al. 2021). Another TelAbortion study, interviewing patients both pre-pandemic and during, explored patient perspectives on the impact of TEMA on them, reported themes include convenience and accessibility, better privacy, and a lack of alternatives (Kerestes et al. 2021). Indeed, 13% of participants said that without TelAbortion they would likely have continued their pregnancies. Perhaps unsurprisingly, participants considered these benefits to be heightened during the pandemic. Aiken and colleagues (2021), exploring why patients chose telemedicine, likewise found factors such as cost, privacy, and distance to clinics to be prevalent. Comparing TEMA and in-person cohorts, Kaller and colleagues found satisfaction to be higher in the TEMA group in terms of satisfaction with the informed consent process and being more comfortable asking questions (2021, 231/2). However, it is important to note that this study reports that 24.9% of those who chose in-person care did so as they felt more comfortable talking face-to-face (2021, 231). This highlights the importance of TEMA not becoming the only option as it grows in popularity—a point that we will highlight throughout this book (see Chapter 6).

Daniel and colleagues (2021) found that, among obstetricians and gynaecologists who had not provided early medical abortion in the previous year, 24% reported that, if able to write a prescription for a patient to collect the medications from a pharmacy,[v] they would offer the service. With 22% being unsure, a greater increase is possible

---

[iv] Northern Ireland Act 1998, s.4.
[v] As noted above, the FDA has now temporarily suspended the in-person dispensing requirement.

(and important to maximse the provider pool. See Chapter 3). Most interestingly, this willingness was consistent across the US, including areas that are traditionally considered more conservative. The data used for this analysis were from a 2016/17 survey, so views may have changed. Indeed, the authors postulate that the pandemic may have increased the likelihood of obstetricians and gynaecologists wanting to provide services with no in-person contact.

The FDA's recent suspension of the in-person requirement, then, may lead more doctors to offer abortion services in the US (at least temporarily). Among those already offering such care, the pandemic has certainly led to service adjustments to reduce in-person contact—even before the FDA acted. Tschann and colleagues (2021) highlight measures introduced at clinics across the US (and Canada), including curbside pickup of mifepristone and the foregoing of some testing requirements in certain circumstances.

As positive as these data are in reinforcing the case for TEMA, Chong and colleagues' (2021) findings do raise a matter that needs addressing going forward. They found that a higher proportion of patients using the TelAbortion service were older, more educated, and white. Improved access to care for any group is a positive, but, equally, it is important that further steps in the direction of telemedicine (both in abortion care and elsewhere) focus on also reaching disadvantaged populations and not leave them behind.

Given ongoing changes to everyday life due to the COVID-19 pandemic, TEMA is receiving increasing research attention—indeed, telemedicine in general is a growing focus. We have no doubt that more great work will be published between us writing this preface and the publication of this book, and it is a shame that we are unable to highlight it.

Jordan A. Parsons & Elizabeth Chloe Romanis
May 2021

Acknowledgements

This book would not have been possible without the unwavering support of many friends and colleagues. First, our gratitude to Nicola Wilson at Oxford University Press for taking a punt on an overambitious pair of baby academics and commissioning this book—we hope you are not regretting it. Thanks also to Lauren Tiley and Adam Breivik at the Press for supporting us throughout the writing process and answering a whole host of stupid questions. Appreciation must go to Patricia Lohr, Elizabeth Raymond, Daniel Grossman, Jason Burkhiser Reynolds, and several other staff from various abortion providers who have helped us out with nuggets of information that saved us hours of research. We are indebted to a veritable army of colleagues who enthusiastically discussed our ideas with us and provided invaluable feedback on earlier drafts: Alexandra Mullock, Chelsea Cox, Dunja Begović, Emma Cave, Emma Milne, Harleen Kaur Johal, India Cole, Marcus Sirianno, Peter Young, and Victoria Hooton. Last, but most certainly not least, kudos to Nathan Chalk for putting up with our endless phone and Zoom calls over the past year distracting him from work during lockdown.

Contents

List of illustrations

In order of appearance

Abbreviations

AA 1967	Abortion Act 1967
BPAS	British Pregnancy Advisory Service
CEDAW	United Nations Committee on the Elimination of Discrimination against Women
COVID-19	Coronavirus disease 2019
D&C	Dilation and curettage
D&E	Dilation and evacuation
EMA	Early medical abortion
FDA	United States Food and Drug Administration
HCP	Healthcare professional
NHS	National Health Service
NICE	National Institute for Health and Care Excellence
OAPA 1861	Offences Against the Person Act 1861
REMS	Risk Evaluation and Mitigation Strategies
SPUC	Society for the Protection of Unborn Children
TEMA	Telemedical provision of early medical abortion
TRAP	Targeted regulation of abortion providers
UK	United Kingdom
US	United States
WHO	World Health Organization

Introduction

Ideas, unless outward circumstances conspire with them, have in general
no very rapid or immediate efficacy in human affairs. (Mill 1845, 370)

Mill's shrewd observation well over a century ago perfectly encapsulates the reality
of Great Britain's regulation of the telemedical provision of early medical abortion
(TEMA). Despite overwhelming evidence that TEMA is as safe and effective as early
medical abortion (EMA) delivered in person—and favoured by many patients—it
took a global pandemic and the resulting near impossibility of providing adequate
abortion services to finally push those in power to make changes that enabled TEMA
provision. In Northern Ireland and the United States (US), even a global emergency
has proven insufficient to force lawmakers to address systemic problems with abortion
access that TEMA can *begin* to address.

* * *

It is a fact of life that people experience unwanted pregnancies. Inevitably, then,
people have a need for abortion services. Demand cannot be denied when one
considers that 209,519 abortions took place in England and Wales in 2019
(Department of Health and Social Care 2020a, 4). Of these, 207,384 were provided to residents of England and Wales, representing 1.8% of women between
the ages of 15 and 44 *in a single year*. It must be recognised that official statistics
use *recorded* abortions as the numerator and *all* women as the denominator. They
do not account for abortions accessed clandestinely or women who are unable
to conceive. If the statistics were adjusted to reflect *all* abortions in England and
Wales in relation to the number of people who *can get pregnant* (including those
who do not identify as women), the abortion rate would be higher. Abortion prevalence is also significant elsewhere, such as in Scotland (Public Health Scotland
2020) and the US (Kortsmit et al. 2020)—the Guttmacher Institute estimates that
roughly 73,000,000 abortions take place globally each year (2020). Abortion is,
then, a form of healthcare that a significant proportion of people will access at
some point in their lifetime.

Despite how commonplace abortion is, it has long been a politically charged area
of healthcare. Indeed, some disagree that abortion is healthcare altogether. Even
amongst those who do characterise abortion as healthcare, some refer to most abortions as 'elective' procedures on the basis that they are not necessary to prevent death
or serious physical harm. This characterisation is, in many ways, problematic (Janiak

Early Medical Abortion, Equality of Access, and the Telemedical Imperative. Jordan A. Parsons and Elizabeth Chloe Romanis,
Oxford University Press. © Oxford University Press 2021. DOI: 10.1093/oso/9780192896155.001.0001

and Goldberg 2016), and we will revisit it shortly. With abortion being so politicised, there exist barriers to access not found elsewhere in healthcare systems. There may be waiting lists for operations and long distances to travel for specialist care in various specialties, but only in the context of abortion care is it common for the law to impose strict time limits on accessing services that increase the stakes of these barriers. The additional control that the law exerts over the bodies of pregnant people can be characterised as abortion exceptionalism, as we will come to highlight. It stems from a notion that a person seeking to end a pregnancy must be experiencing difficulty, which is ultimately rooted in the storied political history of abortion and heavy religious influence enforcing abortion as a moral wrong. In short, abortion is frequently (and inappropriately) not recognised as routine healthcare.

In this book, our focus is EMA. A more precise explanation is provided in Chapter 1 but, for now, an EMA is an abortion procured by use of pharmaceutical agents during the first trimester—usually in the first 10 weeks of pregnancy. With EMA not requiring any surgical procedures and instead entailing the taking of two drugs, it is (or, clinically speaking, *can* be) a relatively straightforward treatment.

Some of the most significant barriers to EMA imposed by regulations in both the United Kingdom (UK) and US are those requiring pregnant people to visit abortion clinics in person. In many cases several clinic visits are required. Such regulations are problematic for myriad reasons, though most notably because, for many people, the nearest abortion clinic is a significant distance from their home—these clinics are not as plentiful as general practices and pharmacies. Whether face-to-face interaction with a healthcare professional is required for consultation, counselling, ultrasound scanning, or to physically hand over the drugs used to procure an EMA, making it mandatory to access care in person immediately creates divides along the lines of socioeconomic status and race. This is where telemedicine comes in as a potential solution.

TEMA is not a speculative proposal. As we will come to explore, abortion providers have successfully implemented TEMA services for almost two decades.[1] As a result, there is a wealth of evidence supporting the position we will advance in this book. TEMA presents an opportunity to remove unnecessary in-person requirements on accessing abortion, thereby moving in the direction of equal access for all. Not only can TEMA benefit those who would previously have been unable to access care, but it also provides an additional choice of care pathway for patients who *can* relatively easily access traditional, in-person care. As such, it fits squarely within the principles of patient-centred care that are now rightly guiding developments across healthcare. The benefits of TEMA even extend beyond the patient level, by improving the efficiency of services (Aiken et al. 2021a) and making cost savings (Hawkins et al. 2021). One can justifiably say that TEMA is positive across the board, and we will demonstrate this in the proceeding chapters.

The year 2020 was noteworthy in the history of abortion—particularly TEMA. Due to the COVID-19 pandemic, many healthcare systems rushed to implement various forms of remote care where possible. However, in many jurisdictions, the highly

[1] Possibly longer, depending on the flexibility of one's definition of TEMA.

politicised nature of abortion policy meant socio-legal barriers to access were maintained, and abortion exceptionalism prevailed even in such extreme circumstances. Elsewhere, the exacerbation of access barriers was recognised, and efforts made to address it. Great Britain might be seen as a shining beacon of hope on this front—many readers will no doubt already be aware of the (temporary) approval of home use of mifepristone that enabled fully remote TEMA services to be established in England, Wales, and Scotland. However, with the arguable exception of Scotland, these approvals are only temporary. Unless the public consultations that closed in early 2021 result in changes to the law being made permanent, this shining beacon of hope may unfortunately prove to have a halogen bulb rather than LED.[2]

Despite Great Britain introducing TEMA, Northern Ireland explicitly did not. Robin Swann, the Northern Irish Health Minister, suggested that there is no need for directly commissioned TEMA services in Northern Ireland because those in need of care can access it through the British Pregnancy Advisory Service (BPAS).[3] However, BPAS' provision in Northern Ireland is on an emergency basis for those who are self-isolating and unable to leave the home (British Pregnancy Advisory Service 2021). It is inappropriate for a healthcare service to not provide routine care on the basis that patients can access it through overseas charitable providers, in part because of such providers' inability to provide as effective aftercare overseas. There is a similar issue with organisations such as Women on Web[4] being relied upon—as much as they do great work to ensure access to abortion, there remains a problem in that 'the medical treatment offered necessarily ends with provoking a miscarriage' (Hervey and Sheldon 2019, 126). It is important that TEMA services are provided through a regulated healthcare system *within* a jurisdiction, and we will proceed on the basis that the availability of alternatives—particularly clandestine options, given the possibility of criminal consequences—does not constitute a valid consideration in the debate surrounding TEMA provision.

A fundamental foundation of our argument in this book is a recognition that abortion *is* healthcare, and that it is *essential* healthcare. We consider the language of 'elective' in the context of abortion to be highly problematic. It is true that few abortions are 'urgent' in the sense traditionally understood within the elective-urgent treatment distinction—with some exceptions, the pregnant person will not die or be caused serious physical harm if the termination is not carried out *immediately*. However, as Beyefsky and colleagues neatly summarise, this 'fails to capture the reality that the non-medical reasons that women exercise their constitutional right to abortion are often as important to them and their families as averting a serious health consequence' (2020, 2).[5] Many report that they do not

---

[2] At the time this book went to press, there had been no announcement regarding the public consultations and any resulting decision on the continuation of TEMA. However, we acknowledge (and hope) that things may have changed by the publication date.

[3] Northern Ireland Assembly Official Report, Committee for Health, 14 January 2021, 'COVID-19 Response: Mr Robin Swann MLA, Minister of Health; Dr Michael McBride, Chief Medical Officer'.

[4] Women on Web is a charitable provider of TEMA that operates globally outside of regulated healthcare systems. The service is detailed in Chapter 6.

[5] Beyefsky and colleagues are writing in the US context, hence the mention of a constitutional right. Nonetheless, the sentiment carries even where no constitutional protection exists.

feel that their abortion, even for reasons characterised as 'social', was a 'choice' at all (Janiak and Goldberg 2016). Beyond the reasons pregnant people choose to terminate pregnancies, abortion must be considered urgent treatment by virtue of the legal restrictions in most jurisdictions. Where there is a gestational limit on abortion, a person's abortion can (or, rather, *should*) be considered urgent. It cannot be delayed in the way elective treatments can—abortion is 'the ultimate time-sensitive procedure' (Hill 2020, 119).

Notes on language

Before delving into the subject matter, we will clarify some of the language that we use.

First, the term 'abortion' itself is not universally preferred. Some people find it to be charged language that can prove more distressing than, for example, 'termination of pregnancy' (Cameron et al. 2017). We continue with 'abortion' in recognition of its prevalence. Providers generally use it, as do various medical organisations including the World Health Organization (WHO). We do, however, use varied terminology throughout to avoid repetition—this is more a clarification that we have not actively avoided the word 'abortion'.

Second, we refer to 'pregnant people'. There is ongoing debate as to the role of gendered language in healthcare, especially in what has traditionally been referred to as 'women's health'. Whilst only those with physiology assigned female at birth can become pregnant and give birth, not everyone with female physiology identifies as a woman. It is, therefore, problematic to talk of abortion as healthcare that is for *only* women, even though most people accessing abortion services are women. This is not the place to engage in this debate, so we simply wish to note here that we use the language of pregnant people throughout this book for inclusivity. In line with this, we also use gender-neutral pronouns unless referring to a specific person whose gender is known.

Finally, we refer throughout this book to 'healthcare professionals' (HCPs) rather than doctors. This is in recognition of the reality that nurses and midwives are, in most cases, heavily involved in abortion care. However, it is important to recognise that certain aspects of abortion care pathways are solely within the powers afforded (legally) to doctors, and we will refer to doctors where this is the case.

Scope and relevance

In this book, we start from a position of abortion being lawful in at least some circumstances (this being the case in the UK and US), and of EMA using mifepristone and misoprostol being an approved method. We develop the case for TEMA as an *additional* service (or group of services) *alongside* existing, in-person provision of both surgical and medical abortion, whereby any changes would be largely procedural in how consultations, prescriptions, treatment, and aftercare take place.

Our focus is primarily on the UK and US. The choice of jurisdictions in based on the authors' familiarity with the legal and policy landscape of the UK, and the dominance of US conceptions of the 'abortion right' in abortion law discourse. Further, despite both the UK and US being common law jurisdictions and having some economic and cultural similarities, they have different modern histories of abortion politics, resulting regulation, and thus the organisation of provision (Halfmann 2011; Romanis 2020a). There remain, however, many similar socio-legal barriers to access in the UK and US—whilst each jurisdiction's regulation is fundamentally different, both are rooted in notions of exceptionalism, which serves to render abortion 'non-essential healthcare'. These reasons make the two jurisdictions interesting points of comparison.

Whilst we focus on these two jurisdictions, we do still reflect on the state of abortion regulation elsewhere. In Chapter 5, for example, we discuss varying models of TEMA internationally. Further, much of our argumentation is broadly applicable—abortion is a global reality, and the barriers to access that TEMA can overcome are not exclusive to the UK and US (Romanis and Parsons 2020a).

That being said, our arguments may prove less compelling in contexts where atomistic conceptions of autonomy are not dominant. We ultimately approach this issue from a Western perspective in which the concept of informed consent is very much focused on what the patient values. One might consider this something of an occupational hazard in research, and we simply did not have space to give equal attention to varying cultural contexts. Nonetheless, even where more relational or communitarian approaches to autonomy prevail, the underlying argument in favour of TEMA that we present remains; improving access and safety in abortion care is equally important across cultural contexts.

A disclaimer

We are both what you might call 'pro choice' (as you will likely already have guessed). We both support the decriminalisation of abortion. This perspective has inevitably influenced us in developing the ideas advanced in this book. However, our central argument is not one concerning decriminalisation, and does not specifically advocate for change to the 'grounds for abortion' within current legal frameworks. As such, it is not necessary to share our position on these debates to engage with and, indeed, agree with the central argument we advance.

Our focus is on demonstrating the need for TEMA to ensure that abortion is safe, effective, and acceptable to patients. TEMA is also necessary to further equal access to abortion, contributing to the overcoming of socio-legal barriers that disproportionately affect minorities and those with little financial means. Even if you are of the opinion that abortion should be criminal except in very limited circumstances—such as to save the life of the pregnant person—you can still agree that when a pregnancy *is* going to be terminated it should be done in the safest, most effective way possible, without causing unnecessary pain or distress, and without access disparities based on structural inequalities.

A roadmap

Each chapter in this book examines an important element of our overarching case for the introduction, retention, or reinstating of TEMA. As a useful point of reference, this section provides an overview of each chapter.

In Chapter 1, we provide an explanation of what EMA is and where it fits on the spectrum of abortion methods (i.e. in relation to surgical methods). In detailing EMA, we highlight the wealth of evidence that demonstrates how the procedure is safe, effective, and acceptable to patients. We also indicate factors that could make a patient prefer a particular abortion method.

Chapter 2 outlines the legal frameworks governing abortion in the UK and US. We argue that abortion regulation in both jurisdictions is predicated on the notion of 'abortion exceptionalism' (Borgmann 2014). Abortion is not appropriately recognised as essential healthcare and is instead subject to a unique set of rules placing limitations on where, when, why, and how abortion can be provided.

In Chapter 3, we illustrate how abortion exceptionalism has constructed legal barriers to accessing abortion that, intersecting with structural factors (e.g. geographical and socioeconomic), have resulted in extreme inequity in access to abortion in the UK and US. Abortion access, because of socio-legal barriers, is most difficult to access for vulnerable and marginalised groups.

Chapter 4 considers the gradual move to permitting home use of misoprostol in the UK. We characterise this as something of a policy stepping stone that, as an unfortunate political reality, was necessary to pave the way for TEMA. Issues with this system are highlighted, and we argue that this policy development can be considered, at best, evidence *informed* (as opposed to *based*), and an example of a highly political use of the precautionary principle.

Chapter 5 details our core case for TEMA. Applying the 'telemedical imperative' framework (Parsons 2021a), we argue that there is a moral duty for TEMA to be introduced where possible. We base this primarily on evidence of the safety, effectiveness, and acceptability of TEMA. Further, we demonstrate how the common concerns raised about TEMA are empirically unfounded.

It is important to recognise that there is not (and, indeed, *should* not be) a strict binary between in-person and telemedical care provision. As such, in Chapter 6 we discuss the range of TEMA models that have been implemented, and posit that each should be conceptualised as existing on a 'telemedical continuum'. We present this not only as a description of TEMA provision *across* services, but also as a normative case for choice *within* services.

When the COVID-19 pandemic began in 2020, the ability of healthcare systems globally to deliver care was hugely affected. Abortion was one such affected area. Chapter 7 demonstrates that the already discussed barriers to 'traditional', in-person abortion care were exacerbated by pandemic circumstances, creating an even more pressing need to implement TEMA.

Chapter 8 examines the legal changes and policy decisions made in the UK in response to abortion access concerns during COVID-19. We demonstrate how, despite an initial period of uncertainty, (temporary) changes to abortion law in Great Britain that enabled the introduction of TEMA substantially improved access. Northern

Ireland, however, has failed to ensure access, with devastating consequences. We argue that legal changes to render TEMA lawful must become permanent, and change is necessary in Northern Ireland to ensure equality of access everywhere in the UK.

Chapter 9 surveys the very different legal and policy landscape in the US in response to the pandemic, characterised by substantive failure by both federal and state governments to remove requirements that preclude TEMA. More concerningly, some states erected further barriers to care that, effectively, resulted in a near total abortion ban. We argue that the legal and policy response in the US has been woefully inadequate, and the impact of this further supports the case for TEMA.

* * *

Hervey and Sheldon argue that the central question in the introduction of TEMA concerns 'the responsible conduct of medical practice in supporting women's reproductive health' (2019, 125). This sentiment perfectly captures the crux of this work. The case we put forward in defence of TEMA is, at its core, concerned with the improvement of reproductive health. Given the strong evidence base for the safety, effectiveness, and acceptability of TEMA—which has become significantly stronger following various (temporary) implementations of TEMA in response to the COVID-19 pandemic—we argue that any society that claims to hold evidence-based healthcare in high regard has a *moral* obligation to introduce, retain, or reinstate (as applicable) TEMA to protect and promote the health of pregnant people.

1

Understanding early medical abortion

The focus of this book is, first and foremost, the use of telemedicine to facilitate early medical abortion (EMA). There are ways telemedicine could improve other abortion services. For example, a remote consultation ahead of a surgical abortion would certainly ease many of the barriers to care that will be discussed in later chapters. Readers may even consider much of the case that we make for telemedical EMA (TEMA) in Chapter 5 as applicable to other services. Indeed, the telemedical imperative framework which we adopt is intended for broad applicability (Parsons 2021a). However, we purposely restrict our focus to fully explore the unique aspects of EMA in relation to telemedicine—in brief, that EMA can be provided *entirely* remotely.

Despite this focus, it is still important to acknowledge the wider context. As such, we explain a range of abortion methods in this chapter. In doing so, we highlight potential reasons why a person may prefer one method of abortion over another. By understanding how exactly an EMA is carried out, one can more accurately recognise how such care might map onto a telemedical care pathway.

We begin by outlining the different common methods of abortion, specifically outlining the difference between medical and surgical methods, before looking to the safety, effectiveness, and acceptability of EMA. Establishing EMA's credentials regarding these three factors will prove essential in our later framing of the case for TEMA around the telemedical imperative (see Chapter 5).

1.1 Methods of abortion

Many methods of abortion are available, with varying levels of invasiveness. Generally, abortions later in pregnancy are more invasive, not only in terms of the method used but also the extent of side effects. It is for that reason that, if someone opts for an abortion, the ability to access it as soon as possible is not only preferable, but important for health reasons. We will consider the importance of abortion care being delivered as early as possible, and the role of TEMA in ensuring this, in later chapters.

Here we will consider different methods under three broad categories: surgical abortion, medical abortion, and EMA. The reason for our distinction between medical abortion in general and *early* medical abortion specifically will become apparent. We address these methods in this order—from most invasive to least—so that we finish with that which is the focus of this book.

Early Medical Abortion, Equality of Access, and the Telemedical Imperative. Jordan A. Parsons and Elizabeth Chloe Romanis, Oxford University Press. © Oxford University Press 2021. DOI: 10.1093/oso/9780192896155.003.0001

1.1.1 Surgical abortion

The most invasive means of terminating a pregnancy—save illicit practices outside of regulated clinical practice—is surgical. Surgical methods of abortion are necessarily more invasive as they are ordinarily reserved for the termination of pregnancies of advanced gestational age relative to nonsurgical methods. Whilst a surgical abortion is certainly an option in the first trimester, less invasive medical methods are usually favoured when possible. World Health Organization (WHO) guidance on the safe provision of abortion care details three methods of surgical abortion: vacuum aspiration, dilation and curettage (D&C), and dilation and evacuation (D&E) (2012).

Vacuum aspiration is a method whereby the contents of the patient's uterus are removed through a cannula, using either an electric or manual vacuum. Where a manual vacuum is being used, suction is applied by a 60 millilitre manual aspirator. This is a brief procedure, taking between 3 and 10 minutes depending on how far through the pregnancy it takes place. Preprocedural cervical preparation may be used to reduce the risk of cervical or uterine injuries. Preparation is more likely to be required at higher gestational ages and may be done medically (using drugs such as mifepristone or misoprostol[6]) or mechanically (using dilators). For the procedure, analgesics or anaesthesia will be used. The WHO guidance does not mention general anaesthetic, although this may be used where vacuum aspiration is being carried out at a higher gestational age. For example, the British Pregnancy Advisory Service (BPAS) uses local anaesthetic for vacuum aspiration up to 14 weeks' gestation, but conscious sedation or general anaesthetic up to 15 weeks (meaning conscious sedation and general anaesthetic are options below 14 weeks' gestation in addition to local anaesthetic, but after that point, the option of general anaesthetic is removed—BPAS uses D&E after 15 weeks) (British Pregnancy Advisory Service a). The recovery time is brief for vacuum aspiration but varies depending on the anaesthetic used—patients are mostly able to leave the clinic after around 30 minutes if local anaesthetic is used, whereas conscious sedation and general anaesthetic usually necessitate a longer recovery period. Further, in some countries it is required that you be accompanied home after general anaesthetic regardless of the procedure performed.

D&C entails the cervix being dilated either medically or mechanically (the same way as with vacuum aspiration) before a forceps or curette is inserted to scrape the walls of the uterus and remove the contents. This method is not as safe as vacuum aspiration, and a systematic review and meta-analysis found that the use of D&C increases the risk of subsequent preterm birth (Lemmers et al. 2016). It is also generally more painful for the patient. For these reasons, the WHO recommends that vacuum aspiration be practiced instead of D&C (2012, 41). Further, a Cochrane Review noted a statistically significantly shorter duration of procedure with vacuum aspiration as compared to D&C (Kulier et al. 2001 [2009 update], 4), which is likely to affect both patient and provider preferences if both are available.

The final surgical abortion procedure, D&E, is recognised by the WHO as the 'safest and most effective surgical technique for later abortion' (2012, 41). Kapp and Lohr

---

[6] These same drugs are used without the surgical procedure for the purposes of medical abortion, which we will come to explain shortly.

note that it is a method used from 14 to around 24–26 weeks' gestation (2020, 38). As with D&C (and sometimes vacuum aspiration), this method first requires that the cervix be either manually or medically dilated. Electric vacuum aspiration is then used alongside forceps to evacuate the uterus. As this method is largely used later in a pregnancy—after the first trimester—the cannulas used for the electric vacuum aspiration have a greater diameter (between 12 and 16 millimetres) than when vacuum aspiration is a stand-alone method (between five and 16 millimetres). With this method being more common at high gestational ages, it can take a significant amount of time for adequate cervical dilatation to be achieved. According to the WHO guidance, it can take between two hours and two days (2012, 42). Whilst a lengthier procedure, D&E does not usually take more than 30 minutes. The WHO recommends the use of local anaesthetic or conscious sedation (2012, 42), but general anaesthetic is also used (British Pregnancy Advisory Service a).

In addition to these three methods, hysterotomy is still sometimes (though rarely) performed for the purposes of abortion. This procedure involves an incision being made in the uterine wall via the person's abdomen and the contents of uterus being removed through the incision. In the US in 2018, 46 abortions were carried out by hysterectomy/hysterotomy (Kortsmit et al. 2020, 25).[7] Whilst hysterotomy for the purposes of abortion does still happen, WHO guidance quite firmly notes that it 'has no role in contemporary abortion practice' due to its morbidity and mortality both being significantly higher than those of the other surgical methods detailed or medical methods (2012, 42). Given that hysterotomy is not generally considered an appropriate method of abortion today, future mentions of surgical abortion throughout this book should be taken as referring to vacuum aspiration and D&E.

Whilst surgical abortion methods are invasive and carry risks such as uterine perforation (Kulier et al. 2001 [2009 update]), infection, and the risks associated with anaesthesia (Craig and Kitson 2010), there are certain benefits. First, these surgeries are less painful than medical abortion because of the use of anaesthesia. There may be some residual pain for a few days, but the procedure itself will not be painful. Second, surgical abortion is more definitive. Following the procedure, the doctor examines the products of conception to rule out the possibility of ectopic pregnancy and confirm abortion completeness (World Health Organization 2012, 42). Someone may, then, prefer a surgical abortion because of the immediate reassurance that it has worked—and if it has not, this will be discovered by the doctor at the time and dealt with.

1.1.2 Medical abortion

Where surgical means are not clinically necessary to procure an abortion, the procedure will likely be performed medically. Note that in such circumstances it is *likely* that the person will undergo a medical abortion, but the surgical route may still be chosen. Good practice requires that the option of surgical abortion—notably vacuum

---

[7] This does, of course, make up a tiny proportion of total abortions carried out in the US. Indeed, in the report these 46 equated to 0.0%. Of note, the only states in which abortions by this method were reported were Florida and New York (New York City, specifically).

aspiration—be available alongside medical abortion where clinically appropriate. In England and Wales, guidance provided by the National Institute for Health and Care Excellence (NICE) recommends that patients be offered a choice between medical and surgical abortion up to and including 23 weeks and six days' gestation (2019)[8]— meaning up to the gestational limit on accessing abortion under the Abortion Act 1967 (AA 1967) (this will be explored in greater detail in Chapter 2). There are myriad factors that a pregnant person might consider in deciding how to terminate their pregnancy. Some will prefer medical abortion and others surgical for a variety of reasons that might relate to the procedures themselves (and the associated risks) and/or the possible side effects (Kapp and Lohr 2020). Preference may also vary depending on the reason for the abortion; in one study about choice of abortion method when treatment is because of fetal complication, one participant in later gestation favoured medical abortion because it allowed her to see and spend some time with the fetus (Kerns et al. 2018, 1862). A medical abortion—in essentially inducing a miscarriage—enables this.

For medical abortion, two drugs are used. The first—mifepristone—is an antiprogestogen, meaning it acts to inhibit the hormone progesterone. Without progesterone, the lining of the uterus begins to break down, thereby preventing the continuation of pregnancy. Mifepristone is taken orally, with the recommended dose being 200 milligrams regardless of gestational age (World Health Organization 2012, 43).

The second medication—to be taken after mifepristone—is misoprostol. Whilst there are alternative pharmaceuticals that can be used to medically procure an abortion, misoprostol is the most commonly used. This is often for matters of ease, with the alternative of gemeprost, for example, requiring refrigeration and only being able to be administered vaginally (Electronic Medicines Compendium 2019). Misoprostol (or equivalent) is a prostaglandin analogue. It is used to trigger uterine contractions, thereby causing the expulsion of the products of conception (whether embryo or fetus[9]). The process triggered by misoprostol is like that which occurs in a spontaneous miscarriage in early pregnancy.

Of note, the protocol adopted in the administration of misoprostol varies slightly across the world in terms of dose, route, and timing. Whereas mifepristone is ordinarily taken at the same dose and by the same route regardless of gestational age (200 milligrams, orally), recommendations for misoprostol vary. Misoprostol can be taken orally, vaginally, buccally,[10] or sublingually.[11] The recommended route(s) vary/ies with gestational age. Further, individual providers may favour certain routes based on contemporary evidence. A 2013 systematic review found that there was a higher risk of abortion failure (defined by most included studies as a need for surgical intervention

---

[8] This guidance is also legally supported. In English law, persons have a right to choose between treatments that are reasonable alternatives—which surgical and medical abortion are in this context—based on their own subjective values, wishes, and preferences. See *Montgomery v Lanarkshire Health Board* [2015] UKSC 11.

[9] These different terms are both used to describe the human entity during the process of gestation. The 'embryo' refers to the product of conception before eight weeks' gestation (Findlay et al. 2007). The 'fetus' is the term used to refer to the gestating entity before birth, but after this eight-week point. The distinction is made because it is significant in terms of the physiology of each of the two entities.

[10] Buccal administration requires the patient to place the drug between their gums and cheek (the buccal cavity), leaving it to dissolve and be absorbed into the bloodstream.

[11] Sublingual administration requires the patient to place the drug under their tongue, leaving it to dissolve and be absorbed into the bloodstream.

to complete the termination) when misoprostol was administered orally rather than by one of the nonoral routes (Raymond et al. 2013, 30–1). BPAS, for example, only instructs its patients to administer the drug vaginally or sublingually for medical abortions up to 10 weeks' gestation, and vaginally or buccally for those at later gestations (British Pregnancy Advisory Service b).

The recommended dose of misoprostol is 400 micrograms if administered orally (only up to seven weeks' gestation) and 800 micrograms if administered by another route. If the gestational age has not exceeded nine weeks, this initial dose is usually sufficient. At higher gestational ages, however, further doses of misoprostol are needed. According to WHO guidance, additional doses of 400 micrograms should be administered every three hours up to a maximum of four doses for gestational ages between nine and 12 weeks, and up to five doses for gestational ages between 12 and 24 weeks (2012, 43). After 24 weeks, the dose should account for the increased sensitivity of the uterus to misoprostol, but the WHO does not provide specific recommendations because of a lack of clinical studies.[12] Further, whilst medical abortion is possible at later gestations, D&E has been found to cause less pain and result in fewer adverse events during the second trimester (Grimes et al. 2004).

As for the timing of misoprostol—meaning the first dose if several are to be taken— it is usually recommended that the drug be taken between 24 and 48 hours after the administration of mifepristone. It is possible to take misoprostol near enough immediately after mifepristone, and this has sometimes been the preferred method where abortion regulations present barriers to access. For example, before home use of misoprostol was approved in Great Britain for the purposes of EMA (see Chapter 4) it was necessary for both mifepristone and misoprostol to be taken under supervision at an approved clinic. To remove the need for an additional appointment in 24–48 hours, patients would often take both in the same appointment. Whilst this is still safe and effective, with only a slight decrease in the rate of successful abortion (Wedisinghe and Elsandabesee 2010; Shaw et al. 2013), there is evidence that side effects are more common when the two drugs are taken in quick succession (Creinin et al. 2007). As such, throughout this book we will be considering EMA as the ideal of a 24–48-hour gap between mifepristone and misoprostol.

It is possible for a medical abortion to be procured by use of misoprostol alone, and the WHO highlights several studies that have suggested this to be safe and effective (2012, 45–6). Nonetheless, the use of both medications in combination is more so safe and effective, as well as quicker and less likely to cause side effects. As such, we take (early) medical abortion to refer to a regimen including both mifepristone and misoprostol.

1.1.3   Early medical abortion

Where a medical abortion is procured early in pregnancy it is referred to, unsurprisingly, as an EMA. Treatment is generally considered EMA when carried out in the first

---

[12] At the time of writing, updated guidance from the WHO is expected soon which may provide recommendations on misoprostol doses after 24 weeks.

trimester. Exact gestational limits vary between jurisdictions, usually falling between seven and 12 weeks.

EMA is broadly the same as medical abortion carried out later in pregnancy. Both utilise the same medications—mifepristone and misoprostol—to procure a miscarriage. It is the most common means of procuring an abortion in many countries. In England and Wales, 73% of abortions carried out in 2019 were performed medically—a percentage that has been steadily rising for more than a decade (Department of Health and Social Care 2020a, 4). The figure is similarly high in Scotland (Information Services Division Scotland 2019). In the US, EMA is common, though as a percentage of total abortions there is significant variation between states (Kortsmit et al. 2020, 25).

In essence, the more specific terminology of 'EMA' is used to denote what is ultimately a far more straightforward treatment. As already discussed, the dose and route of medication may vary with gestational age. EMA, then, requires a simpler process with only one dose of misoprostol. That is not to say, however, that medical abortion is not a simple process later in gestation—in general, it is.

1.2 Safety, effectiveness, and acceptability of early medical abortion

In the past, abortion was often performed as a clandestine, 'back-street' procedure by unqualified persons and was associated with dangerous methods and high mortality (Keown 1988; Sheldon 1997; Goodwin 2020). In Great Britain, prior to the AA 1967 (which came into force in 1968), pregnant people with unwanted pregnancies were forced to procure terminations illicitly, often in ways that presented a great risk of harm without even proving effective. In the period 1930 to 1934 at a hospital in London, the mortality rate for abortions was reported at 1.8% (Parish 1935, 1110). For patients whose abortion was complete on admission, this was higher at 4.5%—as would be expected where it was carried out without medical assistance in a time before medical abortion. This reality was attributable to both the state of medical technology at the time and the legal standing of abortion. Nonetheless, it can be considered predominantly a result of the law, for the mortality rate in Parish's study decreased the earlier in the abortion process the patient was admitted to hospital; whilst the methods available to doctors were not as safe as those used today, it was still possible to procure an abortion with a low risk of mortality if the patient was seen early in pregnancy.

Whilst not yet perfect, the legal standing of abortion in both the UK and the US has improved since the 1930s (see Chapter 2). This, in combination with advances in medicine, has resulted in a significant drop in abortion mortality rates. Lohr and colleagues (2020) provide some useful comparisons to put this into perspective. In the UK, taking abortion mortality at 0.15 per 100,000,[13] they highlight that a person is at greater risk of dying in a road traffic accident (2.8 per 100,000) or of being murdered (1.2 per 100,000) (2020, 40). Indeed, as is often highlighted in abortion discourse, the

---

[13] Based on Parish's study from 1935, the mortality rate was 1,800 per 100,000. This demonstrates just how far things have come in the safe provision of abortion care.

risks (including mortality) associated with childbirth are significantly higher than those with (legal) abortion (Raymond and Grimes 2012; Gerdts et al. 2016).

The approval of medical interventions, including pharmaceuticals, largely hinges on their safety and effectiveness. Whilst perhaps slightly less important, there is also some weight placed on acceptability. Certainly, in the move towards patient-centred medicine the role of acceptability may well grow. Given their importance, we will here explore how EMA fares against these criteria.

Readers should note that in this section we are concerned with the safety, effectiveness, and acceptability of EMA delivered *in person* at a healthcare facility. This is important information to establish before discussing EMA carried out by patients at home (including TEMA), and we will come to explore the safety, effectiveness, and acceptability of this more specific care pathway in Chapter 5. However, as will become apparent, several key studies include results from home use of misoprostol—we will distinguish results where possible. Further, we are here only discussing a regimen of mifepristone followed by misoprostol; misoprostol alone can be used, but the combination is preferable and more common in the jurisdictions with which we are concerned.

1.2.1   Safety

A 2013 systematic review (Raymond et al. 2013) examined the safety of first trimester (early) medical abortion using 200 milligrams of mifepristone and various doses of misoprostol. 87 trials were included, comprising 36 randomised trials and 51 prospective cohort or case series studies. They were conducted across 35 countries, and evaluable data was provided for 45,528 participants (96% of the total of 47,283).[14] Of these 45,528 participants, just 119 (0.3%) were hospitalised, with reasons including vaginal bleeding, pelvic pain, and infection (2013, 28). Some hospitalisations were for reasons unrelated to the abortion itself, such as ectopic pregnancy. Blood transfusions were needed for 45 participants (0.1%) (2013, 30). These figures are for the combined at-home/in-clinic administration of misoprostol. Looking specifically at in-clinic misoprostol, the rates of hospitalisation and blood transfusion were slightly higher at 0.45% and 0.14%, respectively (2013, 30). The in-clinic rates are still extremely low such that it can be deemed safe, but it is worth noting that at-home administration was found to be safer.

A more recent systematic review (Chen and Creinin 2015) focused specifically on buccal administration of misoprostol up to 70 days' gestation,[15] with all 20 included studies having a dosing interval of between 24 and 48 hours. Rates of hospitalisation

---

[14] We noted earlier that we are primarily concerned with EMA regimens involving an interval of between 24 and 48 hours between mifepristone and misoprostol. The studies included in this systematic review did not all prescribe such an interval. However, only 16 of 120 trial groups included intervals outside this range (total range of 0–72 hours), of which some still included intervals between 24 and 48 hours.

[15] Whilst their inclusion criteria allowed for studies up to 70 days' gestation, Chen and Creinin do acknowledge that there were limited data on the use of mifepristone and buccal misoprostol beyond 63 days' gestation (2015, 20). As such, these results should be considered as applicable to EMA up to 63 days but taken with caution at later gestations.

and blood transfusion were again found to be low, at 0.04%–0.9% and 0.03%–0.6%, respectively (2015, 19). This systematic review also reported on infection and emergency department visits, which were found to be between 0.01% and 0.5% and between 2.9% and 3.7%, respectively (2015, 19). There was significant variation across included studies in which measures were reported, with emergency department visits being reported in only two of them. Nonetheless, these findings support the conclusions of the earlier systematic review (Raymond et al. 2013) regarding the safety of EMA. The findings of these systematic reviews are also supported by more recent data that show low rates of adverse events up to 70 days' gestation with misoprostol administered sublingually, with just two blood transfusions and three hospitalisations in a study population of 703[16] (Bracken et al. 2014, 183).

A person who has an EMA is likely to experience various side effects. Some are drug related, such as diarrhoea, fever, rash, and a change in blood pressure. There are also side effects experienced as part of the abortion process itself, such as lower abdominal pain. Some patients will experience relatively little by way of side effects, whilst others will be quite significantly affected. Chen and Creinin's systematic review, for example, found that rates of diarrhoea and vomiting ranged from between 1.9% and 61.2% and between 16% and 47.6%, respectively (2015, 18–9). Further, whilst all routes and doses carry the possibility of these side effects, research has found that certain side effects are more common with certain misoprostol regimens (Honkanen et al. 2004). In addition to those side effects related to the drugs and the abortion process, some patients may experience pregnancy-related side effects in tandem—for example, nausea, vomiting, and breast tenderness—which can increase discomfort, although these symptoms are likely to largely alleviate once the abortion process has started (Honkanen et al. 2004, 719–20).

The evidence is, then, quite overwhelming in suggesting that EMA provided by medical professionals in licensed medical premises is safe. We provide these qualifiers for the reason that EMA may not be universally safe, as the broader safety of EMA is about more than just the lack of serious risks and side effects of the drugs involved. It may be the case, for example, that in some contexts there could be instances in which a lack of appropriate follow-up services could result in relatively minor complications becoming serious. Overall, however, the data show that EMA is safe when provided within a medical model.

1.2.2 Effectiveness

Raymond and colleagues' (2013) systematic review found EMA to be highly effective in regimens using a dose of at least 600 micrograms of misoprostol. Rates of abortion failure ranged from 1.3% (600 micrograms, sublingually) to 8.2% (600 micrograms, orally), and rates of ongoing pregnancy ranged from 0% (600 micrograms, sublingually) to 3.7% (600 micrograms, vaginally) (2013, 29). Regimens using a dose of 800 micrograms or more administered vaginally accounted for 43 of 120 trial groups

---

[16] Enrolment was 714, but nine were lost to follow-up and two to withdrawal.

included, and in these 43 the average rates were 3.4% for abortion failure and 0.5% for ongoing pregnancy (2013, 29). These findings demonstrate that medical abortion is highly effective, and that rates of abortion failure and ongoing pregnancy might be reduced by the choice of dose and route—nonoral routes with a dose of 800 micrograms or more appear to be most effective. Further, as highlighted earlier in this chapter, Raymond and colleagues also noted a lesser rate of abortion failure when misoprostol was taken at least 23 hours after mifepristone; 4.8% versus 5.4% (2013, 29).

This evidence is also supported by Chen and Creinin's (2015) more recent systematic review. Based on 20 studies, the average rate of successful abortion was found to be 96.6% (2015, 13). Unsurprisingly, the success rate gradually declined at higher gestational ages, ranging from 98.1% with gestational ages of 49 days or fewer to 93.1% with those between 64 and 70 days. Again, these data are supported by Bracken and colleagues' trial concerning sublingual misoprostol—successful abortion was reported in 94.8% of participants in the 57–63 days' gestation group and 91.9% in the 64–70 days group (2014, 183). Surgical evacuation for continued pregnancy took place in only 2% of cases (1.8% 57–63 days; 2.2% 64–70 days) (2014, 183). In comparing the different gestational age groups, the notable difference was in rates of surgical evacuation for excessive or prolonged bleeding—from 0.5% (57–63 days) to 2.5% (64–70 days) (2014, 183). At most, however, this difference suggests that additional caution should be taken in providing care in the tenth week of pregnancy—indeed, Blumenthal, in a response to Chen and Creinin (2015), suggested that such caution should 'simply take the form of counseling' so that patients can decide based on the data (2015, 1107).

A recent study in Singapore (Tan et al. 2018) further supports the effectiveness of EMA up to 70 days' gestation.[17] Of 125 participants, 121 (96.8%) had a successful abortion (2018, 146). This again varied based on gestational age, from 94.9% (50–56 days) to 100% (36–49 days; 64–70 days). Nonetheless, even the lowest rate—94.9%—is sufficiently high to describe the treatment as effective.

There is some evidence that surgical abortion is more effective than medical abortion (Creinin 2000), but that does not detract from the fact that medical abortion is highly effective. It need not be viewed as an either-or situation, and, as is recommended in the guidance of various medical bodies, patients should be offered a choice. Even if there is a slightly higher chance of an incomplete abortion using medical methods, a patient may be happy with this given the other benefits of medical abortion (in particular, that it is less invasive).

Overall, then, EMA is a highly effective method of terminating a pregnancy. Provided patients are informed of the very small risk of an incomplete abortion that would then mean further treatment, it is clear that EMA is effective such that it should be an option for those seeking to terminate an unwanted pregnancy.[18]

---

[17] Some of the participants in this study took both mifepristone and misoprostol at home, though the majority took mifepristone in a clinic.

[18] Based on this evidence, EMA satisfies the threshold for being considered a reasonable treatment alternative, for the purposes of the law in the UK, that supports patient choice. See *Montgomery* (n8).

1.2.3   Acceptability

Even if a procedure serves its medical purpose, the acceptability of that procedure to patients is an important consideration. In general, there are many instances in which burdens that may be associated with medical treatments are such that they would not be tolerated if not *necessary*, and thus they are only considered tolerable in the circumstances because of the outcomes they can procure and the lack of alternatives. Other times, however, when a particular treatment is not necessary, the burdens associated with it might be such that the patient would rather not have it—for example, if they consider the side effects disproportionate to the ailment. It remains, therefore, that acceptability to patients is at least a factor of some relevance, because this will influence the appropriateness of treatment from the patient's perspective. Even in circumstances where acceptability is not believed to carry significant weight—for example, because the ailment is serious and there are not yet available alternatives—patient acceptability still is important to consider as part of the overall perception of a treatment and its appropriateness.[19] In the context of abortion, then, the acceptability of EMA to individuals is important to consider as there are alternative methods as outlined above.

Medical abortion using mifepristone and misoprostol has consistently been found to be highly acceptable to patients. Ngo and colleagues' (2011) systematic review reported consistently high satisfaction levels across the included studies. For those taking the drugs in a clinic, satisfaction ranged from 72% to 97%, and at-home EMA satisfaction ranged from 84% to 99% (2011, 365). Interestingly, patients who took misoprostol at home were seven times more likely to opt for medical abortion in future when compared with those who took the drug in a clinic. This is important to highlight as it does clearly raise the question of whether it is appropriate to require patients to take misoprostol in a clinic, but we will explore this in later chapters.

A more recent study in Singapore of medical abortion performed up to 70 days' gestation found similarly high levels of patient satisfaction, with 94.4% reporting being either very satisfied or satisfied (Tan et al. 2018, 146). In particular, most patients in this study found the side effects (with 78.4% experiencing at least one side effect) either acceptable (68.3%) or neutral (26%) (2018, 146). Unsurprisingly, then, only 10.4% expressed a preference for surgical abortion if they were to terminate a future pregnancy. Largely similar findings were reported in a Nepalese study (Karki et al. 2009).

In terms of qualitative research—which offers interesting and important depth of understanding when it comes to patient experiences of abortion that quantitative projects cannot—several studies have supported these findings of high acceptability. We must acknowledge, however, that they do not all concern the standard misoprostol-mifepristone regimen that we have so far discussed—we specify when this is the case.

Most relevant is an interview study in Canada following the 2017 introduction of medical abortion using mifepristone and misoprostol (LaRoche and Foster 2020). Participants reported that the reasons for them choosing medical abortion—largely privacy and convenience—proved to be positive aspects of the process (2020, 63). One participant captured the general feeling in explaining: 'it was just more relieving to be

---

[19] We will return to this point in Chapter 5 in relation to telemedicine.

able to do the second part with my partner, in a place that I knew I felt safe and comfortable' (2020, 63). Many, however, highlighted the length of the process as a possible negative, in one case drawing a comparison to a previous surgical abortion that was 'done and dusted' in just one day (2020, 63). Overall, LaRoche and Foster reported how participants wanted more information, with most of those who expressed negative feelings about the abortion also describing feeling unprepared (2020, 64). Of note, several suggested that they would have appreciated hearing personal stories of previous patients in addition to the medical information (2020, 64).

Exploring experiences of pain during medical abortion more specifically, Grossman and colleagues (2019) interviewed participants in Nepal, South Africa, and Vietnam.[20] This study, in line with others already discussed, clearly demonstrated variation in experiences, with participants reporting a range from '[i]t wasn't painful at all, not even a little' to '[i]t hurt terribly, it hurt in a way that it's very unlike any normal pain' (2019, 5). Some participants explained that the pain they did experience was less intense than previous (surgical) abortions (2019, 6). Another study (Tousaw et al. 2018) conducted interviews with users of a community-based misoprostol distribution programme (misoprostol-only regimen) along the Thailand-Burma border. Participants were overall positive about their experiences accessing this care, with one remarking: '[i]t is just like having a period with back pain' (2018, 124). This study also found that all participants, including those with an unsuccessful abortion, would recommend the programme to others (2018, 126).

This body of qualitative research supports the quantitative data from the systematic reviews discussed. Taken together, these studies make a compelling case for the acceptability of EMA. Clearly, the vast majority of those who access this care find it acceptable, in many cases to the extent that they would recommend it to others in similar situations. What does become apparent from the qualitative data is that being fully informed of what to expect is important to the acceptability of EMA. Experiences of the process are subjective, so it would not be appropriate to inform a patient being consulted about EMA only that most patients find it highly acceptable. To enable an informed decision, it is necessary to make it clear that the process can be unpleasant for some—the suggestion of some of the participants in LaRoche and Foster's (2020) study that accounts from previous patients could be shared may be an appropriate way. Overall, EMA can be considered suitably acceptable. Whilst the process can be very unpleasant for some, that is not reason to deny care to those who acknowledge this and still wish to proceed.

1.3 Summary

This chapter has explained what different abortion procedures actually entail, which is an important precursor to the arguments in this book. It is quite common for non-medical literature concerning abortion to provide a somewhat superficial overview of only the method of concern and, often in the literature concerning telemedicine

---

[20] This study was conducted as part of a randomised controlled trial in which the three arms received different pain management drugs (one being a placebo arm).

and home use of abortifacients, to assert medical abortion as preferable for reasons of safety, effectiveness, and acceptability with little discussion of the underlying evidence. We are certainly not criticising authors for doing so. We, ourselves, have done just this in previous work in this area. It is often necessary to omit these details for simple reasons such as journal word limits. Nonetheless, we think it important to make clear the realities of these procedures as the differences between them are central to some of our discussions in later chapters. Further, we believe that discussing the different methods of abortion gives some important context about the treatment alternatives that might (or should) be available to those seeking abortion.

In addition, this chapter has also served to demonstrate that, on balance, it is easy to see why medical methods of abortion would be preferred by most. There are certainly reasons why someone may prefer surgical methods—for example, less pain, fewer side effects, and a more definitive procedure. But, of course, this depends on the individual; some may value the flexibility in terms of time that is afforded by medical abortion (depending on regulations in the country in question) more than reducing the burden of side effects. How side effects are perceived and thought of as acceptable is dependent on individual subjective preferences. For this reason, choice of method is of huge importance in abortion care. Indeed, the paramountcy of choice is very much a running theme in this book both at the level of abortion method and the level of precise care pathway.

It should, however, be acknowledged that the UK and US, which are the primary jurisdictions we consider in this book, are in a position of privilege when it comes to offering choice in abortion care. This privilege has not always been exercised, but, as high-income countries, there is at least a realistic ability to offer patients a choice of abortion method. Certain methods may or may not be clinically appropriate (or, indeed, possible) in some settings (Zhou et al. 2020). There is certainly an issue of significant global variation in access to abortion care, but that is a discussion beyond the scope of this book.

Medical abortion has done a significant amount to revolutionise care in the UK and US (and, indeed, globally) since the drugs were introduced. Testament to this significance is the fact that misoprostol features on the WHO's Model List of Essential Medicines. However, whilst it is listed without caveat as essential for reasons other than abortion, its use in combination with mifepristone (meaning for the purposes of medical abortion) is listed with the qualifier of '[w]here permitted under national law and where culturally acceptable' (2019, 47). That the function of this medication in procuring abortion is distinguished from its essential functions is a feature of how abortion is still treated as a contentious aspect of healthcare. The next chapter considers how this idea of abortion as different from other aspects of healthcare has been ingrained in the fundamentals of the legal frameworks regulating abortion in the UK and US.

2

Abortion exceptionalism and the law in the United Kingdom and United States

In this chapter, we outline the legal frameworks governing abortion provision in the UK and US, and we demonstrate *how* abortion is 'exceptionalised' by the law. In both jurisdictions, abortion is distinguished from other aspects of healthcare and is subject to a distinct regulatory regime allowing for increased supervision and limitations on access. This has the effect of labelling abortion 'nonessential healthcare', even though abortion is increasingly being appropriately recognised as essential healthcare (Sheldon and Wellings 2020).

Abortion is subject to a 'wholly distinctive regulatory regime' in the UK (Jackson 2001, 71) and US. In most of the UK (Great Britain) abortion remains a criminal offence. Abortion is only lawfully performed under the terms of the Abortion Act 1967 (AA 1967), which is constructed as an exhaustive list of exceptions to the criminal prohibition of abortion. Although abortion was recently partially decriminalised in Northern Ireland, it remains difficult for people living in Northern Ireland to access care locally (Kirk et al. 2020). We will consider the law in Northern Ireland separately as it differs from the rest of the UK.

In the US, there is significant variation in abortion regulation between individual states. However, state laws are all subject to the constraint that abortion is recognised as encompassed within a person's constitutional right to privacy.[21] States must ensure that their regulatory regime does not 'unduly burden' access to abortion before foetal viability (i.e. the point at which the fetus is deemed capable of an independent existence if it were born).[22] Despite its status as a recognised constitutional right, however, abortion remains subject to 'unique, and uniquely burdensome, rules' (Borgmann 2014, 1048) that set it apart as distinct from other constitutional rights.

In both jurisdictions, we argue, abortion is legally *exceptionalised*; that is, set apart from other areas of healthcare for exceptional and considerable oversight. This is despite the fact that 'exceptionalism' (Borgmann 2014), and the restrictions on access that it enables,[23] is not medically necessary because abortion is safe and routine (see Chapter 1). The excessive regulation of abortion remains because pregnant bodies are treated as a site of public and political contention. This belief—underlying the regulatory approaches to abortion in the UK and US—perpetuates the notion that abortion decisions need state and/or medical supervision.

---

[21] *Roe v. Wade*, U.S. 113 (1973).
[22] *Planned Parenthood v. Casey*, 112 U.S. 2791 (1992).
[23] These will be discussed in Chapter 3.

Early Medical Abortion, Equality of Access, and the Telemedical Imperative. Jordan A. Parsons and Elizabeth Chloe Romanis, Oxford University Press. © Oxford University Press 2021. DOI: 10.1093/oso/9780192896155.003.0002

2.1 Great Britain

Abortion remains a criminal offence in Great Britain. In Scotland this is by virtue of the common law,[24] and in England and Wales abortion is criminalised in two statutes: the Offences Against the Person Act 1861 (OAPA 1861) and the Infant Life (Preservation) Act 1929. Section 58 of the OAPA 1861 criminalises the procurement of a miscarriage, which is committed when an individual unlawfully attempts to procure the miscarriage of any pregnant person,[25] with the intention of procuring the miscarriage.[26] A person who believes they are pregnant only commits the offence if they attempt to procure a miscarriage whilst they are *actually* pregnant, whereas another person commits the offence where they attempt to procure miscarriage even if the person is not actually pregnant. Section 59 criminalises the supply of drugs or other instruments that can be used to procure miscarriage knowing that they are intended for that use, or with the intention that they are used to procure miscarriage. Section 58 carries the harshest punishment for abortion in any European country—life imprisonment (Sheldon 2016a). In addition, section 1 of the Infant Life (Preservation) Act 1929 criminalises 'child destruction', committed when a person 'by wilful act' intentionally causes the death before birth of a 'child capable of being born alive'. A fetus is presumed capable of being born alive at 24 weeks' gestation.[27] There are two significant differences between procuring miscarriage and child destruction. First, 'unlawful procurement of miscarriage' can be committed at any point during a pregnancy, whereas 'child destruction' can only be committed later in pregnancy after the fetus is 'viable' (Grubb 1990). Second, 'child destruction' is only committed where the fetus dies before birth, whereas the language in the OAPA 1861 does not necessarily require that the fetus be killed during the termination of a pregnancy (Romanis 2020b; Milne 2020). As this book is about EMA, we will focus on the offences contained in the OAPA 1861.[28]

In 1939, it was established in common law that some instances of abortion do not constitute criminal procurement of miscarriage. In *Bourne*,[29] MacNaghten J interpreted 'unlawful procurement of miscarriage' in the OAPA 1861 as meaning that some procurement of miscarriage must be lawful, the logic being that the inclusion of the word 'unlawful' must presuppose some instances in which procurement of miscarriage must be 'lawful' (Sheldon 1997; Romanis 2020b). However, 'one may

---

[24] The Explanatory notes to the Scotland Act 1998, J1 explain that, 'at common law in Scotland it is a crime to procure or attempt to procure an abortion'. Chalmers and Leverick (2016) note that the crime of procuring miscarriage in Scottish common law can be committed at any point between conception and birth and by any means including, but not limited to, drugs or instruments.

[25] S.58 does refer specifically to pregnant *women*, but we believe that the statute should be read to mean any pregnant person.

[26] Miscarriage is not defined in the statute. In *R (On the Application of Smeaton) v Secretary of State for Health* [2002] EWHC 610 (admin) it was interpreted as meaning 'the termination of an established pregnancy' (para 17). For an analysis of the some of the problems of the terminology in this offence see Romanis (2020b).

[27] Human Fertilisation and Embryology Act 1990, s.37.

[28] One of the common arguments of those opposed to the establishment of TEMA it that it might enable pregnant people to administer abortifacients at home far later in their pregnancy, at which point the offence of child destruction could be relevant. We address this in Chapter 5.

[29] *R v Bourne* [1939] 1 KB 687.

question historically whether the word was intended or realised by the legislature to imply what MacNaghten J saw in it' (Dickens 1966, 39). *Bourne* established that abortion would not be an *unlawful* procurement of miscarriage where a doctor deemed it necessary for the purpose of preserving the person's life. MacNaghten J determined:

> if the doctor is of the opinion, on reasonable grounds and with adequate knowledge, that the probable consequence of the continuance of pregnancy will be to make the woman a physical or mental wreck, the jury are quite entitled to take the view that the doctor who, under those circumstances and in that honest belief, is operating for the purpose of preserving the life of the mother.[30]

Whilst only a High Court judgment, *Bourne* sufficiently affirmed the legality of therapeutic abortion such that it enabled some abortions—subject to doctors' discretion, and usually only accessible to wealthier people—to be conducted lawfully (Sheldon 1997). It remained the case, however, that most people (because they did not have access to either a doctor willing to perform the procedure or sufficient funds) continued to have clandestine abortions.

The AA 1967 was passed to provide clearer statutory parameters to the crimes in the OAPA 1861 (and Infant Life (Preservation) Act 1929) in England and Wales, and the common law in Scotland. A doctor can lawfully perform an abortion without facing criminal sanction if they do so in compliance with the terms of the AA 1967. Section 1 of the AA 1967[31] stipulates that a registered medical practitioner will not be guilty of a criminal offence if they provide treatment after two medical practitioners have formed the opinion, in good faith:

- That the pregnancy has not exceeded its twenty-fourth week and continuance of the pregnancy would involve risk, greater than if the pregnancy were terminated, of injury to the physical or mental health of the pregnant person[32] or any existing children of their family—section 1(1)(a);
- That the termination is necessary to prevent grave permanent injury to the physical or mental health of the pregnant person—section 1(1)(b);[33]
- That the continuance of the pregnancy would involve risk to the life of the pregnant person, greater than if the pregnancy were terminated—section 1(1)(c); or
- That there is a substantial risk that if the child were born it would suffer from such physical or mental abnormalities as to be seriously handicapped—section 1(1)(d).

---

[30] Ibid, at 694 per MacNaghten J.

[31] As amended by the Human Fertilisation and Embryology Act 1990, s.37.

[32] The Act uses gendered language, but we believe that the statute would be interpreted as applying to any pregnant person, however they identify.

[33] If abortion is provided under this ground then the treatment need not be certified by two registered medical practitioners provided that one is satisfied that 'the termination is immediately necessary to save the life or to prevent grave permanent injury to the physical or mental health of the pregnant woman': Abortion Act 1967, s.1(4).

All abortions performed in England and Wales must be reported to the Chief Medical Officer.[34] In the report form that must be completed,[35] the grounds on which a termination is provided must be specified.[36] Scotland has the same requirement to provide information about the lawful grounds for every termination on a specified form sent to the Chief Medical Officer in Scotland.[37] The report form in both England and Wales and Scotland stipulates five grounds (labelled A–E) which map onto the requirements of the AA 1967, but are distinguished so that more specific information about the reason for termination can be recorded:

A. The continuance of the pregnancy would involve a greater risk to the life of the pregnant person—section 1(1)(c).
B. The termination is necessary to prevent grave permanent injury to the physical or mental health of the pregnant person—section 1(1)(b).
C. Before 24 weeks where the continuance of the pregnancy would involve a greater risk to the physical or mental health of the pregnant person—section 1(1)(a).
D. Before 24 weeks where the continuance of the pregnancy would involve a greater risk to the physical or mental health of any existing children of the pregnant person's family—section 1(1)(a).
E. There is a substantial risk that, if born, the child would be seriously handicapped—section 1(1)(d).

Owing to the requirement to report abortions, and the specific grounds on which they are provided, there are considerable data available about abortion provision in Great Britain. Most abortions are provided under section 1(1)(a) of the AA 1967, known as the 'social ground' for abortion (Brazier and Cave 2016, 404). In 2019, 98% of abortions in England and Wales (204,020) were performed under ground C. In most of these cases, it was recorded that the pregnancy constituted a greater risk to the person's mental health than termination (Department of Health and Social Care 2020a, 10). Similarly, in 2018, 98.8% of abortions in Scotland (13,121) were performed under ground C (Information Services Division Scotland 2019, 25).

It has been argued that section 1(1)(a) 'operates in practice to render every pregnancy legally terminable within the first 24 weeks' (Jackson 2001, 80). Most doctors take the view that early abortion will *always* carry fewer risks than childbirth, therefore abortion—particularly EMA—can always be justified under section 1(1)(a) on 'statistical grounds' (Williams 1983; Keown 1988; Grubb 1991; Jackson 2000; Brazier and Cave 2016). Whilst the British Medical Association initially flagged this as cause for concern shortly after the enactment of the AA 1967 (Keown 1988), today the Association supports the complete decriminalisation of abortion (British Medical Association 2019). The Association recommends that section 1(1)(a) should be interpreted as meaning that there are always legal grounds for abortion early in pregnancy

---

[34] Abortion Regulations 1991, regulation 4(1)(a).
[35] The form is available in the Abortion Regulations 1991, schedule 2.
[36] Regulation 4(1)(b) requires that the form be completed in full.
[37] Abortion (Scotland) Regulations 1991, regulation 4(a). The reporting form is contained in schedule 2.

because of the evidence regarding comparative risks between abortion and childbirth (British Medical Association 2007).

Although the statistical argument means few people will have their request for abortion early in pregnancy refused, the AA 1967 does not allow for abortion on demand. The construction of section 1(1)(a) still means that 'ultimately, the doctors must form an opinion that the ground applies to *this individual* [emphasis added] and not solely on the basis of abstract statistics' (Grubb 1991, 661).[38] The Act instructs that doctors should, in determining whether continuing a pregnancy would involve risk of injury to health, take account of 'the pregnant woman's actual or reasonably foreseeable environment'.[39] This mandates the consideration of the person's socioeconomic circumstances (Sheldon 1997). David Steel, who initially brought the private members bill to Parliament that eventually became the AA 1967, explained that the drafting deliberately encompassed 'the concept of socio-medical care' (Steel 1971, 7), affording doctors wide discretion to attend to patients' social circumstances in decision making. In practice, doctors are afforded the space to interpret the AA 1967 liberally (Sheldon 1997; Priaulx and Jones 2018). The effect of section 1(1)(a) is that abortion was made lawful and reasonably accessible early in pregnancy for most people who need it in Great Britain (Sheldon 1997). Sections 1(b)–(d) are also important to recognise as meeting the need for abortion later in pregnancy.[40] We concentrate our analysis on section 1(1)(a) since this is the ground under which EMA is overwhelmingly performed.

As well as being provided in compliance with one of the grounds in section 1, for abortion to be lawful, treatment must be performed by a medical practitioner,[41] and only in a National Health Service (NHS) or other premises specifically approved for the purpose by the Secretary of State or devolved health ministers.[42] The intent of these provisions was to ensure that abortion was provided in safe conditions.[43] There have been substantial changes to the law in Great Britain between 2017 and 2020 regarding

---

[38] To avoid prosecution (though rare) a doctor must establish that they have formed their opinion based on the person's individual circumstances, rather than relying on the 'statistical argument'. In *R v Smith (John)* [1973] 1 W.L.R. 1510, a doctor's conviction was upheld on the grounds that he did not act in good faith when providing an abortion because he had not formed a bona fide opinion as to the balance of risk between termination and the continuance of pregnancy on the ground for termination under section 1(1)(a) of the Abortion Act 1967. Sheldon observes, however, that British courts are unlikely to see a similar prosecution (or see or uphold a conviction) again because 'it seems now to be widely accepted that some doctors are very liberal in their interpretation of the Abortion Act' (1997, 86).

[39] Abortion Act 1967, s.1(2).

[40] We do not claim that they do so adequately.

[41] Throughout this book we will have cause to interpret the meaning of 'terminated by a medical practitioner' in the AA 1967, since there might be questions about whether a doctor can be said to have performed the treatment where, for example, a nurse practitioner is involved in parts of treatment provision, or where a pregnant person self-administers medication that has been prescribed by a doctor. The House of Lords determined that 'terminated by a medical practitioner' should be understood as meaning that a doctor is accepting responsibility for all stages of abortifacient treatment even if they do not perform all the actions involved in the process of termination themselves. *Royal College of Nursing of the United Kingdom v Department of Health and Social Security* [1981] 1 All ER 545, at 569–70 per Lord Diplock; at 575 per Lord Keith; at 577 per Lord Roskill.

[42] Abortion Act 1967, s.3.

[43] This was discussed in the House of Lords: HL Deb 23 October 1967, vol 285, cols 1396, 1419–20.

where abortion can take place, which will be discussed in later chapters. We raise the issue here to demonstrate how closely abortion is regulated.

Consideration of the historical and social context of the AA 1967 (and the conditions under which it was debated and enacted) is necessary to ground contemporary discussion of its provisions. In carving out exceptions to criminal abortion, it was hoped that the Act might bring an end to the extremely high mortality and morbidity associated with 'back-street abortion' at the time (Sheldon 2016a). The Act was essentially a public health measure (Jackson 2001; Sheldon 2014). It was also enacted to 'bring under control' the persistent and widespread criminal behaviour amounting to 'de facto female resistance to the law' (Sheldon 1997, 24). The instillation of abortion as a closely regulated health matter in which doctors, a socially revered and male-dominated profession, could act as gatekeepers was thus appealing to parliamentarians (who were entirely male) as a way of having more control over the who, why, and when of abortion (Sheldon 1997). Moreover, when the Act was passed, abortion necessarily constituted an invasive surgical procedure, the safe performance of which necessitated appropriate expertise.[44]

The AA 1967 is a product of its time. It has been in force for more than 50 years and has only been amended once in its lifetime in 1990 (Sheldon et al. 2019). The changes that have been made to abortion law since 1990 are all secondary legislation, issued by individuals—government (and devolved government) ministers—under specific powers afforded to them by the Act.[45] This secondary legislation has all related to the practicalities of *how* care can be delivered (specifically *where* it can take place), and thus has made no changes to the overall framework. It is unsurprising, therefore, that the statute is ill-suited to evolve with contemporary best practice in abortion and healthcare more broadly. Sheldon (1997) and Jackson (2000) have both observed that the framework of medicalisation the AA 1967 adopted was necessary to 'depoliticise' abortion provision enough to pass the Bill through Parliament. Today, however, it is outdated and, in effect, 'exceptionalising'. The Act remains framed around the notion that abortion must be limited to those instances where *medical practitioners* believe it to be appropriate in line with one of the criteria in the Act, and otherwise it is criminal. Abortion is the only form of healthcare *expressly* prohibited by statute except where performed by medical practitioners. The offence of assault is committed by any individual who provides any medical treatment where they do not obtain proper informed consent from the victim,[46] and this will include those instances in which the victim has not provided proper informed consent because they were unaware that the person performing an exam or a particular treatment was not medically qualified.[47] It is also an offence in Great Britain to wilfully and falsely pretend to be a registered medical practitioner or to have medical qualifications.[48] Abortion is uniquely subjected to

---

[44] Medical abortion became available in July 1991 with the licensing of mifepristone. Whilst we cannot source this original license, it was referred to later that month in the House of Lords by then Parliamentary Under-Secretary of State for Health, Baroness Hooper: HL Deb 25 July 1991, vol 531, col 880.

[45] Abortion Act 1967, ss.1(3) and (3A). We discuss these powers in more detail in later chapters.

[46] Consent to harm is not generally accepted as permissible in English law, though there is an exception for medical treatment: *R v Brown* [1993] UKHL 19.

[47] *R v Tabassum* [2000] 2 Cr App R 328.

[48] Medical Act 1983, s.49(1).

regulation beyond this. It is criminal for a person who is not a doctor (meaning specifically a *registered* doctor),[49] to supply abortifacients to another person, even where they do not purport to be medically qualified and the person who is being supplied the medication is aware that they are not medically qualified.[50] It is also unlawful for a doctor to provide abortion in a manner noncompliant with the provisions of the AA 1967, even if the patient consents. Thus, it is evident that the AA 1967 is out of step with the regulation of medical treatment more broadly.

Even though it is a criminal offence for a person to unlawfully obtain abortifacients for themselves—online, for example—and to self-administer them, prosecutions are rare in Great Britain. They only tend to take place where abortifacients are self-administered *later* in pregnancy (Sheldon 2016b; Milne 2020; Milne 2021b). There have also been few prosecutions of doctors for failing to comply with the AA 1967. The lawfulness of abortion depends on whether doctors, acting in good faith, *believe* a pregnant person's circumstances to satisfy one of the grounds in the AA 1967, not whether they actually do (Jackson 2001). It is notoriously difficult to prove that doctors did not form their opinion in good faith (Harpwood 1996; Sheldon 1997). That there are few prosecutions does not detract from the status of abortion as 'exceptionalised', but might be described as a buffer against the effects of it being marked out as distinct from other aspects of healthcare.

Further, there is a reluctance on the part of juries to convict and judges to uphold a conviction under the OAPA 1861 where it is not immediately obvious that the doctor was knowingly and deliberately behaving 'criminally' (Romanis 2020b). In one case, the Court of Appeal overturned a doctor's conviction for unlawful procurement of miscarriage, explicitly stating that 'a verdict against a doctor is likely to be unsafe' where their actions were not clearly in violation of the reasonable boundaries of good medical practice.[51] Nevertheless, that abortion is a crime in Great Britain perpetuates stigma surrounding ending a pregnancy, and deems such care 'nonessential' in marginalising the practice from the rest of healthcare—even if the crime is almost never prosecuted. Cook explains that '[c]riminal abortion, like crime generally, is a legal and social construct […] [t]he criminal essence of abortion then implicates the social construction of those who actually and potentially seek abortion and those who provide and assist in its provision. By framing abortion as a crime, societies ascribe deviance to those seeking and providing it' (2014, 348–9). The criminal law instils a concept of electiveness in making the decision to terminate abnormal.

Abortion is further exceptionalised in that it is an area in which Parliament has expressly intervened in the doctor-patient relationship, specifically to install the doctor as the decision maker where there is no reason to presuppose that the person seeking care does not have capacity to make decisions. That abortions are only available in a certain set of circumstances is at odds with the primacy that is increasingly afforded to patient autonomy in UK healthcare law (Jackson 2000). An

---

[49] Ibid, s.2. Doctors who practice in the UK must be registered with the General Medical Council (and hold a licence to practise).

[50] Both persons (if the person receiving treatment is actually pregnant) would be guilty of offences under the OAPA 1861, sections 58 and 59.

[51] *R v Smith* (n38), at 1516 per Scarman LJ.

adult patient with capacity is legally entitled to accept, refuse, or choose any treatment that is clinically indicated for any or no reason based on their own preferences and values.[52] The law affords the patient 'an absolute right to choose whether to consent to medical treatment, to refuse it or to choose one rather than another of the treatments being offered'.[53] Further, the right to make one's own autonomous decisions about one's health 'exists notwithstanding that the reasons for making the choice are rational or irrational, unknown or even non-existent'.[54] As Lady Hale observed in 2015: 'Gone are the days when it was thought that, on becoming pregnant, a woman lost, not only her capacity, but also her right to act as a genuinely autonomous human being'.[55]

The AA 1967, however, adopts a different approach, in that it only allows people to choose to end their pregnancy in circumstances that have been deemed 'rational' by the legislature. Sheldon (1997) argues that the grounds in the AA 1967, which constitute the circumstances in which termination is legally 'justifiable', are constructed in a way that reinforces the norm of maternity on female bodies. A female cannot reject their destiny of motherhood, but they can reject a particular pregnancy where the state has deemed the circumstances such that they might not make the 'best' mother (Sheldon 1997). Jackson notes that whilst it is possible to argue that the AA 1967 is merely a 'harmless legal fiction because in practice doctors usually just give their approval for decisions that have already been taken' by the pregnant person for whatever reason, this is not quite right (2001, 81). It remains the case that people must explain their circumstances in a way that satisfies their doctor that their circumstances fit within those described in the Act. There are no other areas of healthcare where patients are, by virtue of legal requirements, required to present their case for treatment in particular terms to be permitted treatment. This requirement in the case of abortion can sometimes lead the doctor to mould a consultation so that the patient's experiences are discussed into the terms required by the Act. Lohr and colleagues have expressed concern about the extent to which the AA 1967 encourages the consultation to be focused on creating 'narratives which fit into the legal framework' (2020, 45). This could come at the expense of discussion that would better benefit the patient's wellbeing. That the abortion must be explained in this way perpetuates stigma, but also potentially prevents honest and open discussion between patient and provider. Abortion is also treated differently from other aspects of healthcare in that it is not treated as a private matter between patient and doctor. Abortion law, in requiring the patient's reasons and situation preceding their choice to match those deemed permissible by the legislature, and to be validated by a medical professional, is entirely out of step with the approach taken elsewhere in healthcare law.

The AA 1967 specifically installs the doctor as a gatekeeper to abortion (Sheldon 1997; Keown 1998), which has entrenched an uncomfortable power dynamic in the abortion decision that might affect the consultation (Lohr et al. 2020). We will

---

[52] *Re T (Adult: Refusal of Treatment)* [1993] Fam 95; *Montgomery* (n8).
[53] *Re T* (n52), at 102 per Lord Donaldson.
[54] Ibid.
[55] *Montgomery* (n8), at para 116 per Lady Hale.

discuss the impact that this has on access in Chapter 3. We raise it here to highlight that this is another way in which abortion is legally 'exceptionalised'. In modern medicine and the law, the tendency is to conceptualise the relationship between the doctor and patient when it comes to making decisions as a partnership (Cave and Milo 2020). In this partnership, the doctor is responsible for providing the necessary information to a patient about potential treatment alternatives,[56] and the risks and benefits associated with each,[57] such that the patient can decide for themselves based on their values and preferences. Whilst the doctor provides expert information about the clinically appropriate options,[58] it is the patient who is the decision maker. Sheldon emphasises that the AA 1967, however, reinforces a problematic notion that doctors remain the best judges of people's reproductive decisions, 'even when the abortion decision involves not an understanding of medical factors so much as a close knowledge or scrutiny of the woman's broader environment and her ability to cope as a mother within it' (2014, 195). Whilst the AA 1967 is subject to 'increasingly liberal interpretation by doctors' (Sheldon 2014, 195) and there has been some legal recognition that the perspective of the person seeking treatment must 'be at the heart of the matter' if medical practitioners are 'to arrive at a decision in good faith',[59] the AA 1967 still prevents doctors from completely centring the patient to comply with legal requirements. It remains a clear demarcation of abortion, compared to other areas of healthcare, that a patient's decision to have an abortion is not lawful by virtue of their informed consent alone, but by their doctor's determination that the abortion is appropriate in line with a fixed list made by politicians in the 1960s.

2.2 Northern Ireland

The AA 1967 has never applied in Northern Ireland. As such, until 2019, the only statutes governing abortion were the OAPA 1861 (and the offences therein already described) and the Criminal Justice (Northern Ireland) Act 1945, which, mirroring the Infant Life (Preservation) Act 1929 in England and Wales, criminalised the intentional destruction of a 'child capable of being born alive'.[60] Before 2019, abortion was only lawfully permissible in Northern Ireland where the common law had carved out exceptions to the crime of procurement of miscarriage. The *Bourne* defence at common law[61] applied in Northern Ireland. However, the defence was much more narrowly understood when applied by judges in Northern Irish cases. Abortion was not found unlawful for the purposes of the OAPA 1861 where it

---

[56] *Montgomery* (n8), at para 46 per Lords Kerr and Reed.
[57] Ibid.
[58] The law still broadly recognises that the doctor can define the relevant treatment options based on what is clinically appropriate. The question of whether they have identified the clinically appropriate options might still be determined by reference to whether the options they identify would be 'accepted as proper by a responsible body of medical men skilled in this particular art': *Bolam v. Friern Hospital Management Committee* [1957] 1 WLR 583, at 587 per McNair J.
[59] *Paton v British Pregnancy Advisory Service Trustees* [1979] QB 276, at 281 per Baker P.
[60] S.25.
[61] *Bourne* (n29).

could be established that continuing the pregnancy constituted a real and serious risk[62] to the pregnant person's health that would be permanent or long term[63] (Fox and McGuinness 2018; Fox and Horgan 2020). These decisions all set a higher bar than that initially outlined in *Bourne*. The effect of the law was such that abortion was only available in narrowly defined circumstances. Abortion was rarely performed in Northern Ireland because pregnant people and their doctors risked prosecution—and life imprisonment if found guilty. Fox and Horgan (2020) explain that, following devolution in 1999, a culture of fear was instilled by government guidance that reiterated the criminality of, and punishment for, healthcare professionals (HCPs) providing abortion. This produced a chilling effect, rendering abortion highly inaccessible. From 2015, several high-profile prosecutions of women who had obtained abortifacients online and self-administered them further entrenched this culture of fear (Fox and McGuinness 2018). This was in stark contrast to the situation in Great Britain where abortion had been made readily available by the AA 1967, and prosecutions were rare in those few instances where people ordered abortifacients online and self-administered them. Until 2019, Northern Ireland had one of the most restrictive legal responses to abortion in Europe, and people in Northern Ireland had no access to care unless they had the means to travel to another country (usually England).

In 2019, abortion was *partially* decriminalised, as the Northern Ireland (Executive Formation etc) Act 2019 repealed sections 58 and 59 of the OAPA 1861 in Northern Ireland.[64] It remains a criminal offence for any person (other than the pregnant person themselves) to abort a pregnancy that results in the death of a fetus 'capable of being born alive'.[65] Of course, this does not criminalise EMA, as the fetus will not be 'capable of being born alive' in the first trimester. In 2020, new abortion regulations came into force in Northern Ireland.[66] They introduce a new criminal offence: the termination of a pregnancy other than in accordance with the regulations.[67] Notably, this offence is not committed by the pregnant person who has a termination, or by a HCP where the termination is performed outside of requirements specified in the regulations (for example, in a place not specifically approved for abortion care) where the HCP forms the opinion in good faith that this is necessary for the preservation of the pregnant person's life or prevention of 'grave, permanent injury' to their physical or mental health.[68]

---

[62] *Re AMNH* [1994] NIJB 1.

[63] *Western Health and Social Services Board v CMB* [1995] NI High Court, unreported 29 September 1995.

[64] S.9(2).

[65] Criminal Justice (Northern Ireland) Act 1945, s.25 as amended by The Abortion (Northern Ireland) (No. 2) Regulations 2020, regulation 13. The 2020 amendment to this offence distinguishes it from that contained in the Infant Life (Preservation) Act 1929 in England and Wales.

[66] The Abortion (Northern Ireland) Regulations 2020 came into force on 31 March 2020 and were later replaced by the Abortion (Northern Ireland) (No. 2) Regulations 2020 on 14 May 2020. There are no major substantive differences between the two sets of regulations, with the second set being introduced for procedural reasons concerning parliamentary time and resources. Chapter 4 provides a more detailed discussion of the procedural aspects of the regulations' introduction.

[67] The Abortion (Northern Ireland) (No. 2) Regulations 2020, regulation 11(1).

[68] Ibid, regulation 11(2).

The grounds for termination provided in the regulations broadly mirror those of the AA 1967 in Great Britain, with some notable exceptions.[69] Part 2 of the regulations provides the grounds for terminations that have gestational limits. Regulation 4(1) enables a registered medical professional to provide a termination where two registered medical professionals are of the opinion, formed in good faith, that the pregnancy has not exceeded 24 weeks, and that 'the continuance of the pregnancy would involve risk of injury to the physical or mental health of the pregnant woman which is greater than if the pregnancy were terminated'. Regulation 4(2) requires that registered medical professionals take account of the person's actual or reasonably foreseeable circumstances—reminiscent of section 1(1)(a) of the AA 1967. Interestingly, however, the Northern Irish regulations are more permissive of EMA than the AA 1967, with regulation 3 stipulating that 'a registered medical professional may terminate a pregnancy where a registered medical professional is of the opinion, formed in good faith, that the pregnancy has not exceeded its 12th week'. Abortion can thus lawfully be provided with the involvement of just *one* registered medical professional, and without justification based on stipulated grounds.

Regulation 8 provides further conditions as to where terminations must be carried out to comply with the regulations (preventing HCPs from committing an offence under regulation 11). Treatment must be provided in general practitioners' premises, health and social care clinics and hospitals, or (*only* for misoprostol) in the patient's home. The Department of Health may also approve further places for treatment.[70] There is more detail provided here than in the AA 1967, largely, we imagine, because lessons have been learnt about more places, outside of hospitals, where abortion can be safely provided. Evolution from the AA 1967 can also be seen in the Northern Irish regulations in *who* can provide abortion care. Whilst the AA 1967 is explicit that there must be a doctor providing or supervising care,[71] the Northern Ireland regulations define a registered medical professional that provides or supervises care as a registered medical practitioner, registered nurse, or registered midwife.[72]

As noted, some aspects of the regulation of abortion in Northern Ireland, particularly regarding EMA, can be considered an evolution of the AA 1967: the regulations allow abortion on demand until 12 weeks' gestation; they create no criminal liability for service users (even where a person accesses EMA outside the parameters of the regulations); home use of misoprostol is explicitly approved; and nurse/midwife prescription of EMA is lawful. However, abortion is still subject to a unique regulatory regime, set apart from other aspects of healthcare for special attention. This still has the effect of exceptionalising abortion in the sense of perpetuating the stigma that surrounds abortion as 'different' from other healthcare, but also in continuing to limit the when, where, why, and how of abortion care in many of the same ways as the AA 1967 in Great Britain.

---

[69] There is insufficient space here to outline all differences on matters beyond EMA. For example, differences in how the grounds for abortion based on fetal abnormality are defined.

[70] The Abortion (Northern Ireland) (No. 2) Regulations 2020, regulation 8.

[71] 'Registered medical practitioner'.

[72] The Abortion (Northern Ireland) (No. 2) Regulations 2020, regulation 2(2). The Explanatory Memorandum to the regulations makes clear the precise choice of language. This is discussed in more detail in Chapter 3.

2.3 United States

Following the Supreme Court case of *Roe*,[73] abortion is constitutionally protected by the right to privacy under the Fourteenth Amendment in the US. *Roe* was decided in a public health context, much like debates surrounding the AA 1967 in Great Britain. Hospitals in the US were treating many abortion-related complications where procedures had been unlawfully provided outside of the healthcare system. Death from abortion was common, especially amongst people of colour (Goodwin 2020). *Roe* constituted some relief for people experiencing unwanted pregnancies, and the 1970s saw a substantial decline in morbidity and mortality associated with clandestine abortion (Cates, Grimes, and Schulz 2003).

Despite the constitutional protection of abortion following *Roe*, this right is best described as a 'mish-mash' (Goodwin 2020, 53), because access to abortion is governed by law at both federal and state level. Many states have passed laws, within parameters set by the Supreme Court, that place substantial obstacles in the path of a person seeking abortion. *Roe* recognised that persons have a limited right to terminate a pregnancy (a negative right based on limiting state interference), though this was qualified by a state's interest in protecting fetal life after viability such that states 'may go so far as to proscribe abortion during that period [after fetal viability], except when it is necessary to preserve the life or health of the mother'.[74] *Roe* was specific that as well as having a right to choose, individuals also have a right to 'obtain abortion' without undue influence from the state. This is properly understood as a negative right because there is no obligation that the state facilitate access, only that they do not legislate to ban abortion. It has been speculated that abortion has become so exceptionalised that it is in no way recognised as a medical matter, but instead as a prominent political issue. Thomson-Philbrook (2014) suggests that this conceptualisation of abortion as political occurred as a direct result of the fact that abortion was declared to be a right exclusively accessed by women (and people with female reproductive physiology). There is a near constant flurry of legal challenges to the constitutional status of the abortion right, which—in some parts of the US—has only increased over time.

Almost two decades after *Roe*, in *Planned Parenthood v. Casey*,[75] the Supreme Court was charged with determining the constitutionality of the Pennsylvania Abortion Control Act of 1982, which introduced several provisions regulating abortion before viability, including a requirement for the patient to confirm that their spouse was aware of the procedure. The Court upheld the construction of a person's constitutional right to privacy as encompassing a right to terminate a pregnancy, but equally recognised that the state had an interest in the fetus *before* viability.[76] The judgment emphasises that 'viability marks the earliest point at which the State's interest in fetal life is constitutionally adequate to justify a legislative ban on nontherapeutic abortions'.[77] However, it acknowledges that there can be other legislative interventions in

---

[73] *Roe* (n21).
[74] Ibid, at 163–4.
[75] *Casey* (n22).
[76] Ibid, at 846.
[77] Ibid, at 860.

the abortion decision at any point in pregnancy. In fact, the Court was explicit that *Roe* had 'undervalued the State's interest in potential life in practice' (Soares 2006, 1101). In this sense, *Casey* made a significant departure from *Roe*. The approach to the constitutionality of abortion in the US is now one of a balancing of rights—that of the person's privacy and that of the state to protect fetal life. The status of abortion as merely a negative right is further reinforced to the degree that states have no duty to enable the realisation of an individual's right to abortion before viability. Following *Casey*, states can legislate about abortion at any point in gestation provided that the law does not in 'purpose or effect [...] place a substantial obstacle in the path of a woman seeking an abortion before the fetus attains viability'.[78] The constitutionality of a law regulating abortion turns on whether the law constitutes an undue burden for people seeking abortion prior to viability. This test is applied as a subjective assessment of the facts at issue. The *Casey* decision emphasises that, in considering whether any state law constitutes an undue burden on abortion access, '[t]he proper focus of constitutional inquiry is the group for whom the law is a restriction, not the group for whom the law is irrelevant'.[79] *Casey* clearly further increased the role of judicial interpretation in determining the boundaries of the abortion right (Winkler 2020, 19), which has resulted in some lower courts being willing to apply a deferential standard to uphold laws that 'insert the state into a doctor's relationship with her patient for ideological reasons' (Borgmann 2014, 1077). Thus, the undue burden test, as a way of assessing state laws, has left abortion more susceptible to restriction (Soares 2006, 1104).

The undue burden test has been widely criticised for opening the door 'for state legislatures' exceptional treatment of abortion, as they have piled on restrictions not applied to other medical procedures' (Borgmann 2014, 1086). Goodwin notes that *Casey* welcomed in a 'new era in antiabortion strategy – legislating TRAP [targeted regulation of abortion providers] laws' (2020, 69), which are intended to limit access to abortion. Targeted regulations include what might be termed 'demand-side' laws (Joyce 2011), which seek to regulate the individual seeking abortion and encourage a change of mind—for example, mandatory waiting periods. They also include 'supply-side' laws that regulate abortion providers, such as requirements about the gestational limits of provision and, more specifically, the locations of clinics or their resources (Joyce 2011). In states that are determined to limit access to abortion, the focus has shifted over time from 'demand-side' regulation towards 'supply-side' regulation because it is believed to be more effective (Joyce 2011). These laws intend to limit the capacity of clinics to provide care, and even to ensure that they shut, and in many cases are successful (see Chapter 3). Moreover, 'even where such laws do not succeed in shutting down all clinics [in the state], they aim to make abortion disfavoured in the law' (Borgmann 2014, 1063) by labelling abortion as outside the norm, or more explicitly as wrong (though lawful).

The permissibility of such legislative interventions targeting abortion, Goodwin explains, 'highlights and underscores the weaknesses in current Supreme Court jurisprudence' (2020, 70). *Gonzales v. Carhart*[80] in some ways epitomises how the undue

---

[78] Ibid, at 878.
[79] Ibid, at 894.
[80] 550 U.S. 124 (2007).

burden test does not adequately protect the right to abortion in practice. In *Gonzales*, a federal ban on D&E (which can be performed both pre- and post-viability—see Chapter 1) was upheld on the basis that it did not constitute an undue burden on a person's constitutional right to privacy, despite presented evidence that, in some circumstances, their health might be better preserved by the procedure compared to alternatives. It was held that the ban was pertinent to the federal government's goal to respect human dignity and that their pursuit of this objective 'may, directly, or tangentially, burden the abortion right' (Bridges 2010, 924). *Gonzales* seemingly marked a problematic shift in which the Supreme Court was willing to start from the presumption that a fetus, even pre-viability, is a 'life' that a state has an interest in respecting. In the balancing of rights, the scales are tipped further in favour of states in that it is a high bar to demonstrate that a measure is an 'undue burden' when measured against the 'interest' in fetal life.

More recently, in *Whole Women's Health v. Hellerstedt*,[81] the undue burden test was rearticulated in a way deemed to be a progressive step away from *Gonzales*. The Supreme Court in *Hellerstedt* was tasked with considering the constitutionality of a Texas law (HB2) introducing several supply-side regulations impacting clinics, including requirements that staff have admitting privileges to nearby hospitals and that clinics meet the same standards as surgical centres. The law in question, Goodwin observes, was an attempt to place 'so many barriers in the paths of women seeking abortion in Texas so as to render the right to terminate a pregnancy more illusory than real' (2017, 341). In making its determination, the Court stressed a two-stage test in assessing whether a law constituted an undue burden. As a first limb, it is necessary to consider whether, on the facts, the law has the effect of unduly impacting on pregnant people seeking access to abortion when considered against the potential benefits. In the judgment, Breyer J emphasises that the test from *Casey* 'requires that courts consider the burdens a law imposes on abortion access together with the benefits those laws confer'.[82] In *Hellerstedt*, the Court held that, based on the evidence presented, neither of the measures in HB2 were medically necessary.[83] Breyer J held that the medical evidence was conclusive that abortion was safe to the degree that neither measure had the benefit of better protecting people's health.[84] Both measures therefore constituted an undue burden because they resulted in a significant drop in the availability of care whilst affording little benefit.

The second limb of the test requires that the state's motivation for legislating—and whether they are in fact legislating to assert a legitimate interest—must be considered.[85] That the Court was willing to consider a state's motivations for legislating does seemingly present a step in the direction of ensuring appropriate protection of the constitutional right to choose, because it allows for greater scrutiny of TRAP laws. It has been argued that there are limited interests the Court would accept as legitimate

---

[81] 579 U.S. ___ (2016).

[82] Ibid, at 19.

[83] Ibid, at 32 per Breyer J: 'the record evidence thus supports the ultimate legal conclusion that the surgical-center requirement is not necessary'.

[84] The majority opinion paid close attention to evidence that emphasised the safety of abortion care, including peer-reviewed studies and expert testimony.

[85] *Hellerstedt* (n81), at 19 per Breyer J.

in this context: the health and safety of the pregnant person; to protect the medical profession or its integrity; and the promotion of fetal life (Feltrow 2018). However, even with only these motivations accepted as legitimate state interests, there is significant scope for laws that restrict access. Borgmann argues that laws that 'profess to make abortion safer are in fact an increasingly potent part of the arsenal anti-abortion-rights activists are employing in their fight to make abortion illegal' (2014, 1063).

Whilst *Hellerstedt* was a step towards more thorough interrogation of TRAP laws, Goodwin (2020) argues that it failed to move the abortion right forward. The judgment did not adequately recognise people's interest in ending unwanted pregnancies or their capacity in making the decision, and remained inattentive to the extent to which TRAP laws disproportionately discriminate along the lines of socioeconomic status and race (see Chapter 3). Most significantly, *Hellerstedt* 'rests on perpetuating the notion of abortion as a threat against women's physical and mental health' (Goodwin 2017, 342) in that it emphasises strongly that the potential benefits of laws must be considered. This is an implicit recognition that laws limiting access to abortion have benefits. It reinforces the notion of abortion as 'physiologically regrettable and potentially unsafe to such a degree that women [...] would benefit from' intervention (Goodwin 2017, 350). The unfortunate logic is that various restrictions that force people to rethink their decision, or that limit providers' ability to operate in particular ways, will benefit people because 'abortion is not a good thing for them'.

In 2020, the Supreme Court heard the much-anticipated *June Medical Services v. Russo*.[86] In advance of the decision there was disquiet amongst reproductive rights groups as this was the first case to be heard since the bench had become majority conservative (following the appointment of Justices Gorusuch and Kavanaugh in 2017 and 2018, respectively). Of particular concern, the facts of the case were similar to those of *Hellerstedt*, and so there was confusion as to why the case was being heard in the Supreme Court at all. This case also concerned a TRAP law that required practitioners providing abortion care in Louisiana to have admitting privileges at a hospital within a 30-mile radius of their clinic.[87] Much like in *Hellerstedt*, the legislative intent was not to bring a challenge specifically to the constitutional right to abortion, but to make abortion functionally impossible to access in the state. The District Court and Court of Appeal in Louisiana had both concluded that the admitting privileges requirement constituted a substantial burden in the path of those seeking abortion. In Louisiana, many hospitals are unwilling to offer admitting privileges to those working at abortion clinics. Winkler argues that, given the clear and established precedent that was directly applicable here, that the Court agreed to hear the case 'only after the conservative majority of the Court was strengthened reveals how insufficient separation of powers between the executive and judicial branches are eroding the rule of law' (2020, 17). The Court ultimately found that the law constituted an undue burden and struck it down as unconstitutional. Roberts J—who had dissented from the majority decision in *Hellerstedt*—in this case voted with his more liberal colleagues to follow the *Hellerstedt*[88] decision. Whilst *June Medical* might be viewed positively in that the

[86] 591 U.S. ___ (2020).
[87] Act 620—Unsafe Abortion Protection Act 2014.
[88] *Hellerstedt* (n81).

undue burden test was applied to ensure that this restriction was not upheld, there are still causes for concern.

First, there is a clear willingness in this Supreme Court to reconsider long-standing precedent regarding abortion. This is even more concerning following the 2020 appointment to the bench of Coney Barrett J, another conservative judge who is publicly antiabortion. Second, the case could represent a shift in jurisprudence that will disadvantage many people seeking access to abortion. As Fox, Cohen, and Adashi (2020) have highlighted, Roberts J suggested that a more appropriate application of the test in *Casey* was not to consider both the burdens and benefits of an abortion regulation, but merely to consider the burdens. Roberts J stipulated that this is because the balancing test asks the Court to weigh the state's interests in protecting potential human life and people's health on the one hand, against the values often held by those who believe abortion important for equality. He explained that 'there is no plausible sense in which anyone, let alone this Court, could objectively assign weight to such imponderable values and no meaningful way to compare them if there were'.[89] He further noted that the requirement to consider burdens against benefits is not present in the *Casey* decision as it focuses only on whether there was a substantial burden, rather than whether benefits were outweighed by the burdens. The opinion of Roberts J *potentially* paves the way for courts, going forward, to assume that a state's legislative intervention has benefits (or at least to deter them from examining legislative intentions since this is not thought necessary). It is unclear why this should be the case as we have seen that when the Court scrutinises TRAP laws, few have any benefit (intended or actual) on pregnant people's health and safety when accessing care. These laws often do not state their aim as discouraging abortion or promoting state interest in fetal life, and they will often explicitly state that their aim is to protect patient health and safety.[90] However, this is merely a pretext when they are, in effect, attempts to discourage abortion. If taken forward, this (even very slight) shift in the articulation of the undue burden test could have a significant impact on the kinds of decisions that are made by the Court in future. Assuming TRAP laws provide benefits could result in excessive state deference, and, as such, enable the continuation of the TRAP law strategy. It would also enable the upholding of laws like those in, for example, *Gonzales*, in which the available medical evidence indicates that the regulation is not necessary and/or is actively harmful. This sets abortion out as a form of medical care which the state can legitimately restrict access to, interfering with the patient's relationship with HCPs even where this does not actively promote better health outcomes.

Finally, Roberts J emphasised that he was bound by the common law rules of precedent to reach his conclusion in *June Medical*, because *Hellerstedt* concerned a similar Texas law. He places great emphasis on respect for precedent, and the legal and pragmatic benefits it brings, in his judgment. There is a clear feeling, however, that in other circumstances, even those that are not altogether that different, he would be willing to rule that the law did not constitute an undue burden. This Supreme Court continues to embolden TRAP strategy, and even where TRAP legislation is successfully challenged

---

[89] Ibid, at 6.
[90] Some states are more forthcoming that their TRAP laws are intended to favour childbirth over abortion (see Chapter 3).

it still causes problems at the level of care provision due to significant legal uncertainty. Moreover, litigating against this legislation constitutes a monumental financial burden on reproductive health organisations (Goodwin 2020).

The US legal framework can be summarised as the balancing of rights, but one that favours state legislatures. There is a (negative) constitutional right to abortion as part of the right to privacy, but there is no obligation on the state to facilitate access; there is an obligation only to ensure states do not legislate in such a way that places substantial obstacles in the path of a person seeking abortion. 'Undue burden' is interpreted by courts on the facts of the matter in front of them, and in so doing the Supreme Court may be willing, in future, to assume legislation restricting access to abortion (though less than an undue burden) will be of some benefit to service users, or some other state interest. Despite being recognised as a constitutional right, states are afforded broad discretion to limit access to abortion. Numerous states are extremely hostile to the abortion right protected by the Supreme Court's interpretation of the Constitution in *Roe*. Many pass TRAP laws regularly, including some related to telemedicine (see Chapter 9). At least some state legislatures enact TRAP legislation in the hope that it will come before the Supreme Court and lead to the overturning of *Roe*. There are 10 states that have passed laws specifically banning abortion if *Roe* is overturned in the Supreme Court.[91]

2.4 Summary

In both the UK and US abortion is exceptionalised—distinguished from other forms of healthcare for inappropriate reasons. In Great Britain, this is the result of abortion's special status as a crime, which provides only a doctor a defence when providing care in line with a certain set of conditions. That the doctor is framed as a gatekeeper in matters of a person's reproductive healthcare also sets abortion aside as distinct from the movement in UK law towards centring the patient as the decision maker when it comes to their own health. In Northern Ireland, the same might be said of how abortion is exceptionalised given that it remains a criminal offence for HCPs (but not the pregnant person themselves) to provide care outside of the parameters dictated by the 2020 regulations—though these regulations are in some ways more permissive than those in Great Britain. In the US, although there is a negative constitutional right to abortion, abortion is still exceptionalised in that this right has become increasingly diminished with the development of a highly unique set of constitutional rules allowing state legislatures to implement TRAP laws. The Supreme Court's decisions, combined with the current political climate, have granted state legislatures the power 'to construct the types of proxies for constitutional obstructionism and discrimination' (Goodwin 2017, 351). Abortion is uniquely recognised as an instance in which states do not always have to prove their motivations in interfering with people's private lives.

In the next chapter, we highlight the socio-legal barriers to the provision of EMA in the UK and US. These restrictions have their roots in abortion exceptionalism. That

---

[91] Arkansas, Idaho, Kentucky, Louisiana, Mississippi, Missouri, North Dakota, South Dakota, Tennessee, and Utah.

abortion is treated as distinct from other healthcare, and is subject to increased surveillance in the law, prevents it from being recognised as normal and essential care. This is an expression of structural violence manifesting, in a very real way, in control exerted over the bodies of people with the physiology to become pregnant (Nandagiri et al. 2020).

3
Socio-legal barriers to early medical abortion

In the previous chapter, we detailed how the legal frameworks regulating abortion in the UK and the US are predicated on 'abortion exceptionalism'. In this chapter, we demonstrate how exceptionalism has erected legal barriers to abortion in regulating the when, where, who, and how of abortion in the UK and US. The barriers presented are not exhaustive. We point to those resulting directly from exceptionalism, and that have, arguably, the most significant impact on abortion access.

Whilst the AA 1967 is, 'in large measure [...] working well' in Great Britain to extend people's access to safe and legal abortion (Priaulx and Jones 2018, 281), the medical model the Act embodies erects barriers to access, and the effective organisation of service provision. We do not (and cannot) know how many people in Great Britain are unable to access abortion because of legal barriers, but there is evidence that people are accessing abortifacients online due to access concerns (Aiken et al. 2018). The new legislative framework introduced in Northern Ireland is in some ways more progressive than the AA 1967, but it maintains significant legal barriers to care. In the US, abortion is protected only as a negative constitutional right. Consequently, federal and state laws that limit access to abortion are permissible, so long as they do not place an 'undue burden' on those seeking access.[92] The crux of the matter is that federal and state legislatures pass laws that *do* interfere with a person's access by placing (largely procedural) requirements in the path of people seeking care. Legal barriers to abortion access vary significantly between states.

We also highlight how social factors and circumstances intersect with the law to further limit access to care, even where abortion is legal. Whilst a legal framework that permits abortion is important, it is on its own insufficient (Ross and Solinger 2017). Attention must be paid to broader social conditions of persons experiencing unwanted pregnancy to ensure that they are *actually* able to access care that they are entitled to. We therefore consider some of the relevant social factors limiting access, including geography and socioeconomics. Considering how legal rules operate against their social context allows us to review the extent to which abortion is both available and accessible, because the 'law is a living thing, which needs to be studied as it is interpreted and takes effect in practice, rather than merely as it exists on the statute books' (Sheldon et al. 2019, 19–20). Understanding how the law intersects with broader structural factors will also aid our discussion throughout this book in examining how abortion access can be improved with telemedicine.

There have long existed inequities in accessing abortion that impact on people differently along axes of socioeconomics, race, and other factors; these inequities 'are sustained and reproduced by the underlying historical, social, political and cultural

---

[92] *Casey* (n22).

Early Medical Abortion, Equality of Access, and the Telemedical Imperative. Jordan A. Parsons and Elizabeth Chloe Romanis, Oxford University Press. © Oxford University Press 2021. DOI: 10.1093/oso/9780192896155.003.0003

contexts that shape access to [sexual and reproductive health]. Collectively, these entrenched inequalities and fault lines are "structural violence" ' (Nandagiri et al. 2020, 83). This violence is experienced in the denial of care and the perpetuation of abortion stigma at the intersection of law and social structures.

3.1 When pregnant people can receive care . . .

3.1.1 . . . in the United Kingdom

The AA 1967 does not afford people in Great Britain access to lawful abortion 'on demand'. In reality—as explained in the previous chapter—most pregnancies before 24 weeks are legally terminable because the risks associated with childbirth are always more significant. In fact, the Act specifies only that the doctor is satisfied that in their opinion the pregnant person's circumstances fit the statutory grounds for abortion—not on whether they actually do (Jackson 2001). There is considerable deference in the law towards the professional discretion of doctors in determining whether abortion is terminable under the AA 1967—especially section 1(1)(a). We can see this in that few prosecutions are brought against doctors under the OAPA 1861, and where questions are raised about the legality of abortions provided by doctors there is significant judicial deference to medical judgement about the appropriateness of abortion (Sheldon 1997; Brazier and Cave 2016; Romanis 2020b; Romanis 2020d). In the *Paton* judgment, it was remarked that any judge who interfered with the discretion of doctors to provide abortion under the AA 1967 would be both 'bold and foolish' except where there were a clear 'and obvious attempt to perpetuate a criminal offence'.[93]

More recently, there have been instances in which the judiciary have made more pointed remarks about how the medical discretion in the AA 1967 is exercised. In the sentencing of Sarah Catt, found guilty of criminal miscarriage for self-administering abortifacient medication later in her pregnancy, Cooke J remarked that the AA 1967 is often, 'wrongly, liberally construed in practice so as to make abortion essentially on demand prior to 24 weeks with the approval of medical practitioners'.[94] This is illustrative of some hostility towards the broad exercise of medical discretion (Sheldon 2014, 106). Further, whilst abortion is readily lawful earlier in a pregnancy, section 1(1)(a) still constructs a legal barrier to services because individuals must justify their abortion in terms that satisfy two doctors that their circumstances fall within those deemed legally permissible.

Whilst there is no indication that medical professionals *are* refusing to provide EMA on the grounds that they believe a person's reasons are inadequate, it remains concerning that this is one area of healthcare in which medical professionals are *required* to examine a person's social circumstances and reasons for making a particular decision. We noted in the previous chapter that this step—being completely separate from the doctor's responsibility to ensure that the patient has necessary information about the nature of abortion to make a decision—is wholly out of step with the requirements

[93] Paton (n59), at 282 per Baker P.
[94] *R v Sarah Louise Catt*, Sentencing Remarks (Crown Court Leeds, 17 September 2012), at para 15.

of informed consent in healthcare law.[95] There is the potential for interference with a person's access to abortion in the rare event that a doctor were to refuse to certify that a person's abortion was sought—or was permissible—on health grounds. That the law enables this possibility, even if it is not something that we believe HCPs are regularly doing, is concerning. As Sheldon notes, 'the limitations of the medical frame as a basis for defending and furthering women's reproductive rights should nonetheless be apparent [...] the provision of abortion services remains restricted by clinically unnecessary requirements' (2014, 207).

Since the introduction of new regulations in Northern Ireland in 2020, access to abortion before 12 weeks need no longer be contingent on the abortion being framed in health terms. This is an important step towards the recognition that abortion is normal and is usually sought for personal and social reasons. It also better ensures that there are not unnecessary legal barriers in the path of persons seeking abortion. After 12 weeks, however, the same concerns described in respect of Great Britain are applicable for people seeking abortion in Northern Ireland. The requirements in the 2020 regulations for abortion between 12 weeks and one day and 24 weeks mirror those in section 1(1)(a) of the AA 1967.[96]

In addition to the legal requirement that there be a socio-medical reason for an abortion, there are also legal limitations on the gestational age at which the two abortion medications can be administered in the UK. Where one or both abortion medications are to be administered in the pregnant person's home, in England and Wales the pregnancy must not have exceeded nine weeks and six days.[97] In Northern Ireland, where the second abortion medication is to be taken at home the pregnancy must not have exceeded 10 weeks.[98] These limitations might, in some circumstances, present a barrier to access, specifically where there is a delay in accessing care that might result from a number of circumstances discussed later in this chapter. In Scotland, the situation is slightly more complicated, as neither the 2017 approval order (see Chapter 4) nor the 2020 approval order (see Chapter 8) stipulates a gestational limit. Both Scottish approval orders are accompanied by professional guidance that contains a gestational limit—nine weeks and six days in 2017 (Scottish Government Chief Medical Officer Directorate 2017), and 11 weeks and six days in 2020 (Scottish Government Chief Medical Officer Directorate 2020). In a legal challenge, it was noted that such guidance does not form part of the approval order and can, therefore, be departed from by doctors.[99] Whilst there is no reason to believe that doctors would act outside of the professional guidance, it appears that there is nothing in law preventing the provision of mifepristone and misoprostol for home use in Scotland up to 24 weeks' gestation (the only technical legal constraint being section 1 of the AA 1967). We will proceed

---

[95] *Montgomery* (n8).

[96] The Abortion (Northern Ireland) (No. 2) Regulations 2020, regulation 4.

[97] The requirement is the same in the 2018 approval orders in both England and Wales that allow home use of misoprostol only (Department of Health and Social Care 2018a; Welsh Government 2018a), and in the 2020 temporary approval orders in both England and Wales that allow home use of mifepristone and misoprostol (Department of Health and Social Care 2020c; Welsh Government 2020).

[98] The Abortion (Northern Ireland) (No. 2) Regulations 2020, regulation 8(2)(c).

[99] *SPUC Pro-Life Scotland Limited v Scottish Ministers* [2018] CSOH 85. This legal challenge was to the 2017 approval order, but the same point of law regarding the accompanying guidance would—we suggest— be equally applicable to the 2020 approval.

on the basis of a professionally respected gestational limit of 11 weeks and seven days in Scotland.

3.1.2   ... in the United States

Several US states that have created substantial barriers by passing 'demand-side' TRAP laws, designed to regulate when a person can have an abortion (Joyce 2011). The most common of which, termed 'informed consent requirements' (see Table 3.1), are often enacted in statutes called 'Women's Right to Know' Acts. These laws mandate that, before abortion, pregnant people are informed about alternatives to abortion, and information about the abortion, in ways that are intended to propagate the state's (constitutionally recognised) interest in promoting childbirth over abortion,[100] rather than aiding people in making an informed decision. These provisions require that pregnant people be instructed directly by their doctor, directed to state websites, and/or provided with printed materials that contain the following information:

- That there exist state medical assistance benefits for prenatal care and childbirth;
- That local services provide medical and financial support for prenatal care and for new parents (in some states, contact information for these agencies must be provided);
- That the other genetic parent will be legally required to pay child support (in some states, it must be specified that this is the case even if that person offers to pay for abortion);
- A list of local adoption agencies; and
- That adoptive parents can assist with the costs of pregnancy and childbirth.

In some states, directive statements are made about pregnant people engaging with support or adoption agencies. In Alabama, for example, preabortion materials must include the following statement: 'The State of Alabama strongly urges you to contact those agencies before making a final decision about abortion'.[101]

So-called 'informed consent laws' also stipulate that biased information be given about the process of abortion itself, and the potential implications of abortion. In many states, it is compulsory that information be provided about the physiological development of fetuses throughout gestation, in many cases using colour photographs. This often includes a description of 'the probable anatomical and physiological characteristics of the unborn child *at the time* [emphasis added] the abortion is to be performed'.[102] Some states even include information about fetal pain in provided materials.[103] Much of the information people must be provided with about fetal development for consent to be (legally) considered informed, however, is inaccurate.

---

[100] *Casey* (n22).
[101] AL Code §26-23A-5(a)(7) (2019).
[102] KS Stat §65-6709 (2019).
[103] For example, in Georgia: GA Code §31-9A-3 (2019), and Louisiana: LA Rev Stat §40:1061.17 (2019).

Table 3.1 Demand-side TRAP laws in the United States[1]

Legal barrier	States implementing	
Informed consent requirement (biased materials)	Alabama, Alaska, Arizona, Arkansas, Florida, Georgia, Idaho, Indiana, Iowa, Kansas, Kentucky, Louisiana, Michigan, Minnesota, Mississippi, Missouri, Nebraska, North Carolina, North Dakota, Ohio, Oklahoma, Pennsylvania, South Carolina, South Dakota, Tennessee, Texas, Utah, West Virginia, and Wisconsin	
Mandatory waiting period	*18 hours:*	Indiana
	24 hours:	Arizona, Florida, Georgia, Idaho, Kansas, Kentucky, Michigan, Minnesota, Mississippi, Nebraska, North Dakota, Ohio, Pennsylvania, South Carolina, Texas, West Virginia, and Wisconsin
	48 hours:	Alabama, and Tennessee
	72 hours:	Arkansas, Iowa, Louisiana, Missouri, North Carolina, Oklahoma, and Utah
	72+ hours:	South Dakota

[1]The sources of these regulations are detailed in Appendix 3.

A 2013 study that reviewed informed consent materials from states with such requirements found that 31% of statements about fetal development were 'medically inaccurate'. Inaccurate statements were disproportionately about development in the earliest weeks of pregnancy (Daniels et al. 2016, 191).

The language used in the legal requirements, which is often provided for verbatim use, is loaded. This is sometimes implicit, for example referring to the 'unborn child' rather than the 'fetus', which might be an attempt to elicit a particular conception of the fetus and evoke a certain emotional response. In many states, the direction on this is more explicit. In Missouri, for example, abortion counselling materials must include the statement: 'The life of each human being begins at conception. Abortion will terminate the life of a separate, unique, living human being'.[104]

There are also requirements that people be informed of risks to *themselves*. In Kansas, for example, people must be informed of 'risk of premature birth in future pregnancies, risk of breast cancer and risks to the woman's reproductive health'.[105] Empirical evidence suggests no link between medical abortion and preterm birth in subsequent pregnancies (Malosso et al. 2018) or breast cancer (Collaborative Group on Hormonal Factors in Breast Cancer 2004). Lohr and colleagues note that asserting a causal relationship between abortion and longer-term health outcomes is dubious because abortion is generally under-recorded, and there are many (impossible to quantify) confounding factors that can determine future pregnancy or health outcomes (2020, 42). In Michigan, pregnant people must be informed that abortion results in

[104] MO Rev Stat §188.027(2) (2019).
[105] KS Stat §65-6709(3) (2019).

some people experiencing 'depression, feelings of guilt, sleep disturbance, loss of interest in work or sex, or anger'.[106] This statement lacks appropriate situational nuance, including acknowledgement that mental health issues after abortion are no more likely than following the continuation of unwanted pregnancy (Major et al. 2009). As Dickens (2014) observes such a statement is predicated on the alleged condition 'post-abortion syndrome', for which there is little scientific support. It is 'deeply problematic for the state to mandate that physicians provide inaccurate medical information to a patient' (Daniels et al. 2016, 201). 'Informed consent' requirements in the US are in stark contrast to the standard in the UK. In the UK, a person will be considered to have given informed consent to abortion where they understand the medical information necessary to consent to the procedure.[107]

Whilst these requirements do not literally prevent a person from choosing abortion, forcing a person to engage with biased counselling can become a barrier to abortion by interfering with individuals' decision making. The overwhelming majority of people seeking abortion are sure of their decision soon after realising they are pregnant (Rowlands 2008), and before they make contact with a provider (Gatter et al. 2014). For those who are uncertain, biased counselling can be catastrophic. It prevents individuals from making a decision that aligns with their own values and subjective preferences based on *accurate* information. Further, biased counselling is associated with an increased negative emotional response in those who choose abortion after counselling (Berglas et al. 2017).

These requirements were introduced and are enforced with the intention of persuading people *not* to have an abortion. In Louisiana, the legislature specified that the purpose of the informed consent provisions is to 'protect unborn children from a woman's uninformed decision to have an abortion'.[108] These laws are, in substance and effect, a deliberate attempt to erect a barrier to care, because a person must listen to antiabortion narratives about having an abortion. To describe such requirements as being necessary to ensure an individual's informed consent is, at best, disingenuous. The information that must be supplied is either misleading (and thus a danger to the procuring of true consent), or unnecessary to obtain informed consent. Further, when the information being delivered feels hostile to the pregnant person's subjective experience, this can make it more difficult for them to raise any concerns that they may have. Again, this reduces the likelihood of truly informed consent.

The Supreme Court has held that the 'Women's Right to Know' laws are constitutional because they enable states to assert a legitimate interest. In *Danforth*,[109] it was emphasised that it was 'desirable and imperative' for pregnant people to make the decision about abortion 'with full knowledge of its nature and consequences'.[110] Equally, in *Casey*, the Court found that informed counselling measures 'should not be invalidated if their purpose is to persuade the woman to choose childbirth over abortion',[111] and that states could introduce laws that they believe to be necessary to ensure that

---

[106] MI Comp L §§333.17015(11)(b)(iii) (2019).
[107] *Montgomery* (n8).
[108] LA Rev Stat §40:1061.17(A)(5)(b) (2019).
[109] *Planned Parenthood v. Danforth*, 428 U.S. 52 (1976).
[110] Ibid, at 67.
[111] *Casey* (n22), at 878.

a decision to abort was 'thoughtful and informed'.[112] As such, biased counselling requirements continue to constitute a real barrier to access to, and informed decision making about, abortion in much of the US.

An additional barrier often enacted alongside biased counselling requirements is a mandatory waiting time between counselling and treatment. All states with a mandatory waiting period also have counselling requirements, so these waiting periods are an extension of the state interference into abortion decisions that the 'informed consent' provisions embody. Only two states have mandatory biased pre-abortion counselling with no accompanying waiting period.[113] Mandatory waiting times vary from 18 hours to 72 + hours (see Table 3.1). South Dakota has the most extreme waiting period (described as 72 + hours) because '[n]o Saturday, Sunday, or annually recurring holiday [...] may be included or counted in the calculation of the seventy-two hour minimum time period between the initial physician consultation and assessment and the time of the scheduled abortion procedure'.[114] Thus, if a person undergoes mandatory counselling on Friday at 4pm, they could not have their abortion until the following Wednesday at 4pm (and this is assuming that no public holidays fall in this time). This requirement appears premised on the absurd notion that people are incapable of making decisions about their personal life on nonworking days. Delays because of mandatory waiting periods are often reported as a source of extreme difficulty for many because individuals are forced to sit with biased information about abortion despite having already made their decision. This is exacerbated by desperation for the abortion to be over, the escalation of nervousness about the procedure, and feeling anxious or frustrated—many have even reported this resulting in physical symptoms, such as nausea/vomiting (Roberts et al. 2016). Further, 'forced waiting undermines women's agency and autonomous decision-making ability' as it infantilises their capacity for decision making (Rowlands and Thomas 2020, 581) and prevents them from accessing care quickly when this is their preference. In stark contrast to much of the US, in England and Wales, NICE advises providers *not* to require patients to undergo compulsory reflection time before abortion (2019, 1.1.8). This guidance portrays a sense of importance in providers ensuring that those who are seeking abortion do not exceed legal limits on care or become subject to an increased risk of complications, instead recommending that patients are only referred for support when they request it.

As well as increasing the stress a person experiences, these waiting periods constitute real barriers to care. In most cases, there are requirements that both the consultation and the treatment take place in the clinic,[115] which means that a person must make two trips. Many states rigorously enforce this. In Texas, the law is explicit that if the pregnant person lives within 100 miles of the clinic they must make two trips (one for counselling and one for treatment), and counselling materials can only be provided by post (meaning only one mandatory clinic visit) if the

---

[112] Ibid, at 916.

[113] Alaska and Iowa.

[114] SD Codified L §34-23A-56 (2019).

[115] There are exceptions, with some states allowing counselling to take place over the telephone or materials to be posted. In Chapter 9, we explore state laws regarding where abortions can take place in more detail.

person lives more than 100 miles from the clinic.[116] There is an observed correlation between the distance a person must travel and the time interval between their first appointment for counselling and second for treatment; the further the distance, the longer the interval between appointments (White et al. 2017). Travelling long distances to clinics presents substantial difficulties for many, which are only exacerbated by having to make the journey twice: managing the logistics of long trips to and from clinics; taking time off work; the cost of an overnight stay near the clinic; and making alternative arrangements for other responsibilities, such as childcare (Rouland et al. 2019). The further the distance a person has to travel, the more difficult it is for them to be able to do this twice in quick succession (White et al. 2017). The logistics of travel are most difficult for people from disadvantaged backgrounds who struggle to meet the costs, and who may find it much harder to get or afford time off work (Romanis et al. 2020a).

Waiting periods, and the difficulties they present, often create delays for people accessing abortion. This is especially problematic when delay takes the person beyond any legally-imposed gestational limits—they may then have fewer care pathway options or be denied abortion entirely (Rowlands and Thomas 2020). This can force people to access abortion through unlawful channels, which are more likely to impact negatively on their health (Hervey and Sheldon 2019, 126).

There are gestational limits on medical abortion that were introduced, and are enforced, at the federal level. The US Food and Drug Administration (FDA) has the authority, under the FDA Amendments Act 2007, to issue a 'Risk Evaluation and Mitigation Strategy' (REMS) to enforce a specific set of requirements on the use of a medication, including who can prescribe it and where it can be used, where necessary to ensure that the benefits of a medication outweigh its risks.[117] 'Elements to Assure Safe Use' can be imposed on specific drugs where they are shown to be effective, but because of their 'inherent toxicity or potential harmfulness' they are 'associated with a serious adverse drug experience'.[118] The FDA has a range of available enforcement mechanisms to ensure compliance, including inspections, withholding drug supply, and financial penalties. Of all the medications currently licensed on the US market, only 60 are subject to a REMS (United States Food and Drug Administration a)—including mifepristone. Even in states that do not have an anti-choice executive or legislature, the REMS restricts access.

This program requires that mifepristone only be administered prior to 10 weeks' (70 days') gestation (United States Food and Drug Administration 2019). This has a significant impact on people's access to medical abortion because 10 weeks can quickly pass in the time that a person takes to find out they are pregnant, and to surpass all of the requirements of demand-side TRAP laws—as well as supply-side TRAP laws that limit 'where' abortion can take place.

[116] TX Health & Safety Code §171.012 (2019).
[117] 21 U.S.C. §355-1(a)(1).
[118] Ibid, §355-1(f)(1)(A).

3.2 Where care can be provided . . .

3.2.1 . . . in the United Kingdom

In Great Britain, sections 1(3) and (3A) of the AA 1967[119] specify that treatment for the termination of pregnancy must be carried out in a hospital or class of places approved for the purposes of terminating a pregnancy by specific government ministers. That is, the Secretary of State for Health and Social Care in England, the Cabinet Secretary for Health and Sport in Scotland, and the Minister for Health and Social Services in Wales. Only approved places are deemed *legally* 'suitable' places for abortion, except where a registered medical practitioner forms the opinion in good faith that it is an emergency.[120] As will be explored in Chapter 4, these powers were exercised in Great Britain in 2017 and 2018 to allow the second abortion medication (misoprostol) to be administered at home. Before these changes, people had to attend a clinic twice to have their abortion because both medications had to be administered in this environment. This constituted a significant access issue, but also had the impact of causing significant distress to many who experienced their miscarriage in public places whilst travelling home from clinics (Parsons 2020). A 2011 legal challenge, launched by BPAS, failed on the grounds that Parliament had made clear law that abortion could only be performed in clinics.[121] The marking out of abortion as a treatment that must be performed in a particular place constitutes a part of the 'political case for tight regulatory control of abortion, even where particular restrictions find no basis in medical necessity. The restrictions were accepted as necessary by the High Court in 2012 simply because abortion is 'controversial"' (Sheldon 2014, 202–3).

Changes made in Scotland in 2017, and subsequently in Wales and England (in that order) in 2018, were to approve the home as a class of places where abortion can legally take place. In these orders, the 'home' was carefully defined as the place where the patient was 'ordinarily resident' in Scotland/Wales/England (Scottish Government Chief Medical Officer Directorate 2017; Welsh Government 2018a; Department of Health and Social Care 2018a). The changes to the law in 2020 that allowed both abortion medications to be taken at home in response to the COVID-19 pandemic, which we discuss in more detail in Chapter 8, contain the same definitions of home. Similar provisions were made in the 2020 Northern Ireland regulations, which specify that treatment must be carried out in a hospital, clinic, or primary medical services premises, or, in the case of misoprostol, the home.[122] The home is similarly defined as the 'place in Northern Ireland where the woman has her permanent address or usually resides'.[123]

The definition of home utilised within these approval orders 'means that some women who ought to be offered the choice of medical abortion at home are denied it or are forced to return to a less appropriate environment to comply with the law' (Lohr

---

[119] As inserted by the Human Fertilisation and Embryology Act 1990, s.37.
[120] Abortion Act 1967, s.1(4).
[121] *British Pregnancy Advisory Service v Secretary of State for Health* [2011] E.W.H.C 235 (Admin).
[122] The Abortion (Northern Ireland) (No. 2) Regulations 2020, regulation 8(1).
[123] Ibid, regulation 8(6).

et al. 2020, 50). Examples of some particularly vulnerable groups of people who might be impacted by the restrictive definition of a person's 'home' include students in temporary accommodation, people in temporary homeless shelters, people who are victims of domestic abuse, those living in a particular location unlawfully, and minors in foster care or living between different families (Lohr et al. 2020). There are also groups of people who might prefer to administer medication in places other than their home for support—for example, staying with a friend or family member.

That a person must reside in the same jurisdiction as they are receiving treatment prevents people in Northern Ireland who have travelled to Great Britain to access care from using medications outside of clinics—for example, at a relative's home or in a hotel. This regulation might also technically prevent a person from lawfully being prescribed drugs for use at home from their nearest clinic if this is clinic is located over the border from their home. For example, a person living in North East Wales may find that their nearest clinic is in England. Tight criminal regulation of where abortion can be provided prevents the evolution of services to meet the needs of patients as they become apparent.

3.2.2 … in the United States

The REMS for mifepristone requires that the medication must be 'dispensed to patients only in certain healthcare settings, specifically clinics, medical offices and hospitals by or under the supervision of a certified prescriber' (United States Food and Drug Administration 2019). The patient must also sign a Patient Agreement Form, which suggests that the prescriber and the patient be in the same location on its completion. It states (just above where the provider must sign): 'the patient signed […] In my presence after I counselled her and answered all her questions' (United States Food and Drug Administration 2019). A patient in any part of the US, therefore, must attend a clinic or doctor's office to obtain the medication. Some providers have interpreted this requirement as requiring only the *patient* to be in a specified healthcare setting to be prescribed mifepristone, allowing the doctor to be present digitally—Planned Parenthood in Iowa, for example, requires the patient to attend a clinic in person whilst the prescribing doctor videoconferences in (see Chapter 6). Whilst the REMS does not specify *where* the medication must be taken once collected, at the time of writing 17 states require either that a doctor be physically present during the administration of mifepristone, or that the abortion take place in a hospital, doctor's office, or clinic.[124] This reinforces the problematic notion that abortion needs supervising.

In addition, 30 states have passed significant supply-side TRAP laws, which place further limitations on where abortions can take place by requiring clinics to comply with certain conditions to remain licensed. This introduces a limitation on where abortion can take place—that is, only in facilities that comply with the requirements. As such, doctors who may be willing to provide abortion as part of their primary general practice, for example, may be prevented from doing so. This has worsened access

---

[124] See Chapter 9 for discussion of the specifics of this.

issues by limiting the number of clinics in states with such regimes. At their most extreme, TRAP laws require that abortion clinics have the facilities of, in essence, small hospitals, with requirements for surgical operating facilities on site[125] as just one example. In many states, the legislative framework allows for broad interference to pass a significant amount of regulation. In South Carolina, the legislature specified that the South Carolina Department of Health and Environmental Control is afforded significant discretion. It is specified that they:

> shall promulgate regulations concerning sanitation, housekeeping, maintenance, staff qualifications, emergency equipment and procedures to provide emergency care, medical records and reports, laboratory, procedure and recovery rooms, physical plant, quality assurance, infection control, and information on and access to patient follow-up care necessary.[126]

In other states, very specific requirements are given in the law. For example, clinics in Missouri must have corridors that are six feet wide, procedure rooms must be of specified minimum dimensions and have no windows, and there must be utility rooms with particular facilities.[127] In many states, clinics must be located within 'a reasonable proximity' of a hospital,[128] some of which specify that this means within 30 miles.[129] Some states require that the nearby hospital has specific services available (often obstetrics and gynaecology),[130] or that the clinic have a written agreement with the hospital and ambulance service.[131] This adds to the difficulties in opening, or keeping open, a clinic because external factors determine where they can be located. Providers must find premises within a limited geographical radius that is capable of satisfying specific requirements. Facility requirements are expensive to comply with and limit the ability of providers to keep open multiple clinics in the state. This compounds problems of access because fewer clinics increases the likelihood of people having to travel longer distances. The closure of even one clinic can significantly impact on the service availability in any given state (Jones and Jerman 2014). Even where TRAP laws do not force clinics to close, or do not stand the test of time when legally challenged, they remain costly and result in a decrease in availability.

Supply-side TRAP laws do not better protect patients' health—abortion is already safe. The Supreme Court, however, has been willing to allow restrictions even where it is shown that abortion can be performed in a different way (if there were no restrictions) that is beneficial for pregnant people's health.[132] Many state legislatures openly

---

[125] For example, in Connecticut: Conn. Agencies Regs. §19-13-D54, and Tennessee: Tenn. Comp. R. & Regs. 1200-8-10-.06(1).

[126] SC Code §44-41-75 (2019).

[127] Mo. Code Regs. Ann. tit. 19, §30- 30.070.

[128] For example, in Indiana: ID Code §18-608 (2019).

[129] Including Kansas: KS Stat §65-4a09 (2019), Missouri: MO Rev Stat § 188.080 (2019), North Dakota: N.D. Cent. Code §14-02.1-02.1-04 (2019), Ohio: Ohio Rev Code §3702.3010 (2019); and Wisconsin: WI Stat §253.095 (2019).

[130] For example, in Arkansas: AR Code §20-9-302 (2019); North Carolina: NC Gen Stat §90-21.82 (2019); and Texas: TX Health & Safety Code §171.0031 (2019).

[131] For example, in Kentucky: KY Rev Stat §216B.0431 (2019).

[132] *Gonzales* (n80).

embrace that their laws need not necessarily be written with the aim of ensuring that abortion is safe, but can go further to potentially place unnecessary (in terms of health) barriers provided that these are not an undue burden. The Michigan Code, for example, states that 'the legislature recognizes that under federal constitutional law, a state is permitted to enact persuasive measures that favour childbirth over abortion, even if those measures do not further a health interest'.[133]

3.2.3 Abortion geography

In both the UK and US, legal requirements necessitate people travelling significant distances for abortions, which can be both time-consuming and expensive. Evidence in the US suggests that the greater the distance from an abortion clinic, the lower the incidence of abortion in an area (Bearak et al. 2017). Seven US states have only one abortion clinic,[134] all of which have enacted onerous supply-side TRAP laws. In 2017, 38% of women aged between 15 and 44 lived in US counties with no abortion clinic (Jones et al. 2019). Whilst the median distance that a person had to travel to a clinic was 10.79 miles in 2014, in states known for being particularly antichoice the median was considerably higher—in North Dakota, for example, it was 151.58 miles (just over 14 times the national median) (Bearak et al. 2017). Further, the average is increasing—only slightly at the national level (+0.32 miles), but strikingly in states such as Montana (+46.21 miles), North Dakota (+14.46 miles), and Missouri (+7.45 miles) (Bearak et al. 2017).

Geographical barriers may be thought less problematic in Great Britain because it is far smaller and there is less antichoice regulation. However, there have long been concerns about regional variation in access. Disparities have decreased over time (Sheldon 1997), because charitable providers have made a concerted effort to establish themselves in metropolitan areas where abortion had proved difficult to obtain due to the hostility of local NHS services (Sheldon 2014). With clinics largely concentrated in cities, they can be difficult to access for people living in rural areas (Lord et al. 2018). In a recent study, one woman reported: 'my nearest clinic is over 100 miles away and I have no idea how I would get there and back home after the abortion' (Aiken et al. 2018, 180). It remains the case that most people needing abortion in Northern Ireland must still travel to Great Britain for care despite the recent (partial) decriminalisation of abortion (Kirk et al. 2021).

Even for those who do not live far from their nearest clinic, geography can still present a barrier. In US states requiring separate attendance for in-person counselling and, following a mandatory waiting time, treatment, the distance is, in effect, doubled. For example, a clinic 30 miles away would entail 120 miles of travel in total (Bearak et al. 2017). Individuals' circumstances will affect how difficult a distance is for them to travel. For example, public transportation rarely follows a direct route from A to B, so what is a manageable distance for a person with a car becomes more convoluted (and likely more costly) for the person using public transportation. Further, 'the presence of

---

[133] MI Comp L §§333.17014 (2019).
[134] Kentucky, Mississippi, Missouri, North Dakota, South Dakota, West Virginia, and Wyoming.

one nearby clinic does not necessarily show that the clinic meets the needs of all prospective patients, that it is open daily, or that it has the capacity to meet demand' (2017,
e498). Where clinics serve large areas (such as in US states where TRAP legislation
means that there are few clinics), patients are likely to have to wait for an appointment.

Finally, travel is not just about distance, but broader logistical matters, such as
taking time off work. There is also the matter of childcare or, indeed, the care of other
relatives that may be the responsibility of someone needing an abortion. Those with
limited socioeconomic resources may also struggle to afford travel (we will return to
this later), and structurally disadvantaged individuals—such as those with a disability
or chronic illness—may require assistance. In addition, some people in Great Britain
have reported partner and family intimate violence as a significant barrier to clinic
attendance, regardless of distance (Aiken et al. 2018). One woman in a recent study
reported: 'I'm never allowed to go anywhere alone without my husband or a member
of his family escorting me. I don't have a normal life since getting married. Abortion
is against his family's religion and I'm very anxious about what would happen if I was
caught' (Aiken et al. 2018, 181).

These factors combined illustrate how US TRAP laws and the regulation of where
abortion can take place in the UK increase difficulty in accessing abortion because
of the geographical barriers they create. It is unsurprising, therefore, that such regulation is associated with an increase in gestational age at presentation (Austin and
Harper 2018).

3.3 Who can provide care . . .

3.3.1 . . . in the United Kingdom

In Great Britain, the AA 1967 specifies that a pregnancy must be terminated by a registered medical practitioner, after two medical practitioners are satisfied (forming their
opinion in good faith) that one of the grounds for termination is applicable.[135] A registered medical practitioner means a doctor[136] registered with the UK General Medical
Council.[137] The law is clear that a 'doctor must accept responsibility for all stages of the
treatment for the termination of the pregnancy' and direct 'the carrying out of such
parts of the treatment as in accordance with accepted medical practice' that might be
carried out by others.[138] There is no requirement in the AA 1967 that either doctor
certifying the abortion must have directly consulted, met, or examined the pregnant
person before they can make a determination in good faith that they meet the criteria
for lawful abortion. Department of Health and Social Care[139] guidance issued in 2014
acknowledges this, but specifies that 'it is good practice' for at least one of the doctors
to have seen the pregnant person before making a decision (Department of Health

---

[135] Abortion Act 1967, s.1(1).
[136] *Royal College of Nursing of the United Kingdom v Department of Health and Social Security* (n41).
[137] Medical Act 1983, s.2.
[138] *Royal College of Nursing v Department of Health and Social Security* [1981] 2 WLR 279, at 828 per Lord
Diplock
[139] At the time, it was called the Department of Health.

2014, 5). The guidance continues: 'with technological advances, this may well mean that a doctor does not physically see the woman, e.g. there could be a discussion by phone or over a webcam' (2014, 5). NICE recommends that 'abortion providers should maximise the role of nurses and midwives in providing care' (2019, para 1.1.11).

In practice, it has been the case for some time in Great Britain that nurses and mid-wifes conduct consultations with people seeking abortion, and doctors approve treatment by reviewing the information collected. It is legally permissible for doctors to rely on information obtained by other staff to certify abortion. In these circumstances, the doctor must 'review the [collected] information before reaching an opinion, for example by considering the paperwork or speaking to members of the team' because the doctor must be able to justify that they 'reached their decision in good faith if later challenged' (Department of Health 2014, 9). The Department of Health and Social Care considers the 'signing of forms without consideration of any information relating to the woman to be incompatible with the requirements of the Abortion Act' (Department of Health 2014, 8).

Despite the Department of Health and Social Care's insistence that the certification of abortion not be a 'rubber stamp exercise' (Department of Health 2014, 8), the process is entirely bureaucratic (Sheldon 2016b). The additional layer of bureaucracy in doctors approving treatment prevents providers from ensuring the most efficient organisation of services, as service provision can be delayed where there is a shortage of doctors to review and sign paperwork (Lohr et al. 2020). It also costs providers more money to hire doctors to, effectively, complete paperwork. This process seems especially wasteful when there is an established body of evidence that nurse-led abortion is just as safe (Sjöström et al. 2017). Permitting nurse prescribing would 'simplify access and reduce administrative burdens on doctors, thereby enabling doctors to focus on cases that involve more complex management' (Romanis and Parsons 2020a, 481).

In Northern Ireland, the 2020 regulations adopt different terminology to allow a broader range of HCPs to provide abortions. The term 'registered medical professional' is used to mean a registered doctor, registered midwife, or registered nurse.[140] This term was adopted to ensure appropriately qualified professionals, beyond just doctors, can carry out terminations.[141] It better reflects good practice and will enable local service providers in Northern Ireland (as they are being established) to instigate task sharing. Further, that *one* registered medical professional can terminate a pregnancy after having formed their opinion in good faith that the pregnancy has not exceeded 12 weeks (a second opinion is required only after 12 weeks[142]) can improve efficiency, allowing resources to be directed to complex cases.

Finally, there is the question of who can *refuse* to provide care—as this can equally impact on access. Section 4 of the AA 1967 specifies that, in Great Britain, 'no person shall be under any duty, whether by contract or by any statutory or other legal requirement, to participate in any treatment authorised by this Act to which he has a conscientious objection'. An exception is made where abortion is necessary to save the life of,

---

[140] The Abortion (Northern Ireland) (No. 2) Regulations 2020, regulation 2(2).
[141] The particular term is carefully defined to ensure that a 'broader range of practitioners or healthcare professionals, for example, psychologists or pharmacists' are not included.
[142] The Abortion (Northern Ireland) (No. 2) Regulations 2020, regulation 4.

or to prevent grave permanent injury to the physical or mental health of, the pregnant person.[143] In the event of a legal dispute, the burden of proof in establishing that the objection is 'conscientious' is placed upon the doctor refusing to provide treatment.[144] In practice, the right to conscientious objection has been interpreted as narrow in scope[145] (Brazier and Cave 2016). Where a doctor does conscientiously object there is no requirement in the AA 1967 that they refer the patient to another doctor. In Northern Ireland, a right to conscientious objection is also codified in the 2020 regulations,[146] and again does not provide a statutory duty to refer. The General Medical Council, however, stipulates that—as a matter of good practice—those wanting to object *must* 'tell the patient that they have a right to discuss their condition and the options for treatment (including the option that you object to) with another practitioner who does not hold the same objection as you' and ensure 'that the patient has enough information to arrange to see another doctor who does not hold the same objection' (2013, 3). Doctors are instructed to 'bear in mind the patient's vulnerability and act promptly to make sure that they are not denied appropriate treatment or services' (General Medical Council 2013, 3).

The guidance-based requirement to refer may have limited utility. Many doctors can avoid providing abortions without invoking the right to conscientious objection, thereby avoiding the professional expectation that they refer. A doctor can 'simply refuse to certify that a ground specified in the Act is made out. The woman can then only try to find another more sympathetically inclined doctor' (Brazier and Cave 2016, 425). It is unlikely such behaviour occurs frequently because people in the UK can self-refer to dedicated (independent sector) abortion services (National Institute for Health and Care Excellence 2019). We note, however, that this requires a person to have a certain level of knowledge. This may not be the case for those uneducated about sexual and reproductive health and/or without internet access. Further, a patient whose doctor objects to abortion—even if that doctor recommends that they consult another doctor—may interpret the lack of co-operation or unwillingness to discuss as 'an indication of their ineligibility for termination' (Jackson 2001, 86). This is more likely to be the case when the patient is vulnerable, younger, and/or poorly educated (Jackson 2001; Romanis 2020d). In the past, some doctors deliberately delayed referrals to prevent people from accessing timely termination (Sheldon 2016a), which could still be occurring. This can result in the option of EMA being removed due to (legally imposed) gestational limits (Lohr et al. 2020).

3.3.2   … in the United States

Similar restrictions on who can provide abortion exist in the US. At the federal level, the FDA REMS for mifepristone prevents a HCP from prescribing the drug unless they have specific training or experience, or they become a 'certified prescriber'. To

---

[143] Abortion Act 1967, s.4(2).
[144] Ibid, s.4(1).
[145] *Greater Glasgow and Clyde Health Board v Doogan* [2014] UKSC 68.
[146] The Abortion (Northern Ireland) (No. 2) Regulations 2020, regulation 12(1).

become a certified prescriber, the HCP must sign and return a declaration stating that they have the appropriate qualifications to:

- Assess the duration of a pregnancy accurately;
- Diagnose ectopic pregnancies;
- Provide surgical intervention where necessary, or have plans in place to enable others to do this; and
- Have read and understood the prescribing information for mifepristone (United States Food and Drug Administration 2019).

HCPs who are not doctors specialised in obstetrics and gynaecology must undertake additional training to meet these prescribing requirements. Few doctors have become certified prescribers of mifepristone who were not already providing surgical abortion services (Finer and Wei 2009). Primary care doctors play a crucial role in ensuring access to abortion as they are often the first point of contact when a person has an unwanted pregnancy (Holt et al. 2017). However, many do not automatically have mifepristone prescribing privileges because of their training, and lots do not opt to become certified prescribers. Grossman and Goldstone (2015) suggest this could be because of TRAP law facility requirements in some states meaning general practice doctors would have to make substantial alternations to their premises to begin offering EMA. They also note other pressures such as the 'fear of being ostracized by their peers, or much worse targeted by antiabortion protestors' (Grossman and Goldstone 2015, 189). Lacklustre uptake of mifepristone prescribing certification increases the need for patients to travel, as there are limited clinics able to provide the drug. Further, Holt and colleagues found that primary care doctors in the US who did not provide abortion but had patients request it only referred these patients in 62% of cases (2017, 530), leaving 38% having to rely on information sourced themselves about where to access care.

Beyond federal requirements, most state legislatures have placed further restrictions on who can provide abortion: 35 explicitly permit only *doctors* to provide abortion (see Table 3.2). Very few specifically allow nurses and/or midwives to provide care.[147] Of the states limiting providers to doctors, some have (or used to have) yet more onerous requirements, such as providers having to specialise in obstetrics and gynaecology[148] and/or have staff privileges at a nearby hospital. Admitting privileges requirements were struck down as unconstitutional by the Supreme Court in *Hellerstedt*[149] (Texas) and *June Medical*[150] (Louisiana), but similar provisions remain on the books in other states.[151] Such requirements further limit(ed) access by making it harder (and more expensive) for providers to source appropriate staff and premises.[152]

---

[147] For example, in California: CA Bus & Prof Code §2253 (2019).
[148] A requirement of this nature in Arkansas is, at the time of writing, under challenge: AR Code §20-16-606 (2019).
[149] *Hellerstedt* (n81).
[150] *June Medical* (n86).
[151] There remains a requirement of this nature in Missouri, but it contains a footnote recognising that it is 'substantially similar' to the requirement struck down in Texas: MO Rev Stat §188.080 (2019).
[152] In states with requirements concerning nearby hospitals, hospitals can refuse to afford abortion clinic staff privileges.

Table 3.2 Abortion provider restrictions in the United States[1]

States where only a doctor can provide abortion care

Alabama, Alaska, Arkansas, Connecticut, Delaware, Florida, Georgia, Hawaii, Idaho, Indiana, Iowa, Kansas, Kentucky, Louisiana, Maryland, Massachusetts, Minnesota, Mississippi, Missouri, Nebraska, Nevada, New Mexico, North Carolina, North Dakota, Ohio, Oklahoma, Pennsylvania, South Carolina, South Dakota, Tennessee, Texas, Utah, Washington, Wisconsin, and Wyoming

---

[1] The sources of these regulations are detailed in Appendix 4.

As in the UK, there are federal provisions that protect a right to conscientious objection. The Church Amendment—passed shortly after *Roe*—specifies that individuals cannot be required to perform or assist in abortion procedures where contrary to their 'religious beliefs or moral convictions'.[153] Almost all state legislatures (46) have passed their own conscientious objection provisions, further entrenching this right (Guttmacher Institute 2021). The extent of the other barriers to abortion means that 'it is conceptually and pragmatically complicated to sort the contribution to constrained access to reproductive care attributable to conscientious objectors' (Chavkin et al. 2013, S42), though it inevitably contributes to some extent. As there has been limited uptake of doctors becoming certified prescribers, where those who might be automatically certified choose instead to conscientiously object this can have a significant impact. Further, 14% of doctors in one study of primary care doctors reported routinely attempting to dissuade patients from abortion (Holt et al. 2017, 530)—this disproportionately affects those individuals who may not recognise that such dissuasion represents the doctor's own view and not the patient's eligibility for care.

3.4 How abortion is funded . . .

3.4.1 . . . in the United Kingdom

In Great Britain, whilst 74% of abortions are provided by an independent sector clinic, 99% of abortions are funded by the NHS by contract (Department of Health and Social Care 2020a, 4), meaning they are free at the point of access. Since 2017, abortions provided in Great Britain to people who have travelled from Northern Ireland are also publicly funded (Government Equalities Office 2017). Before this, people from Northern Ireland were charged around £900, which made it unaffordable for many. Care being free at the point of access is positive, but there remain other financial barriers to access.

---

[153] 42 U.S.C. §300a-7.

Since the introduction of Northern Ireland's new legal framework concerning abortion in 2020, no funding provisions have been made. On 5 October 2020, Robin Swann, the Minister for Health in Northern Ireland, confirmed:

> My Department has not given instructions to the Health and Social Care Board to commission abortion services. However, abortion is now legal and can be carried out by registered medical professionals.[154]

There is some local service provision in Northern Ireland because of work by the Northern Ireland Abortion and Contraception Task Group, but this has been challenging without funding (Kirk et al. 2021). It has also not been possible for services to be established across Northern Ireland, and some NHS trusts have, due to inadequate funding, suspended services they had begun to establish (Kirk et al. 2021). Consequently, many people in Northern Ireland still must travel to Great Britain for care, despite being legally entitled to it in their own jurisdiction.

At the time of writing, funding for abortion services in Northern Ireland is especially contentious, with campaigners continuing to fight for state-funded services. In October 2020, Claire Bailey challenged Robin Swann in the Northern Irish Assembly:

> The abortion regulations were laid before Parliament and came into force in March [...] Will the Minister tell the House the other lawful medical services for which his Department has refused to provide funding or resource?.[155]

Her challenge explicitly highlights that the failure to commission funded services in Northern Ireland results from abortion exceptionalism.

3.4.2   ... in the United States

Funding for abortion is extremely limited in the US, with most people having to pay for their own care. In 1977, Congress passed the Hyde Amendment, banning the use of federal funds (in the Medicaid scheme) for abortion.[156] The amendment (still in force) allows federal funding of abortion only where pregnancy threatens the person's life or it resulted from rape or incest.[157] Henry Hyde, the congressman who proposed the amendment, was explicit that the purpose of the law was to limit access: 'I certainly would like to prevent, if I could legally, anybody from having an abortion, a rich woman, a middle-class woman or a poor woman. Unfortunately, the only vehicle available' is to limit funding.[158] The amendment 'effectively conditions indigent pregnant women's care on them remaining pregnant' (Goodwin 2020, 67), because

---

[154] Northern Ireland Assembly Deb 5 October 2020, 'Abortion Services: Northern Trust'.
[155] Ibid.
[156] Departments of Labor and Health, Education, and Welfare Appropriation Act of 1977.
[157] Departments of Labor, Health and Human Services, and Education, and Related Agencies Appropriations Act of 1994, §510.
[158] Congressional Record – House, June 17 1977, 19700.

prenatal care is covered but abortion is not. It was *deliberately* engineered in this way. In permitting federal funding of abortion only in specific circumstances, the Hyde Amendment distinguishes between abortions considered essential and those it considers 'elective'. This perpetuates stigma by suggesting a minority of pregnant people have 'worthy' reasons for abortion, and so must be funded, whereas others do not (Janiak and Goldberg 2016, 90).

The Hyde Amendment has withstood several challenges in the US Supreme Court. In *Harris v. McRae*,[159] Stewart J declared that the right to privacy afforded in *Roe*[160] did not equate to a person having a 'constitutional entitlement to the financial resources to avail herself of the full range of protected choices'.[161] The reasoning continued that federal government (or, indeed, state legislatures) cannot create obstacles to a person's exercising of their freedom of choice, but 'it need not remove those that are not of its own creation'.[162] A person's financial resources were deemed not to be a barrier created by the federal government. To describe the failure to allow funding for abortion as non-interference seems disingenuous when the explicit motivation given in passing the Hyde Amendment was to prevent people having abortions.[163] Further, whilst specifics are beyond the confines of this book, it must be noted that there remain substantial wealth disparities on the basis of race in the US (Conley and Glauber 2008), much of which is the result of the legacy of historical legal and societal systematic oppression, as well as contemporary socioeconomic policy that disadvantages people who are not white on the basis of this legacy (Hanks and Colleagues 2018). That the most disenfranchised groups that are likely to struggle to afford abortion are people of colour is not something that we should allow federal and state governments to completely abdicate responsibility for (Goodwin 2020).

The federal Patient Protection and Affordable Care Act of 2010 (known as 'Obamacare') introduced a requirement that states establish a 'Health Benefit Exchange'.[164] These are virtual marketplaces in which people can comparison-shop for health insurance coverage. The Act allows states to prohibit abortion coverage on any plan offered through an exchange if they enact legislation to specify this,[165] which 25 have done (see Table 3.3). Individuals in these states must purchase an optional rider for abortion coverage. Most of these states have enacted legislative provisions similar to the Hyde Amendment in that there is coverage where necessary to save the pregnant person's life or where the pregnancy resulted from rape or incest.[166] Two states—Louisiana and Tennessee—have made no exception. Even in states where exchange policies can cover abortion, it is not always easy for a

---

[159] *Harris v. McRae* 448 U.S. 297 (1980).
[160] *Roe* (n21).
[161] *Harris v. McRae* (n159), at 316.
[162] Ibid.
[163] We appreciate that both authors are from the UK, where public funding for all healthcare is the norm, and this has likely influenced our opinion here.
[164] 42 U.S.C. §18031(b)(1).
[165] Ibid, §18023(a)(1).
[166] Some states only make exception for those cases where the abortion is necessary to save the person's life. For example, Kansas.

Table 3.3 State regulation of exchange health policies in the United States[1]

State health insurance exchange policies exclude abortion coverage

Alabama, Arizona, Arkansas, Florida, Georgia, Idaho, Indiana, Kentucky, Kansas, Louisiana, Michigan, Mississippi, Missouri, Nebraska, North Carolina, North Dakota, Ohio, Oklahoma, Pennsylvania, South Carolina, South Dakota, Tennessee, Texas, Utah, and Wisconsin

[1]The sources of these regulations are detailed in Appendix 5.

person to tell when purchasing insurance which policies do or do not cover abortion (Hasstedt 2015).

Most states have also passed legislative provisions banning the use of state (nonfederal) funds for abortion. Figure 3.1 illustrates the volume of states (including some that might not be described as hostile to abortion in that they have not passed substantial TRAP regulation) that prohibit the use of state public funds except in a narrow set of circumstances. Many mirror the Hyde Amendment, making exceptions only where necessary to save the pregnant person's life, or where the pregnancy results from rape or incest. Others only allow the use of public funds where it is necessary to save the pregnant person's life (see Figure 3.1). Some are explicit in their rationale. The North Dakota provision, allowing for funding only where necessary to save life, for example, reads: 'Between normal childbirth and abortion, it is the policy of the state of North Dakota that normal childbirth is to be given preference, encouragement, and support by law and by state action, it being in the

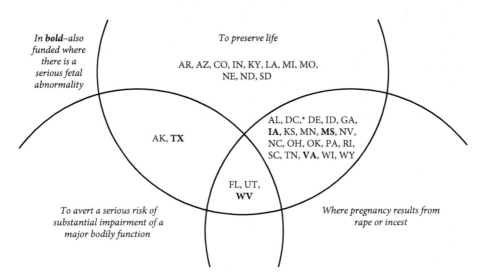

Figure 3.1 Limitations on the use of state funds in the United States[1]

[1]The sources of these limitations are detailed in Appendix 6.

best interests of the well-being and common good of North Dakota citizens',[167] and thus no state funds may be used for abortion. This illustrates the extent to which state policies, even on how abortion can be funded, are built around abortion as non-essential health-care. Some states allow funding in circumstances beyond those in federal law, including where necessary to avert a serious risk of substantial physical impairment of a necessary bodily function, or in cases of serious fetal abnormality.

3.4.3   Socioeconomics and abortion

Whilst abortion is free at the point of access in Great Britain, there are still costs in-volved in accessing care associated with travel, time off work, and childcare arrange-ments. Cost remains a barrier, though less so than in the US because, since 2018, there has been no requirement for patients to attend clinics twice, and the procedure itself is free. That said, the costs of travel for people from Northern Ireland (coming to Great Britain) remain a significant barrier. In Great Britain, those facing travel into cities from rural areas have reported it as such a difficult prospect that they felt they had to access abortion medications unlawfully (Aiken et al. 2018). Inevitably, wealthier people in the UK continue to find it much easier to access services. Much of the analysis below in the context of the US therefore also applies to those who have to travel long distances in the UK.

As Goodwin emphasises, 'if you are poor and cannot pay for an abortion, *Roe v. Wade* may provide little solace' (2020, 64) because for many poor people a federal ban on Medicaid for abortion is the same as banning it altogether (2020, 67). The Hyde Amendment has been devastating in terms of access, as Medicaid provides for the poorest citizens in the US. The cost of EMA varies between providers, but the average cost was estimated at $535 in 2014 (Jones et al. 2018, 215). For a person with an income placing them at the ceiling of Medicaid eligibility, $535 equates to almost one third of their total (taxable) household income for a month (Donovan 2017). Even amongst those not Medicaid eligible, having $535 as immediately avail-able disposable income is simply unrealistic for many. This can force people in need of abortion to 'divert money from other essentials such as food, rent and utilities' (Fried 1997, 38).

The cost is not limited to the medication. For reasons already discussed, many must travel to access care—potentially significant distances. A 2018 systematic review con-cluded that 'if TRAP laws increase out-of-pocket costs to women, […] women of lower socioeconomic position may face greater challenges in obtaining abortions' (Austin and Harper 2018, 132). Those living in rural areas of the US are more likely to have to travel a considerable distance, and are simultaneously those most likely to be living in poverty (Upadhyay 2017). Further costs must also be considered, such as taking time off work or arranging childcare so that travelling to a clinic is possible. Due to this range of costs that accessing abortion entails, poorer people will generally take longer to arrange funds, which may result in fewer choices of procedure (Fried 1997,

---

[167] N.D. Cent. Code §14-02.3-01(1) (2019).

38). Where this delay means the person needs surgical abortion, the cost increases. D&E, for example, can cost between $500 and $3000+ (Cowles 2018). Those seeking care may also turn to abortion funds across the US, which are organisation that exist to fund abortion and associated costs for those in difficulty (National Network of Abortion Funds 2021). However, these organisations have varying resources and eligibility requirements. Further, access requires the person in need being aware of this option.

3.5 Abortion stigma

3.5.1 … in the United Kingdom

To fully understand the impact of abortion law on access, 'it is crucial to unearth the stereotypes that underpin the law, even a law that partially enhances women's ability to access safe abortion' because this enables us to identify 'the negative cultural attitudes about women and abortion' (Pizzarossa 2019, 27). It is only in identifying legally enforced stereotypes and identifying their harm that we work towards eradicating legally sanctioned stigma (Cook and Cusak 2010).

Abortion is—or should be—readily accessible in the UK under the AA 1967 and the 2020 Northern Ireland regulations, but neither of these legislative instruments have relented the degree of control the law exercises over bodies with female physiology. Both continue, to differing extents, to label people seeking access to abortion as innately vulnerable, and decision-making power over their bodies is subject to medical control. This is more so true in Great Britain where a pregnant person still faces criminal consequences for accessing abortion outside of the strict criteria. As described in Chapter 2, this creates stigma by only enabling access in circumstances deemed 'rational' by the legislature. The law requiring that abortion be justified in these terms introduces potential for consultations to be uncomfortable. We have already alluded to this in how consultations with doctors who will not provide abortion can impact on individuals. In some instances, an individual's fear of discussing the social reasons for abortion can prevent them choosing to access abortion through lawful channels (Aiken et al. 2018). Even in Northern Ireland, where pregnant people are not subject to criminal sanctions when terminating their pregnancies, that medical professionals must examine the reasons for abortions taking place after 12 weeks of pregnancy to evade criminal sanction still introduces the possibility of people fearing discomfort discussing their reasons.

There remains a social taboo around abortion in the UK. Love describes how much of this is constructed partly by silence, in 'what is hard, or impossible, to say' (2001, 319). This can impact on many people's comfort in attending abortion clinics, often because there is a fear of being seen. A 2018 study, examining why women in Great Britain had accessed abortion online through unlawful channels, found that 30% of participants had worried about a breach of their privacy or confidentiality in attending a clinic in person (Aiken et al. 2018, 180). These fears are exacerbated by abortion protestors. There are groups that congregate outside clinics as a matter of protest, and, in many instances, to hand out anti-abortion materials to people entering the clinic. In response to a consultation about the creation of a 'no-protest' zone in the London Borough of Ealing, 470 respondents described witnessing protestors threatening patients by explaining that they would go to Hell, referring to them as 'Mum', handing them leaflets, taking photos of them, and not leaving them enough room to easily enter the clinic.[168]

In the UK, there is no statutory regulation of protesting outside abortion clinics. However, the Anti-social Behaviour, Crime and Policing Act 2014 affords local authorities the power to make 'Public Space Protection Orders', to prohibit 'specified things being done in the restricted area'.[169] An order can only be made where the activity to be prohibited 'has had a detrimental effect on the quality of life of those in the locality', the activities are likely to continue having this effect in the public place,[170] and they are of a 'persistent or continuing nature' 'such as to make the activities unreasonable'.[171] Orders last for up to three years,[172] and violating their terms (without reasonable excuse) is a criminal offence publishable by a maximum fine of £1000.[173]

In 2018, Ealing Council became the first local authority to issue such an order around an abortion clinic, creating a buffer zone of 100 metres around it as a designated area in which there could be no protest. The order specified that no protest meant no interference (verbally or physically) with a person entering the clinic, no recording or photographing of individuals, no playing of voice recordings or music, and no displaying of signs depicting any text or images relating to termination in the safe zone.[174]

The order was challenged by the Good Counsel Network, but was upheld by the Court of Appeal.[175] The judgment affirmed that the right to private life[176] of patients of the clinic was interfered with by the actions of the protestors. The protestors argued that there is no reasonable expectation of being able to enter a clinic privately since it is in a public place and entrance is by public highway, and that protests are to be expected because abortion is a 'controversial topic of general public importance'.[177] This argument was, however, rejected with 'no hesitation':[178]

> service users visiting the Centre are women in the early stages of pregnancy. Some are children. Some are victims of rape. Some are carrying foetuses with abnormalities, even fatal abnormalities. Some may not have told friends or family. Their very attendance at the Centre is a statement about highly personal and intimate matters. They may be in physical pain and suffering acute psychological and emotional issues both when attending and leaving the Centre. There is no alternative way of arriving at and

---

[168] The consultation responses were set out in *Dulgheriu and Orthova v Ealing London Borough Council* [2019] EWCA Civ 1490, at para 48.
[169] Anti-social Behaviour, Crime and Policing Act 2014, s.59(4)(a).
[170] Ibid, s.59(2)(a)–(b).
[171] Ibid, s.59(3)(a)–(b).
[172] Ibid, s.60.
[173] Ibid, s.67.
[174] The terms of the order are set out in *Dulgheriu v Ealing Council* (n168), at para 14.
[175] *Dulgheriu v Ealing Council* (n168).
[176] European Convention on Human Rights, art 7.
[177] *Dulgheriu v Ealing Council* (n168), at para 52.
[178] Ibid, at para 53.

leaving the Centre except across a public space, which they would naturally wish to cross as inconspicuously as possible.[179]

The Court concluded that service users would have both 'the reasonable desire and legitimate expectation that their visits to the Centre would not receive any more publicity than was inevitably involved in accessing and leaving the Centre across a public space and highway'.[180] They also determined that the order was justifiable in how it balanced the service users right to access (favouring this) against the right to protest.[181] This protest did not merely cause shock and disturbance, but actively caused psychological and emotional harm to individuals with serious potential adverse health consequences.[182] In March 2020, the Supreme Court refused the claimants' application for permission to appeal. As such, buffer zones in these terms can be lawfully established in the UK.

Similar action to create buffer zones has now been taken by some local councils across England (Elgot and Slawson 2018). However, such policies have not been universally adopted. The Back Off campaign estimates that 42 clinics in England and Wales (and approximately 100,000 people who have attended them for treatment) have been affected by protests since 2018 (Back Off a). This is a substantial access barrier for those concerned with their privacy, which was 30% in one study of women who had chosen to access care unlawfully (Aiken et al. 2018, 180). The Back Off campaign also reports that harassment of staff is causing issues that impact on access. There is at least one instance of an NHS location withdrawing abortion services at the request of staff who were frightened by the protesting (Back Off b). The blanket introduction of buffer zones around abortion clinics would ensure that in-person care, free of harassment, remains an option.

3.5.2   ... In the United States

Fried observes that there is a significant effort by the US antichoice movement—both legally and extra-legally—to ensure that people who obtain abortion are 'portrayed as selfish, sexually irresponsible, unfeeling and morally blind individuals who kill their own children for 'convenience'' (1997, 41). Much legislation is framed around the notion of abortion as 'elective'. This framing is common in state legislation that distinguishes between abortions that, for example, can be state funded or covered by exchange insurance, and those that cannot. The term 'elective' is a thinly veiled 'synonym for "less morally justifiable", as opposed to clearly justifiable abortion' (Janiak and Goldberg 2016, 91). We demonstrated how this affects access as these notions are translated into what is effectively antiabortion counselling and mandatory waiting in many states.

---

[179]   Ibid, at para 58.
[180]   Ibid, at para 60.
[181]   European Convention on Human Rights, art 11.
[182]   *Dulgheriu v Ealing Council* (n168), at para 89.

The Freedom of Access to Clinic Entrances Act of 1994 introduced a federal criminal prohibition on using force, threat of force, or physical obstruction that attempts to (or does) injure, intimidate, or interfere with a person because they have or are attempting to access reproductive health services.[183] It also prohibited damaging or destroying any facility because it provides reproductive health services.[184] The penalty for these offences is (on first offence) a fine or up to one years' imprisonment,[185] and subsequent offences carry a maximum sentence of three years.[186] Whilst the Act prohibits trespassing and blocking the entrance of clinics, it is also explicit that it does not prohibit 'any expressive conduct (including peaceful picketing or other peaceful demonstration) protected from legal prohibition by the First Amendment to the Constitution'.[187] Whilst the Act prohibits certain protest behaviours (that largely would likely have been criminal anyway as assault or harassment), it *actively permits* others, such as distributing pamphlets and being present in large groups outside abortion clinics. As such, abortion protests are a persistent problem. One study found that 84% of clinics offering abortion across the US had experienced at least one form of harassment in 2011 (Jerman and Jones 2014, e422). 80% of clinics faced picketing outside, with 28% reporting picketing involving physical contact with patients, including them being blocked from entering (Jerman and Jones 2014, e422). These figures were all higher at clinics where at least half of patients are seeking abortion services (as opposed to a minority of patients). In response, some clinics have established 'clinic escorts' so that patients do not pass protestors alone (Shah 2019). People have reported the presence and behaviour of protestors as negatively affecting their experience of attending a clinic, causing them to feel both anger and guilt (Cozzarelli et al. 2000). Abortion protests are also undertaken as extreme acts of violence. In 2015, for example, three people were killed outside a clinic in Colorado (Turkewitz and Healy 2015).

Outside-clinic protesting can also negatively affect patients' experiences of consultation, and/or the provider-patient relationship. In one study, a respondent reported being confused about whether the clinic she was attending was actually supportive of abortion, and specifically of her decision to abort, because she 'understood the protestor presence to be evidence that clinic workers did not care about protecting patients like her' (Kimport et al. 2012, 207). Such concerns might deter people from entering. Measures clinics have taken to protect themselves—such as metal detectors on entry—also contribute to an unpleasant experience for patients, making their attendance feel 'like a secretive, shameful thing' (Kimport et al. 2012, 207). Consequently, clinics can be difficult spaces for individuals, and some report travelling further to avoid clinics known for being targeted by protestors (2017).

Abortion protesting limits the establishment of clinics because of the expense of security measures. The US has a long history of violence against abortion providers (Stack 2015). It is, then, understandable that many doctors have reservations (based on their safety) about becoming providers (Grossman and Goldstone 2015). Beyond

---

[183] 18 U.S.C. §248(a)(1).
[184] Ibid, §248(a)(3).
[185] Ibid, §248(b)(1).
[186] Ibid, §248(b)(2).
[187] Ibid, §248(d)(1).

the barriers to access protesting creates, it is unsettling that both providers and patients may feel that they are risking their lives in providing/accessing *constitutionally protected* healthcare.

3.6 Summary

In the US, the landscape of access is devastating. There exist, at both federal and state level, significant access barriers. Measures designed to interfere with a person's ability to make a truly informed decision about abortion, to delay access, to shut clinics, and to limit the number of available providers, create an environment that is hostile to abortion. The result is that people must travel long distances, withstand harassment outside clinics, and struggle to pay out-of-pocket for essential, time-sensitive healthcare. Access to abortion in the US is not reflective of its widely acclaimed status as a constitutional right.

In contrast, in Great Britain, whilst the AA 1967 cannot be described as progressive, there does seem to exist what Lee describes as a 'socio-legal gap' which 'seems to benefit women by allowing them greater access to abortion in practice than the statute might appear to provide, at least in early pregnancy' (2003, 533). The AA 1967 does ensure that most people needing abortion can have one, funded and by skilled providers. However, that the Act contains no affirmative right to accessible services is having a detrimental impact on people's access to and experiences of abortion. Many of the requirements in the AA 1967 'conflict with modern conceptions of healthcare and medical ethics, and interfere with the application of evidence to permit best practice' (Lohr et al. 2020, 43).

We cannot accurately estimate how many people in Great Britain have struggled to access abortion services, but we do have some indication that there are at least some who have sought abortion through unlawful channels, such as the online provider Women on Web, because of their (perceived) inability to access local services (Aiken et al. 2018). Further, despite abortion now being legal in Northern Ireland, 'safe local treatment remains inaccessible to many of those who need it' (Kirk et al. 2021, 3). This makes abortion more expensive and onerous for those who find themselves *still* in the position of having to travel to Great Britain or engage providers like Women on Web.

In the next chapter, we consider the evolution of abortion policy that did result in some progressive changes regarding where abortion can take place in Great Britain between 2017 and 2019. We do so to illustrate some problematic features of public policy, particularly in relation to abortion.

4

Piecemeal progression and home use of misoprostol in the United Kingdom

With abortion regulation—much like many areas of health policy—it is rare for significant shifts in regulatory frameworks to happen all at once. Northern Ireland may be considered somewhat unusual in that respect, having gone from being relatively archaic in its approach to abortion law to partial decriminalisation in 2019 with no steps in between. When this happens, it is often (as was the case with Northern Ireland) because a country has fallen so far behind what can be considered the 'norm' for similar countries, and significant pressure from one or more directions causes a sudden 'correction'. It is far more common for policy to develop slowly, in increments that are perhaps less controversial than a significant regulatory leap, thereby avoiding, as Lindblom describes, 'serious lasting mistakes' (1959, 86). With the exception of Northern Ireland, this is precisely what has happened in recent years with abortion policy in the UK. Since the AA 1967 came into force in the late 1960s, perhaps the greatest shift in abortion policy (and consequently the next step in this gradual progress towards more liberal regulation) was the approval of home use of misoprostol for EMA. It is this series of changes that will be the focus of this chapter.

Starting with an overview of home use of misoprostol as a practice and the nature of governmental powers to approve it, we go on to chart the series of events between 2017 and 2020 which have resulted in home use being permitted throughout the UK. In particular, we highlight how the process was very different when comparing all of the countries in Great Britain with Northern Ireland. Making observations on these developments, we argue that three key and (largely) problematic elements of the progression of abortion policy in Great Britain (and, to a lesser extent, Northern Ireland) are observable. First, abortion regulation in the UK cannot rightly be considered evidence-based policy. Second, there is a clear and political application of the precautionary principle. Third, the constituent nations (specifically of Great Britain) appear susceptible to a political peer pressure that causes their abortion policies to remain largely similar.

4.1 Home use and powers of approval

Prior to the changes outlined in this chapter, there had been a requirement in Great Britain to take both drugs required for a medical abortion—mifepristone and misoprostol—under medical supervision. As we explained in Chapter 2, this was a consequence of the AA 1967 being enacted before medical abortion was introduced. In 1967, abortion entailed a far more invasive procedure. Procuring an abortion

Early Medical Abortion, Equality of Access, and the Telemedical Imperative. Jordan A. Parsons and Elizabeth Chloe Romanis, Oxford University Press. © Oxford University Press 2021. DOI: 10.1093/oso/9780192896155.003.0004

legitimately (meaning legally, through a doctor) meant surgical abortion. As such, it is understandable that the law was written to require the procedure be performed on medical premises. When the bill that became the AA 1967 was being considered, however, it was noted that pharmaceutical methods of abortion were a realistic expectation.[188] Medicine has advanced, and we are now at the point where most abortions carried out in England and Wales (Department of Health and Social Care 2020a, 13) and Scotland (Public Health Scotland 2020, 14) are medical terminations (and mostly EMAs). There is no general need (in terms of clinical necessity) for EMAs to take place on medical premises (see Chapter 1).

Home use of misoprostol for the purposes of EMA generally refers to a care pathway whereby the patient undergoes a consultation and any necessary tests at an approved clinic, mifepristone is administered at that clinic, and the patient then takes home the appropriate dose of misoprostol to later self-administer at home. There will, naturally, be some level of variation in how exactly this process plays out, but we will proceed on the understanding that home use of misoprostol entails mifepristone being administered in a clinical setting.

Where home use of misoprostol is permitted, patients are afforded the ability to complete their abortion in a more familiar environment. Additionally, requiring patients to take both drugs in a clinic means that the effects of the miscarriage can begin when the patient is still travelling home. As noted in Chapter 1, mifepristone alone does not induce miscarriage. It is misoprostol that causes the womb to contract, thereby resulting in the expulsion of the products of conception. As the effects can begin very quickly for some individuals, taking both drugs in a clinic and then leaving results in some experiencing heavy bleeding when, for example, using public transport to get home. Given the geographical barriers to access we outlined in Chapter 3, this potentially traumatising experience is very likely for those living far from a clinic. In Great Britain, many accounts of such experiences have been made public. As part of the Women's Equality Party campaign for home use, Claudia described her experience after taking misoprostol in a clinic:

> I had no idea how quickly it would take effect. I was lucky I had enough money for a taxi - it was a 15 minute drive, but in those 15 minutes I turned pale green and could feel the process starting. I was counting down the seconds until I arrived home. I collapsed almost as soon as I got inside and started vomiting and miscarrying on the bathroom floor. I can't imagine what it would have been like if we had been stuck in traffic for just two minutes longer. Or if, like many women, I couldn't afford to take a taxi. (Women's Equality Party 2018)

This account is not unique, and at the time there were several such experiences reported by various news outlets.

It should be noted that here we are talking specifically about the home use of misoprostol for the purposes of EMA, meaning as part of an *induced* miscarriage. Misoprostol has long been provided for home use throughout the UK as part of the

---

[188] Minutes of Standing Committee F on the Medical Termination of Pregnancy Bill 1 March 1967, col 348.

treatment for a *spontaneous* miscarriage. It is when the decision to end the pregnancy is the pregnant person's choice that regulations have, until recently, presented additional barriers. This is yet another example of abortion exceptionalism. Evidently, the reasons for this additional regulation were not based on medical evidence; if they were, home use of the same drug for what is ultimately the same purpose would not have been permitted when such actions were not considered a matter of choice. The regulatory landscape around misoprostol was quite clearly discriminatory towards those who were considered to be *choosing* to end their pregnancy and was, therefore, politically motivated.

When medical supervision was required for the swallowing of both medications in Great Britain, treatment had to be carried out in a hospital or an approved clinic. However, it had been suggested that it was within the power of the Secretary of State for Health and Social Care—and the relevant counterparts in the devolved nations—to approve a pregnant person's home as a place where a pregnancy could be terminated. Section 1(3) of the AA 1967, which stipulates where the termination of pregnancy must be carried out, includes 'a place approved for the purposes of this section by the Secretary of State'. This, arguably, was insufficient to allow the approval of home use, as it requires 'a place' to be approved; this would require the homes of all people seeking an abortion to be individually approved. However, this legislative hurdle to home use was removed in 1990. Section 37(3) of the Human Fertilisation and Embryology Act 1990 inserted section 1(3A) of the AA 1967, which states:

> The power under subsection (3) of this section to approve a place includes power, in relation to treatment consisting primarily in the use of such medicines as may be specified in the approval and carried out in such a manner as may be so specified, to approve a class of places.

House of Commons debates surrounding the Human Fertilisation and Embryology Bill involved significant disagreement as to whether it was appropriate for changes to legislation concerning abortion to be included.[189] On the matter of the locations at which an abortion could take place, then MP Ann Widdecombe commented in a House of Commons debate that the (proposed) increased powers of the Secretary of State would result in 'legalised back-street abortions with precious little counselling or control'.[190] Nonetheless, the Bill was passed, thereby introducing the language of 'class of places' that would make the introduction of home use possible; rather than having to individually approve the individual homes of those seeking abortions—which, understandably, would never have happened—it would be possible to approve the homes of patients accessing abortion services as a class of place.

In Northern Ireland, the question of where an EMA can take place has not been relevant until fairly recently. As we detailed in Chapter 2, the AA 1967 does not extend to Northern Ireland, meaning abortion remained a criminal offence under sections 58 and 59 of the OAPA 1861 until the applicability of these sections to the law in Northern Ireland was repealed by Westminster in 2019. Without there being any legislation

---

[189] HC Deb 2 April 1990, vol 170, cols 914–85.
[190] HC Deb 21 June 1990, vol 174, col 1196.

equivalent to the AA 1967, discussion of home use would have been somewhat jumping the gun, because abortion was not routinely permissible even at medical premises.

4.2 The home use chain reaction in the United Kingdom

Whilst health is a devolved matter, on many matters all four nations that constitute the UK tend to align. For example, England and Scotland have recently followed Wales in the move to a system of deemed consent for organ donation (Parsons 2021b), with Northern Ireland having closed a public consultation on the policy in early 2021 (Northern Ireland Department of Health 2020). With the exception of Northern Ireland, this is the reality of the regulation of abortion. This has been most recently demonstrated by the response to the question of abortion care during the COVID-19 pandemic, seeing the introduction of telemedical services and the approval of home use of mifepristone (which will be discussed in Chapter 8). Whereas there was significant variation in each nation's general response to the pandemic, on abortion there was something of a united front. Northern Ireland was realistically only able to avoid introducing the same changes as in the rest of the UK by having (partially) decriminalised abortion (though without relaxing regulations to incorporate the home use of mifepristone) around the same time. Later chapters in this book focus specifically on this point. Here, we will chart the series of developments resulting in the approval of home use of misoprostol for the purposes of EMA throughout the UK (see Figure 4.1).

4.2.1   Scotland

Leading the way, the first nation to permit home use of misoprostol was Scotland. In a letter to medical boards in October 2017, the Scottish Chief Medical Officer Dr Calderwood detailed the Government's decision that the requirement for people to attend a clinic to take misoprostol would no longer universally apply (Scottish Government Chief Medical Officer Directorate 2017). The approval came just 10 months after the publication of a report by a coalition of women's rights organisations that called for home use to be permitted to introduce flexibility that would 'be beneficial to many women for a range of factors that include domestic abuse, parental involvement, and work and childcare commitments' (Engender 2016, 24). This was a significant move, and the biggest, in terms of improving access to abortion care in the five decades since the AA 1967. As such, the move was praised by many and calls for the other nations of the UK to follow suit soon followed.

The approval order exercised the power of the Scottish Health Secretary to approve a 'class of places' under sections 1(3) and (3A) of the AA 1967 (this power became vested in the Scottish Health Secretary with the coming into force of the Scotland Act 1998). It specifically stipulated that home use of misoprostol was permitted provided the patient attended a clinic, where they were prescribed both mifepristone and misoprostol, and took the mifepristone in the clinic. Further, for the purposes of the approval, 'home' refers to the place in Scotland (thereby precluding cross-border care) where a pregnant person is ordinarily resident. It is worth emphasising that there are some issues with defining the home as the place a person is ordinarily resident,

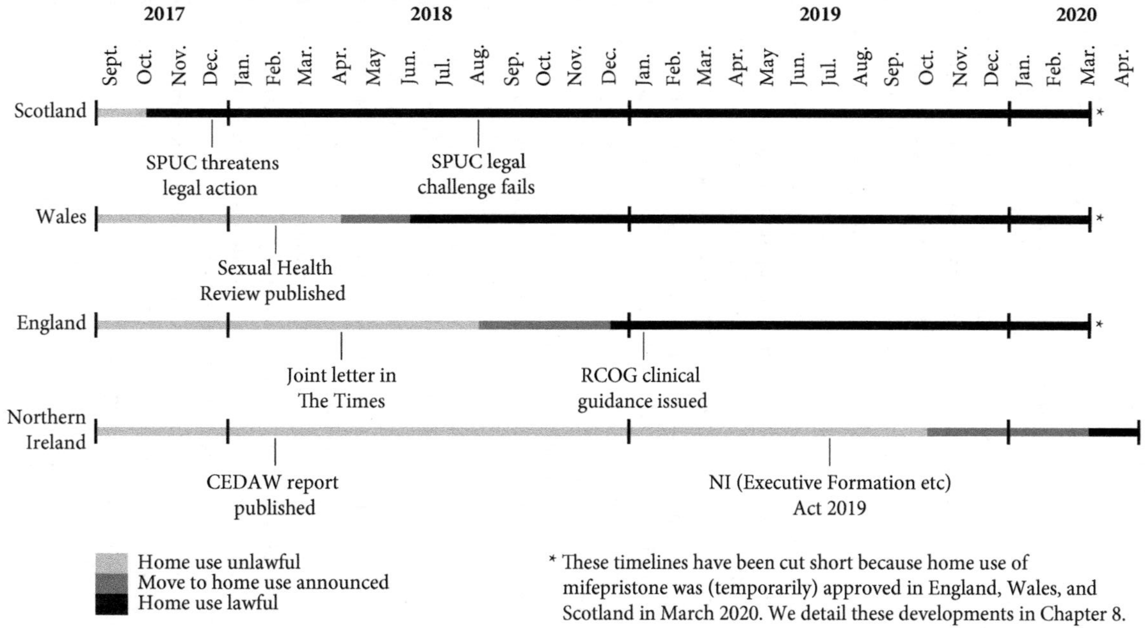

2017
2018
2019
2020
Sept.
Oct.
Nov.
Dec.
Jan.
Feb.
Mar.
Apr.
May
Jun.
Jul.
Aug.
Sep.
Oct.
Nov.
Dec.
Jan.
Feb.
Mar.
Apr.
May
Jun.
Jul.
Aug.
Sep.
Oct.
Nov.
Dec.
Jan.
Feb.
Mar.
Apr.
Scotland
SPUC threatens legal action
SPUC legal challenge fails
Wales
Sexual Health Review published
England
Joint letter in The Times
RCOG clinical guidance issued
Northern Ireland
CEDAW report published
NI (Executive Formation etc) Act 2019
Home use unlawful
Move to home use announced
Home use lawful
* These timelines have been cut short because home use of mifepristone was (temporarily) approved in England, Wales, and Scotland in March 2020. We detail these developments in Chapter 8.

Figure 4.1 The introduction of home use of misoprostol in the United Kingdom

because this excludes some vulnerable people from administering abortion medications in places in which they feel comfortable (see Chapter 3).

Accompanying the approval order were practice guidelines from the Scottish Abortion Care Providers Network. In addition to extensive procedural guidance, these guidelines included a gestational limit of nine weeks and six days for home use of misoprostol, with the day of mifepristone administration having to fall within that limit (meaning misoprostol could be taken at 10 weeks' gestation, given the necessary period between the two drugs being administered). Lists were included of both absolute contra-indications and circumstances in which caution should be exercised regarding home use. Absolute contra-indications listed included inherited porphyria (a group of disorders that can affect the nervous system and/or skin), known or suspected ectopic pregnancy, and uncontrolled severe asthma. Circumstances requiring caution listed included severe anaemia, pre-existing heart disease, and a severe inflammatory bowel disease—in such circumstances, the guidelines note that whoever is providing care should discuss the matter with senior medical staff.

Unsurprisingly, the approval was not unanimously supported. In an online article published soon after the approval (which has since been removed), prolife organisation the Society for the Protection of Unborn Children (SPUC) condemned the move as a '[r]eturn to back-street abortions' (Parsons 2020). Within just two months, in December 2017, the Scottish arm of SPUC threatened the Scottish Government with a legal challenge should the approval order not be revoked within three weeks. In a letter to the Scottish Chief Medical Officer, SPUC stated that they were of the view that the approval was unlawful and that it acted to remove the 'stringent medical oversight from the process, thereby endangering the lives of women' (Society for the Protection of Unborn Children 2017).

The Scottish Government did not reverse its decision, resulting in a judicial review being petitioned by SPUC Scotland.[191] SPUC submitted that the approval was unlawful on the bases that (i) 'a home is not a permissible class [of place] for the purposes of the legislation' and (ii) 'the approval issued runs counter to the requirement in the legislation that abortion be carried out by a medical practitioner'.[192] On the first point, SPUC suggested that a person's home as a class of place was too broad and unrestricted; they suggested that all homes could be considered within such a class of place. On the latter point, SPUC argued that in allowing a person to self-administer misoprostol, the approval did not satisfy the requirements of section 1(1) of the AA 1967, because the termination could not be considered as being 'carried out' by the medical practitioner who provided the misoprostol.

SPUC's legal challenge was unsuccessful. On the matter of a home as a permissible class of place, Lady Wise deemed SPUC's argument that the class was too broad and unrestricted 'misconceived',[193] noting that the case of a person wishing to go to the home of a relative who is providing emotional support in order to self-administer misoprostol (something they would be unable to do under the approval) demonstrates how the terms of the approval relating to the definition of 'home' represent a 'real and substantive restriction on location'.[194] Further, she referenced the commonplace

---

[191] *SPUC v Scottish Ministers* (n99).
[192] Ibid, at para 4.
[193] Ibid, at para 31 per Lady Wise.
[194] Ibid.

self-administering of medication for relatively serious conditions at home.[195] On the matter of the role of the medical practitioner, Lady Wise cited Lord Diplock's judgment in *Royal College of Nursing v Department of Health*,[196] wherein he described the treatment as a 'team effort', and Lady Wise considered whether the person self-administering misoprostol may be considered part of this team.[197] She concluded that as a person would still self-administer misoprostol if required to attend a clinic, it is acceptable that they self-administer it at home; if the former can be considered as carried out by a medical practitioner, there is no reason why the latter cannot.[198] It is, then, she detailed, necessary that the pregnant person be part of the 'team' referred to by Lord Diplock, whether the misoprostol is self-administered in a clinic or at the pregnant person's home.[199]

Aside from the ruling that the approval was lawful, it is important to highlight the matters raised in this case concerning the guidance from the Scottish Abortion Care Providers Network that was issued alongside the approval. We have already noted that the guidance provides a gestational limit, but it also suggests as a criterion for prescribing misoprostol for home use that another adult be at home with the person following self-administration of the medication (Scottish Government Chief Medical Officer Directorate 2017). In her judgment, Lady Wise noted that the guidance did not form part of the approval and therefore had no bearing on the permissibility of home use of misoprostol. Rather, it provides a decision-making aid that may be lawfully departed from by a medical practitioner. Therefore, as neither a gestational limit nor a requirement for another adult to be at home with the person following self-administration of misoprostol is contained in the approval order, these are not legal stipulations. This means that, theoretically, it would have been permissible for a medical practitioner to provide misoprostol for home use to a person up to 24 weeks' gestation. As noted in the previous chapter, it is unlikely that any doctor would depart from the guidance because there are professional incentives not to do so, but it is important to recognise that there is no apparent *legal* prohibition on doing so.

Having introduced this new regulatory landscape first, it was inevitable that opposition to the change in Scotland was significant. As it would be the same legal authority that Wales and England would later exercise to introduce a similar policy change, SPUC's legal challenge was important in reducing the potential for organisations opposed to the change to pursue legal challenges in Wales and England. As such, even though Wales introduced a similar approval order prior to the judgment in SPUC's legal challenge, the Scottish experience very much paved the way for a far smoother implementation of the home use policy in the rest of Great Britain.

4.2.2 Wales

Second in the chain reaction of liberalising misoprostol regulation was Wales. This was first signalled on 17 April 2018, a year after Scotland permitted home use

---

[195] Ibid, at para 33.
[196] *Royal College of Nursing v Department of Health* (n138).
[197] *SPUC v Scottish Ministers* (n99), at para 39.
[198] Ibid, at para 40.
[199] Ibid.

of misoprostol (and before the judgment was issued in SPUC's legal challenge in Scotland). The Welsh Cabinet Secretary for Health and Social Services, Vaughan Gething, made an announcement in the Senedd (Welsh Parliament):

> I have instructed officials to start work immediately on how we can amend the legal framework to allow for the treatment for termination of pregnancy to be carried out at home, in line with recommendation 7.[200]

The recommendation he was referring to was that of Public Health Wales' *Sexual Health Review 2017/2018*, which had published its final report in February of that year (Public Health Wales 2018). This report noted issues such as disparities in service provision across Wales, highlighting variation in gestational limits for EMA across health boards and the fact that inequitable services can lead to people either having to terminate their pregnancies later than intended or being forced to see unwanted pregnancies to term (Public Health Wales 2018, 10).[201] Vaughan Gething's decision followed not only this report, but various campaigns by organisations such as BPAS and the Women's Equality Party, and internal pressure from Members of the Senedd.

These signalled changes came just two months later. An approval order was issued on 20 June 2018, permitting home use of misoprostol with immediate effect (Welsh Government 2018a). The same authority was exercised in issuing this approval as in Scotland, under sections 1(3) and (3A) of the AA 1967.[202] Under the order, a pregnant person's home became an approved class of place for the termination of pregnancy, provided mifepristone was taken in a clinic and only misoprostol was prescribed to take home. The same problematic specification that home means the place where the person is 'ordinarily resident' is also included. A later Welsh Health Circular, issued on 29 June 2018, provided clinical guidance (Welsh Government 2018b). This guidance reflected the Scottish guidance of the previous year with regards to the presence of another adult at the time of the self-administration of misoprostol and the gestational limit of nine weeks and six days (the guidance was almost a perfect replica). It similarly stated that the prescription of misoprostol for home use should not proceed '[i]f there is no adult available to be at home with the patient' (Welsh Government 2018b, 5). However, in the absence of a further legal challenge on this point, this guidance can also be taken as a decision-making aid that may be lawfully departed from by a medical practitioner as per Lady Wise's judgment in *SPUC v Scottish Ministers*.[203]

Whilst opposition to this change in Wales did arise (and from largely the same directions as opposition to the earlier change in Scotland, as was anticipated), there was

---

[200] Senedd Deb 17 April 2018, para 410.
[201] Whilst not pertinent to the discussion of home use of misoprostol, this review also found that obstetrics and gynaecology departments in Wales only managed abortions in the late midtrimester that were sought under grounds A, B, and E of the AA 1967 (see Chapter 2 for an explanation of how the A–E grounds map onto the grounds stipulated in the AA 1967). People seeking an abortion under grounds C and D, therefore, had to travel to England to access services. Given that ground C is by far the most common in England and Wales, this is a particularly concerning finding. In response to questions in the Senedd, Vaughan Gething stated that he was looking into how this might be addressed (Senedd Deb 17 April 2018, para 423).
[202] In this case, the authority was transferred to the Welsh Cabinet Secretary for Health and Social Services by the Wales (Transfer of Functions) Order 1999 and the Government of Wales Act 2006.
[203] *SPUC v Scottish Ministers* (n99).

also plenty of praise for the move. Humanists UK's Campaign Officer Rachel Taggart-Ryan, for example, praised the Welsh Government for bringing abortion care 'into the 21st century' (Humanists UK 2018). Indeed, Humanists UK were one of the several organisations, including Royal Colleges, to call on then Secretary of State for Health and Social Care, Jeremy Hunt, in April 2018, to introduce the same changes in England (Royal College of Obstetricians and Gynaecologists 2018).

4.2.3 England

England only moved towards introducing home use in August 2018. This was, however, only a move *towards* introducing home use, as the approval would not come until later that year. On 25 August 2018, in a somewhat poorly worded announcement, the Department of Health and Social Care stated: 'Government confirms plans to approve the home-use of early abortion pills' (2018b).[204] This heading may be read to suggest that both mifepristone and misoprostol were to be permitted for home use given its use of the plural 'pills'. However, the next line makes it clear that only the regulation of misoprostol was to see a change.

Aside from the clumsy use of language, this announcement only committed to introducing home use by the end of the year, providing a significant four-month window in which to make the change. Given the simplicity of the process required for approval—a formal statement from the Secretary of State for Health and Social Care—such a large window seemed unwarranted.[205] Indeed, the TEMA approval that came a little over 18 months later in response to the COVID-19 pandemic was a far swifter process, as we will come to discuss in Chapter 8. This suggests a recognition by the Government/Department that home use of misoprostol was important, but also a feeling that it was not all that important, thereby warranting a glacial pace. Perhaps most concerningly, the initial announcement in August 2018 referenced clear clinical guidance that home use was safe, yet still afforded the Government such a significant window in which to act.

The announcement also mentioned legal advice making clear that the approval would be lawful. Presumably, this was based on the outcome of the already discussed case of *SPUC v Scottish Ministers*.[206] This case made clear that it was within the powers of the respective ministers of Scotland, Wales, and England to make such an approval. As such, it was inevitable that pressure would mount for the Government to bring England in line with the two devolved nations. One would be forgiven, therefore, for assuming that the only reason for the English approval was the avoidance of bad public relations if the country were to lag behind its neighbours so significantly. Whilst it makes no difference to the approval in practice, it is important as a matter of

[204] Of note, this was soon after the judgment in *SPUC v Scottish Ministers* (n99) was issued on 15 August 2018. It is likely, therefore, that the Department of Health and Social Care was awaiting the outcome of the judicial review before deciding whether to make similar changes.
[205] Four months may sound like a short period for a change of national policy. However, the process for this particular change is simple. Further, with Scotland and Wales already having issued approval orders, England had templates at the ready.
[206] *SPUC v Scottish Ministers* (n99).

principle that the actions of the Scottish Government would be the catalyst for the UK Government to respond to the long-term calls of healthcare professionals to permit home use of misoprostol. This is especially true when one considers the fact that, more than a decade earlier, a call for the introduction of home use came from within Westminster. In 2007, the House of Commons Science and Technology Committee issued a report entitled *Scientific Developments Relating to the Abortion Act 1967*. The report made several recommendations including, interestingly, that MPs should consider the fact that there is no good evidence that the two signature requirement 'serves to safeguard women or doctors in any meaningful way, or serves any other useful purpose' (2007, 55).[207] On the matter of home use, the report invited MPs to consider the following:

> We conclude that, subject to providers putting in place the appropriate follow up arrangements, there is no evidence relating to safety, effectiveness or patient acceptability that should serve to deter Parliament passing regulations which would enable women who chose to do so taking the second stage of early medical abortion at home, or that should deter Parliament from amending the [AA 1967] to exclude the second stage of early medical abortion from the definition of "carrying out a termination". This would enable a trial to take place. (2007, 56)

The actual approval order in England came on 27 December 2018 (Department of Health and Social Care 2018a). That it was issued just days before the self-imposed deadline again highlights a distinct lack of urgency. As with the previous approvals of Scotland and Wales, the English order stipulated that a person may take misoprostol at their permanent address or usual residence, provided mifepristone is taken in a clinic no later than nine weeks and six days' gestation. Clinical guidance was issued the following week, on 3 January 2019 (Royal College of Obstetricians and Gynaecologists 2019). This guidance was produced by the Royal College of Obstetricians and Gynaecologists, in collaboration with the Faculty of Sexual and Reproductive Healthcare and the British Society of Abortion Care Providers.

Whilst broadly similar, the English guidance does differ from that issued in Scotland and Wales. Notably, whereas the Scottish and Welsh guidance states that provision of the medication should not proceed if the pregnant person will be the only adult at home, the English guidance simply reads that people should be advised that 'having a partner or trusted adult companion to give support at home is recommended', but that a decision *not* to have someone else present should be respected (Royal College of Obstetricians and Gynaecologists 2019, 5). Pregnant people in England were, therefore, explicitly permitted to make an informed choice as to whether they wanted to be alone to complete the termination. The guidance noted, by way of a justification, that, prior to the approval of home use, people had not been required to have another adult present when they returned home from the clinic after taking both mifepristone and misoprostol. Further, it highlighted scenarios in which such a requirement would be inappropriate, such as when the person's partner is coercive, or when no one is

---

[207] We discuss the two signatures requirement in Chapter 2.

available to be present when they take the misoprostol and a delay to treatment would be problematic (2019, 5).

4.2.4 Northern Ireland

Unsurprisingly, given the nation's history of opposition to abortion, Northern Ireland was the last to permit home use of misoprostol. Indeed, the law in Northern Ireland has lagged behind the rest of the UK for decades. EMA was not even permitted in a clinical setting until *after* the rest of the UK began permitting it to take place (partially) at the patient's home. What makes the case of Northern Ireland particularly interesting is that the country was in fact set to overtake the rest of the UK in terms of liberal abortion law (albeit because of decisions by Westminster which we have touched on already and will discuss further), but then fell behind again because of the devolved government's failure to effectively respond to the impact of the COVID-19 pandemic on access to abortion care (see Chapter 8).

The way the approval orders of Scotland, Wales, and England were framed was such that they prevented people from Northern Ireland who were travelling to Great Britain to access abortion services from benefitting from home use of misoprostol. Had a person travelled from Northern Ireland to an abortion clinic in Great Britain in the period between the home use of misoprostol approval orders and the later 2020 approval orders[208] and taken mifepristone in the clinic, they would not have been permitted to leave the clinic with misoprostol to take at home. As explained in Chapter 3, this is because the earlier approval orders stipulated that 'home' be interpreted as the place in the respective nation where a pregnant person has their permanent address or is ordinarily resident. As such, a person's place of permanent residence being in Northern Ireland places them outside of the remit of the approval orders. There was, then, a need for a similar policy in Northern Ireland.

The process leading to the approval of home use of misoprostol in Northern Ireland was not triggered by Northern Ireland's devolved government itself but by actions taken by the UK Government. In January 2017, following the resignation of Deputy First Minister Martin McGuinness, the Northern Ireland Executive collapsed. Failed attempts to reform it resulted in Westminster passing the Northern Ireland (Executive Formation etc) Act 2019, to extend the period in which the Executive could be reformed before the UK Government would mandate certain legislative changes. This Act provided for the liberalisation of laws relating to abortion and same-sex couples in Northern Ireland in the event that a new Executive was not formed by 21 October 2019.[209] The requirement to make regulations with respect to abortion required the implementation of the recommendations of the United Nations Committee on the

---

[208] The 2020 approval orders being those which permitted home use of mifepristone, which will be explored further in Chapter 8.
[209] Far less frequently acknowledged, the Act also included, under section 10, a requirement to establish a scheme of victims' payments for those with injuries cause by the Troubles.

Elimination of Discrimination against Women (CEDAW) (2018).[210] These include, per paragraph 85, the repealing of sections 58 and 59 of the OAPA 1861[211] and the expansion of grounds for abortion.

The Executive did not reform by the deadline, triggering the process of changes to abortion law in Northern Ireland. In line with the CEDAW recommendations, these changes went as far as to partially decriminalise abortion. In doing so, Northern Ireland went beyond what the AA 1967 provides in Great Britain. Paragraph 84 of the CEDAW report does note that the focus of its recommendations is Northern Ireland but, given that these recommendations entail legislative changes that make for a situation far more liberal than that in Great Britain, it seems strange that the UK Government would have them pursued in Northern Ireland. Indeed, it might be considered a source of embarrassment for Westminster that in forcing Northern Ireland to respond to the CEDAW report they made the rest of the UK appear *less* progressive. Surely having de facto endorsed the CEDAW recommendations, Westminster should have implemented them in the rest of the UK. Nonetheless, this is a very different discussion that we will not enter into here.

Home use of misoprostol became possible in Northern Ireland on 31 March 2020 by way of the Abortion (Northern Ireland) Regulations 2020. Just two months later, on 14 May 2020, these regulations were replaced by the Abortion (Northern Ireland) (No. 2) Regulations 2020. Both sets of regulations are, in all respects pertinent to our discussion, identical. Before we look more closely at what the regulations stipulate, it is worth outlining the convoluted and confusing way in which they came to be.

The Abortion (Northern Ireland) Regulations 2020 came into force on 31 March 2020. As they had been introduced by way of the made affirmative procedure—in line with section 12 of the Northern Ireland (Executive Formation etc) Act 2019—they were due to 'time out' on 17 May 2020 unless both Houses approved them by that day. 17 May represented the required period of 28 days from when the Regulations were laid before Parliament (25 March 2020), extended to account for periods of dissolution, prorogation, or where both Houses were adjourned for more than four days.[212] These initial regulations were then revoked and replaced by the Abortion (Northern Ireland) (No. 2) Regulations 2020 on 14 May 2020 because, according to paragraphs 3.3 to 3.5 of the attached explanatory memorandum, there was deemed to be insufficient parliamentary time and resources to finalise the March regulations by 17 May 2020 given ongoing debates concerning the COVID-19 pandemic. As such, a further 28 days (with extensions as appropriate) for both Houses to approve the (replacement) regulations commenced on the day they were laid before Parliament (13 May 2020). This final approval came on 17 June 2020, affording the Abortion (Northern Ireland) (No. 2) Regulations 2020 permanence. Given the extensions to both 28-day periods

---

[210] Formally, the 'Report of the inquiry concerning the United Kingdom of Great Britain and Northern Ireland under article 8 of the Optional Protocol to the Convention on the Elimination of All Forms of Discrimination against Women'.

[211] Notably, the recommendations did not include the suggestion that section 25(1) of the Criminal Justice (Northern Ireland) Act 1945 be repealed. The 1945 Act was noted in the Report, but only sections 58 and 59 of the OAPA 1861 were recommended for repeal. See Chapter 2 for more discussion of the nature of these laws.

[212] Northern Ireland (Executive Formation etc) Act 2019, s.12(5).

and the fact that the second set replaced the first immediately, the stipulations therein have technically been in force continually since 31 March 2020,[213] though there has understandably been legal uncertainty.

We will proceed referring to the Abortion (Northern Ireland) (No. 2) Regulations 2020 (unless otherwise stated) as they are the regulations that remain in force, but it is worth readers being aware that the same sections of the first set of regulations provided the same permissions. As noted in Chapter 3, regulation 8(1)(d) permits home use of misoprostol provided the conditions of regulation 8(2)—which are largely the same as the approval orders outlined above—are met. The person undergoing treatment must first attend an authorised medical facility, take the mifepristone when there, and can then be prescribed misoprostol to complete the treatment at home. The pregnancy must not have exceeded its 10th week.[214] As a result of some amendment to the *criteria* for abortion (that we have argued is an evolution from the AA 1967 in Great Britain), it is notable that there is no requirement that two doctors certify the necessity of the abortion on socio-medical grounds in Northern Ireland if the pregnancy has not exceeded its 12th week. Instead, just one registered medical professional (inclusive of registered nurses and registered midwives[215]) must be satisfied, forming their opinion in good faith, that the person is not more than 12 weeks pregnant. Given that home use of misoprostol is only permitted in the first 10 weeks of pregnancy, it will only ever require the involvement of one registered medical professional in Northern Ireland.

With these regulations in Northern Ireland having come into force more than a year after home use of misoprostol was permitted in the rest of the UK (well over two years after Scotland first made the change), it is no surprise that they incorporated this, as lessons were learnt from the implementation of home use of misoprostol in the other UK jurisdictions. However, much like the AA 1967, the Abortion (Northern Ireland) (No. 2) Regulations 2020 do still provide for future approval orders. Regulations 3 and 4 combined grant the Northern Ireland Department of Health the power to approve a 'class of places', establishing the same ability to permit home use of mifepristone as in the rest of the UK.

We earlier noted how the residency requirements for home use of misoprostol contained in the approval orders of Scotland, Wales, and England precluded people from Northern Ireland accessing such care. A similar residency requirement is contained in the Northern Ireland regulations, as stipulated by regulation 8(6). Whilst still benefitting many people who want, or may in the future want, to end an unwanted pregnancy, these regulations are similarly problematic when it comes to some vulnerable people (see Chapter 3). It has not yet been tested in court how far the phrasing of 'usually resides' could be pushed in this respect, and how far from the definition of a 'permanent address' would be lawful for the purposes of home use.

---

[213] This is noted in paragraph 3.4 of the explanatory memorandum to the Abortion (Northern Ireland) (No. 2) Regulations 2020, which explains that the reason for this was to ensure that 'the law on abortion in Northern Ireland continues to apply with no risk of a gap or legal uncertainty for service users or providers'. Whilst there appear to be good intentions, the avoidance of legal uncertainty seems a generous goal given the convoluted process that played out.

[214] The Abortion (Northern Ireland) (No. 2) Regulations 2020, regulation 8(2)(c).

[215] As noted in Chapter 3, the language of 'registered medical professional' was carefully chosen so that only certain professionals were afforded the ability to provide such care.

Whilst the 2020 regulations represent a hugely important point in the history of abortion law in Northern Ireland, they immediately fell behind the rest of the UK if measured by access to services. On the day the initial regulations came into force, both Wales and Scotland approved home use of mifepristone for the purposes of EMA, with England having done so the day before. At the time of writing, Northern Ireland has not followed suit on this. We wish only to briefly note this here for completeness, as the events surrounding the approval of home use of mifepristone will be fully explored in Chapter 8.

4.3 Problematic public policy

That the nations constituting the UK (excepting, as is often the case, Northern Ireland) issued approvals for the home use of misoprostol in *somewhat* quick succession is demonstrative of the very nature of this policy area—highly political, and yet close-knit, with limited reliance on medical evidence as guiding. There is a noticeable level of codependency between the three nations which, we suggest, further highlights the political (rather than medical evidence focused) nature of abortion policy development.

Abortion policy in the UK cannot rightly be described as evidence *based*. At most—and, we suggest, still rather generously—it can be characterised as evidence *informed*. This is because the approval orders (and, in Northern Ireland, the 2020 regulations) that permit(ted) home use of misoprostol were not issued in response to medical evidence. Certainly, when they were all announced there was reference to the medical evidence, but the relevant body of medical knowledge was far from recent. The nature of policy development is such that it is rarely swiftly reactive, but the time between an acceptance in the medical community that home use of misoprostol is safe, effective, and, indeed, appropriate, and the realisation of this in UK abortion policies was more than a decade. Relevant medical knowledge was even acknowledged within Westminster by the already discussed 2007 report of the House of Commons Science and Technology Committee. When the announcement ahead of the approval was made in England, medical evidence was cited, but clearly this was not a leading factor else the approval would have come *far* earlier given the 2007 report.

Politicians have a general desire to characterise their policy as evidence based—it makes them appear 'rational and competent' actors and the 'decision process is symbolized as legitimate' (Radaelli 1995, 162). However, we suggest that such a lengthy disparity between medical evidence and policy on the matter of home use of misoprostol precludes the badge of evidence-based policy. Instead, policy can be (at most) thought of as evidence *informed*; it was inevitably a factor in the decision, because it would never have been permitted without the medical evidence to support it, but political reasoning was clearly at the forefront of the decision. This is further highlighted both by the fact that home use of mifepristone was not approved at the same time, and that misoprostol was able to be taken at home in cases of *spontaneous* miscarriage prior to the approvals. Whereas home use of both medications has been found to be safe and effective, if one were to take issue with home use of either drug from a safety perspective, it would be misoprostol, as it is that drug which actually causes the miscarriage. Therefore, if a government is happy that home use of misoprostol is safe, the decision not to also permit home use of mifepristone can in no way be ascribed to safety concerns—it is instead a matter of unnecessary supervision that strengthens our claim of abortion exceptionalism. On the inconsistency of the regulation of misoprostol, if there were real concerns about the safety of home use of the drug, it would not previously have been permitted in cases of spontaneous miscarriage. That abortion policy in the UK is, at most, evidence *informed* demonstrates the extent to which it is politicised. The delay in these decisions further exemplifies the structural control exercised by the legislature in the UK over the reproductive decisions and capacities of people with the physiology to become pregnant (see Chapter 2).

Given just how politicised it is, it is no wonder that changes to UK abortion policy are not swift. In essence, some manner of precautionary principle is at play. This may be somewhat attributable to the controversy that, unfortunately, still surrounds abortion in the public consciousness. It is no secret that abortion is a divisive issue, and this stretches beyond the simplicity of the prolife versus prochoice dichotomy into the finer details of gestational limits and the roles of various stakeholders in the decision-making process. Given this sensitivity, it is easy to see why a government characterised by realpolitik would seek to avoid too significantly alienating any one positional group. This results in gradual policy development, whereby a small step is taken to minimise any backlash, then, once the dust settles, further steps become politically feasible (Lindblom 1959)—although, the pace of this process is inevitably also affected by the abortion stance of those in power. When home use of misoprostol was approved throughout the UK, it was realistic to have expected home use of mifepristone to have followed. Indeed, this has now happened in Great Britain (but not yet Northern Ireland), albeit far sooner than expected because the conditions brought about by the COVID-19 pandemic somewhat fast-tracked the move.[216] The gradual progression of abortion policy is, of course, not unique to the UK. Abortion is regarded as a controversial policy issue in most countries, meaning this piecemeal pattern is observable throughout the world. In the US, for example, mifepristone was initially approved by the FDA, in 2000, for use up to 49 days' gestation and to be prescribed only by doctors, before that limit was increased to 70 days in 2016 and HCPs beyond doctors were able to become certified prescribers (United States Food and Drug Administration 2016; United States Food and Drug Administration 2019).[217]

Finally, this process has shown that in Great Britain—and we are specifically excluding Northern Ireland here for reasons that will become apparent—the composite nations have a tendency to stay close to one another in terms of abortion policy. Whilst each nation has similar powers to revise its abortion regulations—meaning any one of the three could have permitted home use of misoprostol long before they ended up doing so—the changes swept Great Britain within a 14-month window. It is fair to say that this was no coincidence, but that Wales and England implemented the change in response to Scotland having done so. Indeed, the fact that the announcement that England intended to approve home use of misoprostol came just 10 days

---

[216] As will be explored in Chapter 8, these changes in Great Britain to allow home use of mifepristone are, at the time of writing, only temporary in response to the conditions created by the COVID-19 pandemic.

[217] Additional prescribing privileges were enabled in federal law, and some US states have prevented HCPs beyond doctors from prescribing mifepristone. See Chapter 9.

after the publication of the ruling on the SPUC legal challenge in Scotland suggests that ministers were awaiting the outcome before making a final decision. The reality of this relationship is perhaps better demonstrated by the response to the COVID-19 pandemic in approving home use of mifepristone, whereby all three nations again acted in quick(er) succession, but we will discuss this in Chapter 8.

Undoubtedly, this domino effect is the result of something akin to political peer pressure—perhaps something of a mixture of what Dolowitz and Marsh refer to as voluntary and coercive 'policy transfer' (1996, 344). Given how abortion policy in Great Britain is unnecessarily restrictive in general, if Wales and England had not followed Scotland there would have been significant pressure for them to do so. Certainly, there was pressure at the time, but it would inevitably have grown, particularly if England had not issued an approval following the outcome of the SPUC legal challenge (at that point, perhaps the last real basis on which the approval could be withheld—uncertainty over legal authority to do so without amendment to the AA 1967—was undermined). It is problematic that political reasons meant it took Scotland introducing home use of misoprostol for Wales and England to do so. However, equally, this unofficial copycat system might be viewed as beneficial. Without it, Wales and England may not have issued approval orders. In that sense, then, only one of the three needs to *actually* initiate a progressive change for all three to end up with a more progressive policy. The ideal remains that the whole of Great Britain (and, indeed, every country) follows the medical evidence in progressing its abortion regulations, but, in the interim, it may be at least viewed favourably that a fear of being deemed out of touch or regressive causes Great Britain to move (almost) in sync.

Northern Ireland has been excluded from this close-knit policy progression as it has long had far more restrictive abortion laws. The country had no apparent intention to match the policies throughout Great Britain before it was forced to.[218] Interestingly, Westminster, when making changes for Northern Ireland, went further than the rest of the UK in liberalising its abortion laws by implementing (partial) decriminalisation, and specifically making it so that a pregnant person who has an abortion outside of the parameters of the regulations would not commit a criminal offence. This created a somewhat unusual situation in which the most liberal abortion laws in the UK, particularly for people needing access to early abortion care,[219] were set to be in Northern Ireland. However, as Northern Ireland did not follow the rest of the UK in permitting home use of mifepristone in response to the COVID-19 pandemic, the present state of affairs raises the question of which policy can be considered most progressive—partial decriminalisation for pregnant people who have abortions perhaps sends the better message in *principle* and contributes to the dismantling of legally created and perpetuated abortion stigma (Cook 2014), but home use of mifepristone ultimately improves access in *practice*. Nonetheless, following the events of 2017 to 2020 that we have charted, the four nations of the UK are the closest they have been in decades

---

[218] This might be thought of as a significant concern to many public and administrative lawyers. Whilst the progressive changes in abortion law made in Northern Ireland are important, many may have lingering concerns about the extent to which this move by Westminster was a blatant show of disrespect for devolution in the UK.

[219] Meaning in the first 12 weeks of pregnancy—see Chapter 3.

on abortion policy. Whether or not there will be any movement in Great Britain on the question of (partial) decriminalisation remains to be seen, but it is inevitable that pressure will mount as a result of Northern Ireland's new regulations. Similarly, in Northern Ireland there will be calls for home use of mifepristone to be approved, which may or may not be heeded.

4.4 Summary

This chapter provided a detailed overview of the approval of home use of misoprostol through the UK, which was one of the most significant periods of change in the history of abortion law in the country since the 1960s. With Scotland as a catalyst, a domino effect ensued throughout Great Britain, resulting in drastic improvements to abortion access throughout all three nations by ensuring that pregnant people did not have to be unnecessarily supervised swallowing the first of two abortion pills. In Northern Ireland, the changes came in an altogether different fashion, which was essentially a matter of Westminster intervening to 'bring it in line with' the rest of the UK.

Ignoring how each nation reached this point, it can be viewed as positive that they all did. However, observing the steps that led to the changes reveals a less progressive tale. We thus highlighted several important procedural aspects of abortion policy in Great Britain (and, to a lesser extent, Northern Ireland) more generally. Notably, that this policy development can be considered evidence *informed* at best, that a highly political use of the precautionary principle is employed, and that the individual nations of Great Britain have a tendency to stay within arm's reach of each other on abortion policy.

What has become very much apparent since the approval orders in Great Britain is that there was a desire for this service among those seeking abortion services. Data from Scotland show that in 2018 (the first full year in which home use of misoprostol was permitted), 29.9% of medical terminations were completed at the patient's home by self-administration of misoprostol, with this figure rising to 49.3% in 2019 (Public Health Scotland 2020, 15). Similarly, in England and Wales in 2019 (the first full year in which home use of misoprostol was permitted in both countries), 36% of medical terminations were carried out in this manner. It is, at the time of writing, far too soon to expect any such data from Northern Ireland. Nonetheless, it would be reasonable to expect a similar, if not greater, demand for abortion services involving home use of misoprostol.

Home use of misoprostol is important because it improves the comfort of patients and increases accessibility by removing the need for a patient to make two trips to a clinic (Parsons 2020). However, it does not go far enough, we argue, to begin to address many of the access barriers outlined in the previous chapter. In the next chapter, we consider why there is a moral imperative for TEMA—inclusive of home use of mifepristone.

5

Early medical abortion and
the telemedical imperative

In 2020, there was significant growth in the use of telemedicine globally due to the COVID-19 pandemic. Telemedicine was introduced as part of the virus response in many countries to reduce the risk of exposure to the virus in clinical settings and complement the introduction of social distancing measures in the community. In England, the Secretary of State for Health and Social Care, Matt Hancock, commented during a House of Commons debate:

> We have moved to a principle of "digital first" in primary care and with out-patients: unless there are clinical or practical reasons, all consultations should be done by telemedicine.[220]

Incidentally, it was several weeks after these comments that Hancock applied this principle to abortion care, despite there being no 'clinical or practical reasons' for TEMA not to be introduced. This delay further highlights the abortion exceptionalism we have outlined. We discuss the changes to abortion regulation and care implemented throughout Great Britain in response to the pandemic in Chapter 8, so will not do so here. Suffice to say, following some initial policy confusion, TEMA was introduced in response to the heightened risk of infection presented by in-person services.

However, prior to this reactive 'telemedical rush', remote care provision was limited and often implemented for its system benefits rather than patient benefits. That is not to say that the system benefits of telemedicine are not important, as ultimately system benefits can (depending on the health system in question) have something of a trickle-down effect resulting in benefits to patients—for example, efficient services shorten waiting times for patients. Rather, a focus on patient benefits is equally important.

In previous chapters, we have demonstrated the very real barriers to EMA services that exist in the UK and US. We now turn our attention to the role telemedicine can and, as we will argue, should play in overcoming at least some of these barriers. To do so, we will apply the framework of the telemedical imperative which one of us has previously proposed (Parsons 2021a). The telemedical imperative posits that healthcare systems have a duty to implement telemedical services where possible, provided that four criteria are met: safety, effectiveness, acceptability, and the flexible, catch-all condition of 'no service-specific concerns'.

We do not consider telemedicine to be a silver bullet in the context of abortion care. It is far from being so. However, we do suggest that telemedicine is, in essence, a way

---

[220] HC Deb 11 March 2020, vol 673, col 383.

Early Medical Abortion, Equality of Access, and the Telemedical Imperative. Jordan A. Parsons and Elizabeth Chloe Romanis, Oxford University Press. © Oxford University Press 2021. DOI: 10.1093/oso/9780192896155.003.0005

of enabling *more* people to *access* care that is already *available* to them—services being offered is not the same as services being accessible. Some of the barriers we have outlined in earlier chapters simply cannot be overcome by TEMA. For example, if a patient is identified as being at high risk of an ectopic pregnancy and therefore requires an ultrasound scan, telemedicine cannot entirely remove geographical barriers. As such, we argue here that TEMA should be introduced as one way of contributing to the improvement of abortion services overall. Services provided should be inclusive of the diverse range of experiences, and resulting needs, of those who require access to care.

5.1 The telemedical imperative

The telemedical imperative seeks to promote the realisation of the benefits of telemedicine.[221] Notably, the benefits of overcoming health inequities, improving the efficiency of healthcare systems, and enhancing the autonomy of service users. We stress here that the telemedical imperative's focus is on the introduction of telemedical services *in addition to* the in-person equivalents and not as replacements. Further, it considers the in-person and telemedical options with a particular service to be on an equal footing. Duffy and Lee (2018) instead suggest that in-person services becoming 'Option B' is important in the pursuit of patient-centred care. However, we have concerns with this approach as it seems to presuppose that telemedical options are necessarily better. In reality, some patients may prefer to access certain services in person for myriad reasons, and they may feel pressured to instead receive telemedical services if they are a default. As such, we advocate for telemedicine as *additional* and not substitutionary, with in-person and telemedical provision of the same service being of equal standing—this is particularly important in the context of abortion care, as will become clear.

A significant proportion of telemedical services that have been developed seek to improve health outcomes for disadvantaged patient groups. Barriers to accessing health services are often socioeconomic—or, at the very least, related to socioeconomic factors—and telemedicine can reach patients where they are. For example, many projects exist in low- and middle-income countries to introduce telemedicine, making services available to communities that have historically been unable to access them. Even where geography is less of a barrier, telemedicine has been used to improve access by, for example, removing the need for patients to take time off work or make childcare arrangements for routine consultations. It is also implemented to improve access to more specialist care, such as where there are limited facilities in a country with the expertise. With the barriers that telemedicine can remove often being socioeconomic in nature, telemedical services at least have the *potential* to lessen the impact wealth gaps have on health outcomes globally. In doing so, telemedicine contributes to the wider mission to address health inequities at both local and global level.

---

[221] We will only briefly summarise the telemedical imperative here. Those desiring a more detailed outline can read the original article (Parsons 2021a).

As telemedical services largely utilise the internet and smart devices (such as mobile phone applications), there is a point to be made about the digital divide. After all, the digital divide is largely associated with socioeconomic status, so it could be considered counterintuitive to seek to overcome socioeconomic disadvantage using means that may not be available to those concerned. However, herein lies an important aspect of the telemedical imperative—that it concerns telemedical services as *additional* and not as replacements for in-person services.

A related benefit is that of improved efficiency. This is, as already alluded to, a benefit both to systems and patients in an interrelated fashion. Even if a patient can easily access services, there are often long waiting times. Telemedicine has the potential to reduce waiting times by, for example, minimising the time between patient appointments. Of course, telemedicine has its own issues that prevent a seamless transition between patients, such as connectivity issues, but overall can minimise unused time. Not only will reduced waiting times be appreciated by patients, but they can also improve the safety of services; early signs of disease may be noticed to enable preventative measures and time-sensitive treatments to be provided earlier. Efficiency may also translate into financial savings which could be redirected to improve other, in-person services.

Finally, telemedicine can be considered as autonomy-enhancing for patients. This benefit assumes that telemedical services should not replace in-person delivery (an important foundation of the telemedical imperative) as the patient's autonomy is enhanced by the provision of an additional choice. When a service is only available in person, the patient cannot be considered as having any real choice about *how* they access the care they need; deciding whether to go for the only option available is a false choice. With the introduction of telemedical options, patients have a real choice— the choice between telemedical or in-person provision of the service in question— thereby enabling *meaningful* choice. Of course, those who may be unable to access in-person services, or can access them only at significant cost, may not have their autonomy meaningfully enhanced as the telemedical option becomes the only feasible choice. Similarly, those without access to the necessary technologies may still be considered as having only the option of in-person services. It is important to recognise, however, that there is a continuum between telemedical and in-person services rather than a binary division between the two forms of care provision. Within a care pathway, a patient may be able to engage with some aspects in person and others remotely. We discuss this idea of a telemedical continuum further in Chapter 6, along with discussion of the relationship between autonomy and multiple choices. For our purposes here, it is enough to just note how telemedicine again has the *potential* to enhance autonomy.[222]

Given these benefits, it is important that telemedical provision of services is at the very least contemplated. To consider the introduction of telemedical services, the

---

[222] Our consistent highlighting of telemedicine's *potential* rather than assertions of what it *will* do is important for the simple fact that it will vary hugely across contexts. For example, remote monitoring to remove the need for patients with chronic conditions to attend regular consultations may be considered less autonomy enhancing than a range of choices for patients receiving primary care consultations (in person, telephone, videoconferencing, or online messenger). As such, these benefits will arise to varying degrees across telemedical services, and in some cases may not arise at all.

telemedical imperative provides a framework of four factors as explained below. The first three are of consistent importance, whereas the fourth allows room for adjustment depending on the service in question.

5.1.1 Safety

If a service is unsafe and harms patients, its introduction would not generally be considered ethically permissible whether delivered remotely or in person. Derse and Miller nicely capture the importance of telemedical services being safe in writing that telemedicine 'should not be allowed to expand access at the expense of creating substandard practice' (2008, 457). This first criterion arises from the duty of doctors not to harm their patients.

The telemedical imperative proposes a relative standard for considering safety. As it perceives telemedical services as additional, those considered will already have an in-person equivalent against which to be assessed. As such, to satisfy the safety criterion a telemedical service must, statistically, be roughly as safe as (or, of course, safer than) its in-person counterpart.

A factor in the safety of a telemedical service inevitably relates to the quality of the connection, be that telephone or internet. In a case discussed by Freudenberg and Yellowlees (2014), a patient quietly made a verbal indication of his intention to self-harm, but his webcam did not register this, so his doctor was unaware. It is likely that this patient's doctor would have heard this—or would at least have heard a mumble that would prompt a request for him to repeat what he said—if the consultation had taken place in person. A poor connection, then, can raise safety concerns. It is for this reason that a clinician should cut short a consultation with a poor connection and re-schedule it. Even if a telemedical service is deemed safe at the commissioning level, it remains a duty of doctors to protect their patients and this may even mean insisting on in-person services if, for example, a patient has a poor internet connection.

As one of us has previously argued in first proposing the telemedical imperative, the safety criterion may be less important in certain, very limited, circumstances (Parsons 2021a). In extreme cases—for example, submarine crew and astronauts in space (Chaet et al. 2017, 1137)—the standard of care may be justifiably lowered. However, this is largely irrelevant in the case of EMA so we will not dwell on this exception.[223]

5.1.2 Effectiveness

In addition to being safe, it is important that a telemedical service is effective. These two criteria go somewhat hand-in-hand; an effective but unsafe service is ethically problematic, as is a safe but ineffective service. Without both criteria being met, there is a risk of harm to the patient that brings into question a service's ethical defensibility.

---

[223] It is possible that someone could need an EMA in one of these scenarios. Nonetheless, it is fair to say that such a scenario would be extremely rare—in part because of pregnancy testing requirements prior to submarine deployment in some armed forces.

As such, it is necessary that a telemedical intervention can, in general, achieve its purpose in addition to being safe.

Of note, this necessity being *in general* reflects the telemedical imperative's positioning as primarily applicable at a commissioning/policy level. For a telemedical service to be made available at all, it is important that it is mostly effective, but inevitably it will not be effective in all instances. This is where clinical discretion comes to the fore, and a clinician should insist on in-person delivery of a service for a patient if necessary.[224] Established clinical standards remain important, and the American Medical Association's Council on Ethical and Judicial Affairs has noted that telemedicine is not appropriate in circumstances where it prevents these standards being met (Chaet et al. 2017, 1137). Similar stipulations can be found in the General Medical Council's ethical guidance on remote consultations in the UK (General Medical Council a).

Beyond the impact on the individual patient, there is a distributive justice argument in favour of the effectiveness criterion. Should a telemedical service be ineffective, the patient will require further care. Whether a repeat of the same telemedical service, the in-person equivalent of that same service, or an entirely different service in the event of a worsened condition, the ineffective telemedical service creates a need for further resources.

5.1.3   Acceptability

The third criterion is acceptability. Whilst the safety and effectiveness criteria focus primarily on the treatment itself, acceptability looks to the patient's experience of the service. This is of increasing importance with the wider shift towards patient-centred medicine.

Acceptability goes beyond the physiological aspects of a service. Whilst it is important that a service is physically tolerable—so excessive side effects may, in some cases, be reason to only offer the service in person—it is equally important that the experience of patients is not problematic, so as to best preserve mental, as well as physical, health. For example, some patients may have serious concerns about the security of remote consultations, both in terms of the technology not being secure and the possibility of being overheard by someone they live with or a neighbour. This is perhaps more likely when the issue is particularly sensitive or carries significant social stigma, such as a patient seeking mental health support. If telemedical delivery of a particular service causes unnecessary levels of distress to patients, then it may not be appropriate for it to be offered. However, it is important to recognise that other patients may find it distressing to be in a clinical environment. Generalisations about acceptability are problematic.

---

[224] Incidentally, there may also be occasions when it is necessary to insist on telemedical delivery of a service. For example, this has been seen during the COVID-19 pandemic. We do not, however, consider that this will be the case in any but the most exceptional circumstances, and the COVID-19 pandemic might be considered the very definition of exceptional circumstances in healthcare going forward. If a patient wants to access care in person and is willing to travel as needed to do so, then only in the most extreme circumstances would it be appropriate to insist that they access that care remotely. Our thanks to Marcus Sirianno for highlighting this point.

As acceptability can be very subjective, the minimum standard for a telemedical service need not be set high. If studies have found that a particular telemedical service is not acceptable to most patients, but a sizeable minority are very satisfied with it, this criterion should be considered met. In such circumstances, it would be important to inform patients accessing the service of this, perhaps noting any common complaints from those who did not find it acceptable. Ultimately, however, it should be the choice of the patient to decide whether telemedical delivery is likely to be acceptable to them. Here the importance of telemedical services not becoming a default is apparent; acceptability is inherently subjective, and even a patient who considers it acceptable may still prefer to access the service in person (Collins et al. 2000; Chaet et al. 2017, 1137).

The acceptability criterion adds something of a human touch to the telemedical imperative. It reminds us that just because something works, we should not necessarily do it. Humbyrd discusses a case in which a patient and his family were informed of his incurable lung cancer by a doctor unknown to them by video link even though they were in a hospital at the time, which she describes as an example of 'efficiency over compassion' (2019, 2639). A patient may prefer to receive information this way if the alternative is to wait, but without their prior agreement this example further highlights the problems with telemedicine becoming the default.[225]

5.1.4 No service-specific concerns

The final criterion exists to recognise that sometimes a telemedical service being safe, effective, and acceptable is not reason enough to implement it. Sometimes there remains one big sticking point that renders a service inappropriate regardless of its other credentials. Hence, this last step is necessary to consider whether there are any concerns specific to the service in question that cannot be reasonably overcome.

A prime example of a telemedical service that is safe, effective, and acceptable, but may fall at this final hurdle, is the placement of complex medical equipment in a patient's home for remote monitoring. Bauer suggests that where this happens the home becomes a 'de facto ICU', placing significant burden on those who live with the patient (2001, 141). Even if this is safe, effective, and acceptable to the patient, the burden on others *may* be reason to reconsider how appropriate this service is.

The 'de facto ICU' example is rather niche in terms of the burden it places on those who live with the patient. Ordinarily, the patient is first concern and the impact on others is only factored in by the patient themselves. It is for this reason that 'burden on family/friends/carers' would not be appropriate as a criterion, but instead can be encapsulated by this catch-all when relevant. The flexibility of this final criterion is important as it makes the telemedical imperative more broadly applicable. It allows for adaptation so that uncommon concerns can be considered without having to be explicitly listed as criteria.

---

[225] The issue of 'telemedical primacy' has been discussed elsewhere (Parsons 2021a, 304).

5.2 Applying the telemedical imperative

Having outlined the telemedical imperative along the lines it was originally proposed (Parsons 2021a), it now remains for us to apply it to the particular telemedical service in question: EMA. Following the telemedical imperative, the case for TEMA can be made provided it is safe, effective, and acceptable, and that there are no other major concerns specific to TEMA that cannot be reasonably overcome. In Chapter 1, we considered the safety, effectiveness, and acceptability of EMA provided in person. The credentials of TEMA on those three counts are largely the same.

5.2.1 Safety

As the safety criterion employs a relative standard, the safety credentials of EMA delivered in person at a medical facility are relevant. We discussed this in detail in Chapter 1, where we noted that the procedure is extremely safe up to 10 weeks' gestation—that being the period in which it is considered an *early* medical abortion. Indeed, it is safer than the use of various routine medications, such as penicillin, which are not subject to the same level of supervision (Lohr et al. 2020). The procedure is also safe beyond 10 weeks' gestation, though the necessary dose of misoprostol and the risk of side effects both gradually increase—we are, however, concerned only with *early* medical abortion here. The question is, then, how TEMA compares to in-person EMA.

A systematic review conducted by Endler and colleagues (2019) included 13 studies of TEMA,[226] including retrospective cohort, prospective cohort, descriptive, and qualitative studies.[227] Their findings show TEMA to be safe; across the included studies, 0.07% was the highest rate of abortions resulting in a need for blood transfusion, and 2.8% the highest of hospital admission (2019, 1097). It should be noted, however, that the included studies concerned varying forms of telemedicine, some of which were examples of *partial* telemedicine in that they still required an in-person element. For example, that of Hyland and colleagues reported on the service offered by the Tabbot Foundation in Australia, which requires patients to undergo an ultrasound scan to determine gestational age (2018, 336). This is an important consideration as the risk of side effects and incomplete termination increases—albeit gradually—with gestational age. There logically follows, then, a question as to whether there is a greater risk of harm through such side effects when no ultrasound is performed.

TEMA services that are *fully* telemedical and do not have an automatic requirement for an ultrasound scan generally date a pregnancy based on the patient's menstrual history. This relies on the ability of a pregnant person to recall the date of their last menstrual period within a reasonable margin of error. Research suggests that this is something patients can do. A study by Bracken and colleagues (2011)

---

[226] We were unable to engage with one of the included studies (Larrea et al. 2015) because the article is in Spanish.

[227] It is important to highlight that the included studies did not all report against the same measures. As such, some figures presented in this chapter may appear to contradict each other, but this is simply a matter of different reporting measures.

compared patient estimates of gestational age with the results of ultrasound scanning across 10 clinics in the US, with the aim of determining how many would fall within the 'caution zone'. The 'caution zone' was defined as instances where the patient estimated the gestation to be within 63 days, but the ultrasound determined it to be higher (2011, 20). Findings show that patients were very accurate in their own assessment based on the date of their last menstrual period. Of 3,041, just 76 (2.4%) fell within the caution zone and would therefore have been offered treatment when ineligible if self-assessment were relied upon (2011, 20). Further, of these 76, 50 were determined to be between 64 and 70 days by an ultrasound (2011, 20); only 26 (0.8%) would have been outside of the now more common gestational limit of 10 weeks.

These findings are corroborated by a 2014 systematic review (Schonberg et al. 2014). Whilst concluding that further research is necessary when it comes to gestational ages above 63 days, Schonberg and colleagues found low rates of underestimation up to 63 days' gestation (2014, 485). Unsurprisingly, the included studies suggested that estimating gestational age based on menstrual history becomes less reliable as gestational age increases—it becomes more challenging to recall events with accuracy the further they are in the past.

That most patients are likely able to reliably date their pregnancy supports the scan as indicated model, whereby ultrasounds are used only if there is an appropriate reason to. Guidance on abortion care during the COVID-19 pandemic issued by the Royal College of Obstetricians and Gynaecologists (after TEMA was approved) recommends that an ultrasound be provided if the patient is unable to recall the date of their last menstrual period with reasonable certainty or if a high risk of ectopic pregnancy is indicated (2020, 4). Raymond and colleagues (2020) have also published a sample protocol for such services. These models go further to ensure safety by not always placing responsibility on the patient to date their pregnancy. Other services may be considered more problematic in that they do not provide ultrasound scanning in any circumstances, such as Women on Web. Users of the Women on Web service are asked to provide details of an ultrasound scan if possible and are advised of the risk of ectopic pregnancy, but are still able to proceed regardless. However, this is due to the nature of Women on Web in providing a service to people in countries where safe access to regulated abortion care is not possible—users may well be unable to obtain an ultrasound scan, especially if they are seeking to avoid drawing attention to their pregnancy. We are making the case for the lawful introduction of TEMA within jurisdictions that already provides abortion care, meaning reasonable access to ultrasound scanning where indicated. Ultimately, this would mean that the HCP carrying out the consultation could insist on a particular patient undergoing a scan if they have a clinical reason to believe it is appropriate.

At this point, it is pertinent to note that concerns have been raised not only about the accidental misdating of pregnancies, but the possibility of people intentionally deceiving care providers to access abortion services past gestational limits (Christian Concern 2021). If this is occurring, it is on a minute scale (Aiken et al. 2021a), and it is not appropriate to make determinations about the appropriateness of a service based on the tiny proportion of instances in which it may be misused. Further, as Milne (2021a) has noted, irrespective of whether a TEMA service is made available, there will always be a very small number of people experiencing a 'crisis pregnancy'[228] (Milne 2019) who will continue to access abortion past gestational limits. Access to unlawfully sourced abortion medication via the internet has long been a possibility. Thus, potential unlawful use of abortion medications past gestational limits is no reflection of the safety of the service, but rather a reflection of the extent to which crisis pregnancies occur—which we need to provide more support to address. If anything, TEMA being facilitated as a local service might be part of the support offered to reduce unlawful late-term use of misoprostol by enabling many people better access to care earlier in a pregnancy.

More recently—and in response to the challenges COVID-19 presented for abortion care provision—Gambir and colleagues (2020) have considered the safety of at-home EMA compared to that carried out in a clinic through a systematic review. Whilst the focus was not on TEMA, the at-home classification included instances where both mifepristone and misoprostol were taken at home which, in terms of the procedure itself, is the same as TEMA. It should be noted that the at-home classification also included patients who took only one of the drugs at home, but this study is still useful for our purposes. Both services were found to be equally safe, with no statistically significant difference in the rates of side effects between the two classifications (2020, 10).

More directly applicable studies are those of Aiken and colleagues (2021a) and Reynolds-Wright and colleagues (2021). Aiken and colleagues provide early data from TEMA services in England and Wales following temporary approval in 2020.[229] Their cohort study included patients from the three largest abortion providers in England and Wales—BPAS, MSI Reproductive Choices (previously Marie Stopes International), and the National Unplanned Pregnancy Advisory Service—with data covering the two months before and after the change in service model (and including 85% of all medical abortions performed in England and Wales in this period). This study is perhaps more useful than some of those already discussed as the services it evaluates are closer to what might be considered the ideal, by which we mean that they are formal, regulated services offered within a jurisdiction that include (but are not exclusively) a *fully* telemedical care pathway. Other services reported on have largely included some level of in-person care or, in the case of Women on Web, operate across borders and outside of national regulatory frameworks.

Aiken and colleagues found the safety of TEMA to be comparable to in-person care (2021a, 11).[230] In both cohorts (a combined study population of 52,142), there were no instances of infection requiring hospital admission, major surgery, or death. Occurrences of haemorrhage requiring transfusion were just eight (0.04%) and seven (0.02%) in the traditional and telemedicine-hybrid groups, respectively (2021a, 20).

---

[228] Milne uses the phrase 'crisis pregnancy' to refer to instances in which a 'woman experiences her pregnancy as a crisis, to the extent that she feels she cannot accept and respond to her pregnancy' (Milne 2021b, 1). This is often because of complex sociocultural circumstances.

[229] This approval will be discussed in detail in Chapter 8.

[230] It is worth noting that the two cohorts were: (i) patients treated before regulations permitted TEMA, meaning all underwent in-person care (albeit with home use of misoprostol), and (ii) patients treated after regulations permitted TEMA as a 'telemedicine-hybrid' cohort, meaning some (39%) still accessed care in person. Nonetheless, any changes between the two groups can be largely attributed to the impact of TEMA.

These findings illustrate not only that EMA is safe in general, but that there is no greater safety concern when this care is delivered by telemedicine.

Reynolds-Wright and colleagues (2021) provide similar data concerning the Scottish experience of implementing TEMA during the pandemic. Their cohort study included patients accessing abortion care via the TEMA service established by NHS Lothian over a 14-week period from 1 April 2020. Whilst not comparing in-person and telemedical care pathways, the results are still useful in considering the safety of TEMA. Of 663 patients, 16 (2.4%) presented at the hospital after their abortion (2021, 3). Only two were admitted with haemorrhage, neither of which required a transfusion. Others attended with pain and/or bleeding, but only required observation, intravenous fluids, or antibiotics. A significant proportion of patients (18.5%) used the provider's telephone line for advice, but only a minority of these patients were scheduled for a clinic visit—reasons including a positive/invalid pregnancy test, symptoms of continuing pregnancy, or persistent pain (2021, 3).

Overall, then, it appears that the safety of TEMA (or, in some cases, home use of both mifepristone and misoprostol) is comparable to that of EMA in person. Concerns around the estimation of gestational age are overcome by evidence that patients can reliably date their pregnancies based on their menstrual history. As such, the safety criterion of the telemedical imperative is satisfied.

5.2.2   Effectiveness

On effectiveness, the systematic review conducted by Endler and colleagues (2019) is again useful. This review assessed effectiveness by three measures: continued pregnancy; self-assessed abortion completion; and need for surgical evacuation after the medical abortion. Their findings demonstrate that the effectiveness of TEMA is largely similar to the effectiveness of EMA involving in-person care.

Across the included studies that reported on EMA up to and including 10 weeks' gestation, rates of continued pregnancy ranged from 0% to 1.9% (Endler et al. 2019, 1096). Whereas our focus is largely on terminations this early in pregnancy, it is worth noting that they found the rate of continued pregnancy to rise with higher gestational ages. Continued pregnancy when an abortion was performed between 10 and 12 weeks ranged from 1.4% to 2.3% (2019, 1096). This suggests that even if someone were to access the service in this additional two-week period, the procedure would still be highly effective.

On the two other measures of effectiveness, Endler and colleagues (2019) found similarly reassuring results, again in terminations up to and including 10 weeks' gestation. Self-assessed abortion completion was found to range from between 93.8% and 96.4%, and the need for a surgical evacuation after the medical abortion ranged from 0.9% to 19.3% (2019, 1096).[231]

To return to the more recent studies detailed above, Aiken and colleagues (2021a) found effectiveness to be similarly high. In the traditional (in-person) cohort, the

---

[231] The included studies reported on different outcomes. This is why the lowest reported abortion completion (93.8%) and the highest reported surgical evacuation (19.3%) add up to more than 100%.

success rate was 98.2%, increasing to 98.8% in the telemedicine-hybrid group (2021a). Of note, there was no significant variation between the two cohorts in the specific outcomes classified as unsuccessful. Ultimately, these findings suggest that TEMA may in fact be *more* effective than EMA provided in person. Further reflecting on Great Britain's introduction of TEMA in 2020, Reynolds-Wright and colleagues reported that 650 of 663 (98%) abortions performed through NHS Lothian in Scotland were successful (2021, 3).

We can look back to Bracken and colleagues' (2011) study here too, as the 'caution zone' in that study is also when the effectiveness of EMA begins to decrease. That only 0.8% of patients dated their pregnancy as within 10 weeks when an ultrasound placed it at past 10 weeks suggests that we need not be concerned that the overall effectiveness of TEMA will be limited by patients accessing care later in their pregnancies because of unreliable dating based on menstrual history. Almost all patients will, within a scan as indicated TEMA model, undergo their abortion comfortably within the period in which it is highly effective. The evidence is thus conclusive that TEMA meets the effectiveness criterion of the telemedical imperative.

5.2.3   Acceptability

Given that patients have, for many years, left clinics almost immediately after taking mifepristone and misoprostol, it was clear that there was no need for an observation period to ensure safety, nor was there a recognised risk of treatment being ineffective if the process was not carried out entirely in a clinical setting. As such, it was not expected that using telemedicine to provide this care would decrease safety and effectiveness.[232] Acceptability, however, could feasibly decrease in the absence of in-person interaction for a variety of reasons. For example, there have been some concerns about the quality of a consultation that does not take place in person, which may lead to some patients being less aware of what to expect and, therefore, find the side effects distressing. There is not obviously anything innate to the abortion consultation, and discussion specifically of how to use the medications and the potential side effects, that cannot be communicated as effectively by remote means as it might in person. Moreover, there have been no indications, in practice, that people are less informed about their abortion when consulted remotely. There have been several qualitative studies to assess the acceptability of TEMA, as reported in Endler and colleagues' (2019) systematic review. They cover a range of countries and services, and largely demonstrate high levels of acceptability.

Most studies have examined the experiences of people using Women on Web. Two of them do not focus on individual countries (Gomperts et al. 2008; Gomperts et al. 2012) whereas others were concerned specifically with Brazil (Gomperts et al. 2014),

---

[232] Incidentally, it would be reasonable to expect safety to improve with both drugs being taken at home. As we discussed in Chapter 4, patients who were required to take mifepristone in a clinic before returning home to take misoprostol and complete their abortion have reported traumatic experiences on public transport as mifepristone has begun to take effect. Having the whole process take place at the patient's home removes the need to travel and/or be in public when (potentially severe) side effects kick in.

Ireland/Northern Ireland (Aiken et al. 2017), and Hungary (Les et al. 2017). All of these studies reported high levels of satisfaction and acceptability among patients who responded to follow-up questionnaires, reaching 100% in the Brazil study (Gomperts et al. 2014, 131). Of 194 patients in one study, only two answered that they would not have performed their abortion themselves had they known how stressful it would be (Gomperts et al. 2008, 1172–3). In another, 64.1% reported satisfaction and a further 22.5% reported an acceptable level of stress, with only 2.3% finding the process extremely stressful or dissatisfying (Gomperts et al. 2012, 229). More specific data from Ireland/Northern Ireland show that whilst some patients expressed some negative feelings about the process—guilt (17.4%), sadness (11.6%), loss (7.9%), and disappointment (2.6%)[233]—only 0.2% ultimately found the service unacceptable (Aiken et al. 2017, 1211). Some patients in Hungary had some similarly negative feelings after the process, but still 98% stated that they would recommend the service (the other 2% did not answer that question) (Les et al. 2017, 361).

With these reports being in relation to Women on Web, it must be acknowledged that many of these users are unlikely to have had an alternative means of accessing care due to the nature of the Women on Web service. The purpose of Women on Web is to reach those in countries where access is restricted, so it is possible that some of these users would have preferred to have received their care in person had they had the option. Nonetheless, that does not take away from the fact that the majority found the service acceptable *even if* they might have preferred to have accessed care in person. Per the telemedical imperative, we do not consider that the acceptability criterion should be assessed by a relative standard—provided a service is safe and effective, a sizeable minority finding it acceptable is sufficient (Parsons 2021a, 303). This is because acceptability is subjective. Ultimately, it should be a matter for the patient to decide whether they consider TEMA to be the right option for them once presented with relevant information. For example, they might be informed of some of the main aspects of the process that previous patients have raised as reasons for dissatisfaction.

Two of the studies do not concern Women on Web and instead assessed the services offered by the Tabbot Foundation in Australia and Planned Parenthood in Iowa. Both are, as will be discussed in Chapter 6, *partially* telemedical. Nonetheless, many of the pertinent elements of TEMA are relevant; even having to attend some form of health care facility, patients using these two services undergo a remote consultation and self-administer at least misoprostol at home. Patients using the Tabbot Foundation service were overwhelmingly satisfied, with 97% of those who responded to the follow-up question rating it 1 (highly satisfied) on a scale of 1 to 5 (Hyland et al. 2018, 338). Similarly high levels were reported with Planned Parenthood in Iowa (Grossman et al. 2011).

Grossman and colleagues' (2011) study is particularly useful as it compared two cohorts, one using the telemedical service and the other using the more traditional

---

[233] The authors note that the percentages of patients reporting different feelings—some of which we have not mentioned here—do not total 100 because patients were able to provide several responses. Given that at least some patients provided several responses, it is possible (and, we suggest, rather likely) that there was overlap between those reporting feelings of guilt, sadness, loss, and disappointment.

in-person service.[234] They found both satisfaction and likelihood of recommending the service to be higher in the telemedicine group (94% and 90%) than the in-person group (88% and 83%) (2011, 301). Further, 76% of patients in both groups were 'very satisfied' with the conversation with their doctor (2011, 301), which suggests that one of the concerns with TEMA that remote consultation is not as effective as in-person consultation at making the patient feel at ease and as though their questions have been answered is unfounded. Whilst acceptability was high, it should be noted that 25% of the telemedicine group said they would have preferred the doctor be in the room (2011, 301). Nonetheless, that 73% said they would not have preferred the doctor be in the room (2011, 301) is demonstrable of a high level of acceptability, so at most the presence of this notable minority supports the argument that patients should, when making their treatment decision, be informed of the fact that some have not found telemedical services acceptable.

The recent study of Aiken and colleagues (2021a), perhaps unsurprisingly given the results of the many previous studies, also found acceptability to be high. There were responses of very satisfied/very good or satisfied/good from 96% of patients. 80% would opt for TEMA if accessing the service again in future, compared to just 13% reporting that they would choose in-person care. Another recent study already discussed—that of Reynolds-Wright and colleagues (2021)—similarly reported that 94.7% of patients rated the abortion experience as very acceptable (88.2%) or some-what acceptable (6.5%). 86.6% rated the remote consultation itself as very acceptable (83%) or somewhat acceptable (3.6%), and 71.3% would choose a remote consultation if accessing abortion care in the future (2021, 4).

These studies all demonstrate that TEMA is, for the most part, highly acceptable to patients. Even where patients reported negative feelings associated with the process, they still said they would recommend the service, suggesting that those negative feelings were more about the process of abortion in general rather than the specific telemedical pathway chosen. This criterion is not intended to be assessed relative to in-person delivery of the service, nor does it require a majority to find the service acceptable for reasons discussed earlier in this chapter. Nonetheless, the findings of each study discussed would satisfy the criterion of acceptability *even if* we took the standard to be relative. More than 50% of patients found TEMA to be acceptable across the board, and the one study comparing it to in-person provision (Grossman et al. 2011) found satisfaction to be higher in those opting for TEMA.

5.2.4 No service-specific concerns

This final criterion of the telemedical imperative is something of a catch-all. Its purpose is to ensure that there are no major concerns in the implementation of a particular telemedical service, recognising that one that is safe, effective, and acceptable to patients may still present major ethical barriers to its introduction. Given its necessary

---

[234] Patients were not randomised, so those in the telemedicine group had chosen it. Nonetheless, the study still provides useful data as we are proposing that TEMA be introduced as an additional offering. We will come to discuss the importance of choice in more depth in Chapter 6.

flexibility, this criterion's application is somewhat subjective; there may be serious concerns that some would recognise but others would not. We acknowledge, therefore, that those we will now discuss may not be considered exhaustive by some readers. Nonetheless, we believe the three that we do raise—increased clinic closures, ineffective safeguarding, and unreliable dating of pregnancies—are most pertinent and in need of discussion.

First, the matter of clinic closures. Many clinics in both the UK (largely Great Britain, with Northern Ireland only now beginning to establish local abortion services) and the US that offer abortion services exist either to provide only abortion services, or to provide a small range of sexual and reproductive health services. For example, in addition to abortion care, many BPAS clinics in England offer vasectomies, contraceptives, erectile dysfunction services, and, starting in 2021, fertility treatment. Should these clinics see a significant reduction in the number of patients attending in person to access abortion care, it is feasible that some may either cease to provide in-person abortion care or close altogether—TEMA could be managed from a single hub in an area with cheap real estate, as it only requires a call centre and warehouse. This could result in a smaller pool of clinics offering in-person EMA—and, possibly, surgical abortion—which would mean any patient wanting to see a HCP face-to-face before undergoing treatment may end up having to travel further to do so. Consider the fact that, as was detailed in Chapter 3, many already live a significant distance from their nearest abortion clinic, and you have a potential situation in which TEMA necessarily becomes the default. This would go against the importance of telemedical services being introduced as additional offerings and not replacements for in-person care, thereby introducing the risk of the access burden being shifted rather than removed.

Whilst there is no denying that this eventuality is possible at least to some extent, it is unlikely to happen on a significant scale. This is simply because the need for in-person services will remain even if it is reduced. Regardless of what patients want, there are some for whom the option of TEMA will not be available. Most obviously are those who are too far through their pregnancy. The availability of TEMA has been found to reduce the average gestational age at the time of care delivery (Department of Health and Social Care 2020b) by improving service efficiency, meaning it enables some pregnant people to access care sooner. However, there will still be those who do not make the decision to end their pregnancy until well into the second trimester. In-person abortion services—whether medical or surgical—will need to remain to provide for such patients. Even if someone is accessing abortion care within the gestational limit for TEMA, the need for an ultrasound may be indicated. As noted above, it would not be appropriate to forego an ultrasound where there is a high risk of ectopic pregnancy. Further, in many countries abortion services are provided by charitable organisations—such as MSI Reproductive Choices—which are committed to ensuring reproductive choice for pregnant people. It is reasonable to assume, therefore, that they will not make purely financial decisions to remove in-person services following the introduction of TEMA. As noted above, it must also be remembered that many abortion providers offer services beyond abortion—it is unlikely they will choose to cease providing these other services if they introduce TEMA.

Discounting the ethical obligation under the telemedical imperative to continue to provide in-person care alongside telemedicine, in the case of TEMA there are clear practical reasons why widespread clinic closures would not likely ensue. Perhaps the biggest risk is that TEMA would become the default offering. To this, we simply respond that this should not happen and the setting up of TEMA services should account for this risk and have clear treatment protocols that present patients with the options on an even footing—we will revisit this in Chapter 6 when we highlight how TEMA services are not homogenous and very much exist on a continuum. Further, even if clinic closures were considered a realistic prospect in the event that TEMA is introduced, to resist the change entirely on the basis of such a possibility is to invoke the precautionary principle which is problematic in itself—we will come to this momentarily in discussing safeguarding.

The second potential concern sometimes raised by opponents of TEMA lies in the ability to ensure effective safeguarding in the delivery of care. Whereas healthcare professionals in all areas of medicine have some level of duty to promote the welfare of their patients and to protect them from potential abuses, abortion care is an area in which this duty is generally thought to be more significant. This safeguarding concern is rooted in the assumption that there is a greater likelihood of a patient who is accessing abortion services being in a problematic situation in which they may need some assistance to secure their safety and welfare. For example, the patient may be a victim of domestic abuse, of sexual exploitation, and/or may not be freely making a choice to end the pregnancy. In particular, there are concerns about patients aged under 18 (especially those under 16) being victims of sexual abuse. There is also the possibility that an abusive partner or family member may be forcing the patient to terminate the pregnancy. When care is accessed in person, it is possible for the HCP to ensure they speak to the patient alone. This provides an opportunity for the patient to ask for help if they are being coerced. The concern has been raised by some groups that if such care is being accessed through telemedicine, there is no way for the health care professional to definitively confirm that the patient is alone—someone else could be positioned outside of the view of the camera, for example. The concern is that without the 'safe space' of a private consultation room, patients in these situations will be unable to seek help.

This particular concern is distinct from the safety criterion as it is not about the safety of the medical service itself, but an associated aspect of the care pathway. Even if safeguarding cases were to be missed, that does not affect how safe the abortion itself would be. We advance three responses to this concern. First, that safeguarding is still possible in the case of TEMA. Second, even if safeguarding were not able to be performed to the same degree that it might be in person, some of these potentially vulnerable people will need access to abortion care, and it is important that their access to care is preserved. Third, the extent of safeguarding often expected of abortion care providers is unjustifiably high.

Just because a patient is not seen in person, it does not mean that safeguarding concerns cannot be raised. Indeed, BPAS saw an *increase* of 12% in patients undergoing an enhanced safeguarding risk assessment after the introduction of their TEMA service, which they suggest is because patients can find it easier to disclose sensitive issues when in their own surroundings (2020a, 5). This might be particularly likely for groups who might be concerned about their privacy in attending a clinic (as explored in Chapter 3). Certainly, the early data on this particular service suggest that TEMA is at least not a barrier to the identification of safeguarding concerns even if it does not make it easier. There will inevitably be some patients in these situations that are not identified when accessing TEMA, but there is no guarantee that an in-person consultation would have brought about a different outcome. Whilst it is suggested that a patient can be confirmed to be alone during in-person consultations, this does not necessarily ensure that they will feel able to disclose concerns about abuse at home, for example. The reality of these matters is that when accessing TEMA there will be some cases missed that would have been identified in person, and others that will be detected that would not have been in person. In the absence of compelling evidence that a notable drop in safeguarding capabilities would ensue following the introduction of TEMA—especially given the existing data that suggest the reverse to be true—to not introduce the service on the basis of safeguarding concerns is another example of the precautionary principle in action. It is to say that the *possibility* of *some* safeguarding cases being missed is more important a factor than the *guarantee* of enabling and improving access to care for the *majority* of patients. By any metric, this is problematic.

This leads us onto our second response to this concern. Ultimately, that someone seeking abortion care needs some form of welfare intervention does not take away from the fact that they need abortion care. To disallow TEMA might actually prevent more of these people from accessing necessary healthcare. The evidence reviewed in Chapter 3 seems to suggest that many individuals in abusive environments are more concerned about *not* being able to access abortion care in person (Aiken et al. 2017), which on balance means that the provision of care remotely (even if this does not result in an effective safeguarding intervention) will be better for the person than the alternative of them accessing abortion medications illegally or continuing an unwanted pregnancy in an abusive environment. Although it is undoubtedly unfortunate if safeguarding cannot be effectively undertaken, vulnerable people remain in need of abortions, and it is important to ensure they have access. There might also be many instances in which the comparison to in-person care is a misleading counter-factual, since abusers may well not allow their victims to attend environments where there is a risk that they will be left alone with professionals (Aiken et al. 2018). Thus, it may be that these individuals will have *more* interaction with HCPs when TEMA is available to them.

Beyond the feasibility of safeguarding when providing TEMA, it is reasonable to question the extent of the safeguarding expectations placed on providers of abortion services. All HCPs have a safeguarding duty, and with that we take no issue. However, when it comes to abortion care, this duty is often assumed to be far greater. This is another example of abortion exceptionalism without adequate justification. Whilst it remains important that any safeguarding concerns identified by service providers are raised, there is no valid reason why abortion providers should be singled out as expected to go to greater lengths in this respect.

Significant concern around safeguarding in this context is rooted in the assumption that all people accessing abortion services are somehow extremely vulnerable. It stems from the narrative that for a person to be experiencing an unwanted pregnancy something must have 'gone wrong' in their lives, such that they need help. There is no denying that the decision can be challenging and potentially distressing for some, but for others (especially when accessing services early in pregnancy) it is a straightforward decision that is given no more thought than the decision to take antibiotics for an infection. This is evident in how common abortion is globally—even where there are no local services (possibly because of legal restrictions on abortion), organisations like Women on Web continue to enable abortion access. An insistence on checking that patients are sure of their decision further exceptionalises abortion care and fails to recognise it as routine healthcare. Whilst informed consent rightly requires patients to confirm their decision in all areas of medicine, there are fewer hoops to jump through outside of the abortion context where legislation has not been set up to frame the decision as something concerning. This ultimately stems from an innate feeling that the termination of pregnancy is a 'last resort' and that those doing so are in their situation because of some vulnerability that means they need benevolent intervention from a HCP—evident in the framing of the AA 1967 in Great Britain (Sheldon 1997)—or that they should be protected from the remorse that they are somehow expected to feel in accessing abortion care-evident in the so-called 'informed consent laws' in the US. This constitutes inappropriate interference in the autonomous choices of pregnant people. It should be sufficient for a patient to be informed of their options (including the option to continue the pregnancy and the various avenues of support available if the decision is, for example, based on the person's financial situation alone) and provide a straightforward response that they want to proceed with the termination.

Finally, the question of dating pregnancies in the absence of an in-person consultation. A concern has been raised by both HCPs and antiabortion organisations, suggesting that TEMA enables abortion services to be accessed (whether by mistake or deliberately) beyond gestational limits set by law in the absence of ultrasound scanning. With pregnant people being asked to date their own pregnancies based on their menstrual history, there is a worry that such dating will be unreliable, resulting in both safety and legal issues. We have already addressed the safety concern so will not do so again. In brief, EMA continues to be safe beyond the gestational limits set in many jurisdictions (albeit with a gradual increase in side effects), and the scan as indicated model means that ultrasounds are still performed for patients who are in doubt as to their last menstrual period. Here, then, we will look to the legal questions. Our focus here is on such legal questions in the context of England and Wales, and we recognise that there will be different problems across jurisdictions—our discussion is, then, more an example.

As detailed in Chapter 2, abortion remains a criminal offence in England and Wales if obtained outside of the circumstances proscribed in the AA 1967. This includes the provision of abortion medications outside of fixed gestational limits, which in the case of TEMA in England and Wales is nine weeks and six days (Department of Health and Social Care 2020c; Welsh Government 2020).[235] Where it transpires that a pregnancy is misdated (whether accidentally or intentionally on the part of the pregnant person) a criminal offence has technically been committed under the OAPA 1861, which still

---

[235] As noted in Chapter 3, the approval orders in Scotland do not stipulate gestational limits—accompanying professional guidance does. As such, there are no legal penalties where the limit of 11 weeks and six days contained in the guidance attached to the 2020 approval (Scottish Government Chief Medical Officer Directorate 2020) is departed from by doctors.

carries a term of life imprisonment (Milne 2021a). There are concerns, therefore, about the extent to which the criminal law might be engaged in response to TEMA used beyond the gestational limit. Both intentional and accidental use of abortion medications past gestational limits by patients might cause providers anxiety, as in such circumstances the provider may also be criminally liable (on a literal reading of the offence) because they will have provided the means to end the pregnancy without any of the defences in the AA 1967 applying. The AA 1967 does stipulate that it only has to be the provider's *opinion* that the pregnancy is within the 24-week gestational limit to be lawful, rather than it *actually* being within the 24-week gestational limit by virtue of the 'good faith' caveat of section 1(1)(a). However, for the doctor to have a defence to criminal abortion, the abortion need not only be justified under section 1(1)(a), but must also be undertaken in compliance with the protocol in the pertinent approval order.[236] The approval orders in England and Wales (and, indeed, Scotland) contain no such 'good faith' caveat.

Providers have an obligation to report all terminations to the Department of Health and Social Care in England (and relevant departments in the devolved nations).[237] This will include terminations that take place outside of the gestational limit, which could then be reported to the police. Prosecution of a pregnant person who administers abortion medications past the gestational limit is unlikely except in those instances where late administration is clearly intentional as opposed to accidental. However, there are police investigations into the conduct of people who are reported for potentially terminating outside of the gestational limits, and in some instances coroners inquests are initiated. The few prosecutions that have been brought against people for doing so have all been instances in which pregnant people have self-administered later in pregnancy *intentionally* (Sheldon 2016b; Milne 2020). In these cases, the law has responded with harsh consequences—including custodial sentences[238]—despite the questionability of this as a response to people who act in this way (Milne 2020; Milne 2021b).

Although rare, prosecutions in such instances would likely be high profile and could have broader harmful consequences. There might be concerns as to what the possibility of the involvement of the criminal law might do to the relationship between providers and those wanting to access care. Moreover, that a criminal investigation would be conducted (and *how* this would be conducted) to ascertain whether a pregnant person knew that they were past the legal gestational limit might be particularly distressing for them to endure—for example, invasive questioning of friends and family and examinations of personal photographs to look for signs of pregnancy.[239] These concerns are reasons to suggest that greater support needs to be provided to people experiencing crisis pregnancies (Milne 2020; Milne 2021b), and they speak to the extent to which the criminal regulation of abortion care is inappropriate (Milne

---

[236] Abortion Act 1967, ss.1(3) and (3A).

[237] See Chapter 2 for an outline of the reporting obligations placed on providers by the AA 1967.

[238] Sarah Catt, who was found guilty of procuring a miscarriage under section 58 of the OAPA 1861 after administering misoprostol close to full-term pregnancy, was sentenced to 12 years' imprisonment, though this was reduced to five years on appeal, with a third discount (to three years and six months) due to an early guilty plea. *R v Sarah Louise Catt* [2013] EWCA Crim 1187.

[239] Our thanks to Emma Milne for raising these points with us in discussions.

2020; Sheldon 2016b). Finally, it is important to again highlight that these constitute very few cases in the thousands of people who will receive care remotely—Aiken and colleagues' (2021a) study that we discussed earlier in this chapter clearly demonstrates this. Further, later-term administration of these medications does not pose a significant health risk—they are routinely taken during the second trimester in clinics, meaning self-administration may just be far more unpleasant for the patient than expected.

Ultimately, these service-specific concerns that are sometimes raised are insufficient to deny the telemedical imperative in the case of EMA. There is insufficient reason to believe that the introduction of TEMA would cause a notable reduction in the number of clinics offering in-person abortion services, nor is there justification for concerns around the continuation of safeguarding. The various apprehensions associated with a perceived inability to reliably date pregnancies without an ultrasound also largely lack evidential support. In the rare instances where pregnant people access abortion later in a pregnancy, there is no evidence to suggest this will result in serious health consequences. As such, this fourth and final criterion can be considered met, thereby fulfilling all criteria of the telemedical imperative and cementing the case for TEMA.

5.3 Realising the benefits of telemedicine with early medical abortion

TEMA clearly satisfies the criteria of the telemedical imperative. As a service, it is safe, effective, and acceptable to patients, as well as having no significant service-specific concerns that cannot be reasonably overcome. We suggest, therefore, that the case for implementation where it is not yet available (for example, in Northern Ireland and much of the US), and for permanence where it is available on a time-limited basis (for example, in Great Britain), has been made.

The COVID-19 pandemic certainly has made the case for TEMA more compelling. With the additional barriers to access presented by the wider pandemic response (see Chapter 7), the need for positive action to ensure continued access to abortion services has never been greater in many countries. That the pandemic has brought into focus what has been a long overdue change to abortion policy can certainly be viewed as something of a silver lining to a truly awful occurrence. Indeed, it has resulted in the production of rich data on TEMA through what are and have been, in essence, trials of such care on vast scales. We will not dwell on this here as the way(s) in which the regulation of abortion care has thus far been altered (whether for better or for worse) by the pandemic will be explored in detail in Chapters 7, 8, and 9. For now, we note that, even if the pandemic has strengthened the case for TEMA, it was still very much there long before. As such, it should not be viewed as an interim policy, but as an evidence-based means of ensuring access to essential care at all times.

It must also be stressed that the benefits of telemedical services outlined in the telemedical imperative are realised by TEMA. Namely, enhancing patient autonomy, improving the efficiency of wider service provision, and, perhaps most importantly, contributing to the overcoming of health inequities (Parsons 2021a).

TEMA enhances patient autonomy by providing a meaningful choice. Without TEMA, patients are essentially presented with the choice between accessing abortion services in person and not accessing them at all. This is not much of a choice, as a person seeking to end an unwanted pregnancy is not likely (where the circumstances do not force them to) to opt for continuing that pregnancy; in that sense, they are somewhat cornered into accessing care in person, with no choice but to accept the potentially huge disruption to their life. Further, that is those who *can* accept that disruption, as it will simply be infeasible for some. As such, where TEMA is an additional option, patients have an actual choice of services that allows them to pursue the option that most aligns with their subjective values and preferences. At this point, we are talking primarily of the choice between in-person and telemedical care, whereas the ideal is to build in further choice so that care pathways can, within reason, be adapted to suit individual patients. We will come to discuss this further in Chapter 6 when exploring the range of TEMA models that have thus far been established.

A further benefit is improved efficiency of services. This is a far-reaching benefit in that efficiency is not only improved for those who make use of TEMA, but the knock-on effects of this drive efficiency throughout a service, including in-person services. This benefit has been realised quickly in Great Britain. A study including data from BPAS, MSI Reproductive Choices, and the National Unplanned Pregnancy Advisory Service found a substantial drop in the mean waiting time from 10.7 to 6.5 days following the introduction of TEMA (Aiken et al. 2021a, 6). Improved efficiency is in part because TEMA removes some of the short periods of wasted time that are inevitable with in-person care. For example, the time taken for a patient to walk from the waiting room to the consultation room—this may sound insignificant, but when you add together this minute or so from every patient it becomes a period long enough for further consultations. By removing various small delays to service provision, waiting times can be reduced, making a significant difference to those waiting to end an unwanted pregnancy.

Inevitably, reduced waiting times for TEMA can also result in reduced waiting times for in-person care. If TEMA is offered through a central call centre, patients still accessing care in person will join a much shorter queue. The capacity of in-person services may be reduced as staff are redeployed to TEMA services, but, on balance, it is reasonable to still expect waiting times to decrease. As such, the improved efficiency benefits all patients and not only those making use of TEMA.

Perhaps the most important benefit of TEMA is that it improves access to abortion care, thereby contributing to the overcoming of health inequities. In Chapter 3, we highlighted the extent of the barriers faced by many pregnant people in seeking abortion services in both the UK and US. The fact that abortion services are available in a given country does not mean that all of those in need of them are able to access them. For access to be truly equal, the barriers that create geographical and socioeconomic division in access must be addressed. Whilst not the silver bullet it might be thought of on this front, TEMA goes a significant way towards achieving this. There will still be those who require (or even desire) in-person care who do not live near a clinic, and for these people TEMA does not remove barriers. However, for the majority of those seeking to end an unwanted pregnancy, TEMA makes it far easier (and, in the most extreme cases, *possible*) to access services.

5.4 Summary

The overarching purpose of this chapter has been to make the case for the introduction (or continuation) of TEMA in addition to in-person abortion services. Taking the telemedical imperative as a framework for the assessment of TEMA, it is quite clear that all four conditions are met. TEMA has, in several studies of various models, consistently been found to be safe, effective, and acceptable to patients. This includes early data from the services operated in Great Britain, which are perhaps closest to the standard model of TEMA moving forward, as we will explain in the next chapter. Further, there are no serious concerns specific to TEMA that undermine its other credentials; a widespread reduction in the availability of in-person abortion services is unlikely, safeguarding can be carried out just as effectively, and pregnancies can be accurately dated by patients based on their menstrual history.

Beyond satisfying the criteria of the telemedical imperative, TEMA provides several significant benefits. First, it affords patients greater autonomy by offering a meaningful choice. Second, it drives the efficiency of service delivery, not only specific to TEMA but also in-person services. Third, it contributes to the overcoming of health inequities by enabling/improving access to abortion services for a vast number of people. That such important benefits can be realised by the introduction of TEMA strengthens the case.

Having made this case, we emphasise again that we are concerned with the introduction of TEMA *in addition to* in-person abortion services. More specifically, the introduction of TEMA where in-person abortion services are already available. We are not, therefore, suggesting that this chapter has presented the case for a sudden jump from an outright ban on abortion straight to TEMA—although we do believe a compelling case could be made for that. Whereas much of what we have discussed would certainly go some way towards making such an argument, there are many more points to discuss in the context of jurisdictions where abortion is not lawfully available. As such, whilst we certainly would advocate for the introduction of TEMA in all contexts, the scope of what has been argued here is limited to those countries where in-person EMA is available through formal, regulated channels. In the next chapter, we build on this case for TEMA and argue for the availability of several TEMA options along a 'telemedical continuum'.

6

A telemedical continuum for early medical abortion

On hearing 'abortion by telemedicine', many people unsurprisingly envisage a system whereby a patient accesses care without leaving their home. Some form of consultation takes place remotely, the relevant medications are posted to the patient, the patient administers the medications themselves, and, possibly, there is some level of remote aftercare—a patient only need physically attend a medical establishment if something goes wrong. Assuming the personal circumstances of the patient allow for this, it certainly encapsulates many of the benefits of telemedicine already discussed, particularly in terms of convenience and flexibility. As such, it is unsurprising that systems like this have been established.

However, not all TEMA care pathways fit the above description. Some still require that patients attend a clinic for an ultrasound scan, for example. To suggest that TEMA is when a patient never has to leave their home and that the alternative is 'traditional', fully in clinic care is, then, to oversimplify things in a potentially problematic way. There is very much a spectrum of telemedical options in the provision of abortion care, and, we will argue, it is important that such a range of options exists to meet the needs of a range of patients.

In this chapter, we will look to four examples of TEMA services with varying care pathways. The first two—Planned Parenthood in Iowa and TelAbortion—we characterise as examples of 'partial telemedicine' in that they require a patient to attend a healthcare facility for some aspect of care. The second two—Women on Web and BPAS—we characterise as examples of 'full telemedicine' in that a patient can complete the entire care pathway from the comfort of their home (unless, of course, there are contra-indications or complications requiring medical attention). These examples do not represent an exhaustive list of TEMA services. There are far more examples than we could possibly discuss here, with various (slight) differences. Those that we have chosen to explore, however, represent a range of the kind of services that have been established over the last two decades, and highlight some of the key elements of TEMA care pathways. As such, they illustrate how TEMA is possible in not only one way, but there is instead a spectrum of possible pathways that meet the varying needs of patients to varying degrees.

Considering these different examples of TEMA services, we ultimately argue that no single care pathway can be considered the 'best'. At first, it may seem obvious to favour those that can take place without the patient needing to leave their home. However, whilst this may improve access for some pregnant people, it may cause unnecessary anxiety for others. It is important, then, that abortion providers operate a range of options, including both partially and fully telemedical pathways, alongside

Early Medical Abortion, Equality of Access, and the Telemedical Imperative. Jordan A. Parsons and Elizabeth Chloe Romanis, Oxford University Press. © Oxford University Press 2021. DOI: 10.1093/oso/9780192896155.003.0006

the continuation of fully in person care. To do so is to enhance patient autonomy in an era of increasing patient-centricity.

6.1 Partial telemedicine

First, let us consider what we will refer to as 'partial telemedicine'. As the name suggests, services under this heading employ telemedicine for *some*, but not all, elements of the care pathway. There will be some level of in-person interaction between the patient and the service provider, whether for the purposes of consultation, collection of drugs, or other. We stress that partial should not be read as synonymous with worse. As we will come to discuss throughout this chapter, fully telemedical care is not suitable for all patients, so the ideal is to have a range of options.

6.1.1 Planned Parenthood in Iowa

In the US in June 2008, a Planned Parenthood affiliate in Iowa—Planned Parenthood of the Heartland[240]—introduced telemedicine into its service provision to enable patients to obtain abortifacient drugs from clinics that did not have on-site doctors. This may be considered the first recognisable TEMA service established within a jurisdiction and made open to all (eligibility depending). We specify *within* a jurisdiction because Women on Web—which we will discuss later in this chapter—was established in 2005 and provides care globally to people in countries where access to safe abortion is restricted.

Patients using the service established by Planned Parenthood in Iowa make first contact with a central call centre to book an appointment at their nearest clinic, at which point they are told whether that clinic offers telemedical or (fully) in-person appointments.[241] If the nearest clinic offers telemedical appointments, and the patient chooses to proceed (rather than attending a fully in-person appointment further away), they then attend their nearest clinic where they undergo the initial steps in the care pathway in person, before their remote consultation with a doctor. These initial steps include an ultrasound examination to determine gestational age, the taking of the patient's medical history, and the provision of information about EMA. The patient's medical history and ultrasound scan are then uploaded to a secure server by clinic staff who are with the patient in person, to be reviewed remotely by a doctor. A videoconferencing consultation then takes place between the on-site patient and the off-site doctor and, if appropriate, the doctor (in a rather dramatic unveiling) remotely unlocks a drawer in the consultation room in which the patient can find both mifepristone and misoprostol. Still on the videoconference, the patient takes the mifepristone under the supervision of the off-site doctor and an on-site member of staff, before

---

[240] Planned Parenthood of the Heartland is no longer operating under that name, and Planned Parenthood clinics in Iowa now come under the purview of the Planned Parenthood North Central States affiliate.
[241] If the patient's nearest clinic has an on-site doctor, care will be provided face-to-face.

receiving further instructions on completing the abortion—home use of misoprostol is permitted.

This service also includes a follow-up clinic visit as standard, which, as will become apparent throughout this chapter, can be considered somewhat unusual—often aftercare is provided at the patient's instigation if required. Patients accessing TEMA through Planned Parenthood in Iowa are scheduled for their follow-up appointment to take place within a fortnight of them having taken the mifepristone (meaning within a fortnight of their teleconsultation as mifepristone administration must, legally, be supervised[242]). At this appointment, abortion completeness is assessed by ultrasound, and, if the treatment has been unsuccessful, the patient is given several options to proceed.

The Planned Parenthood service in Iowa is significant in improving access to abortion services by reducing the distance patients must travel. Due to the absence of an on-site doctor,[243] many of the participating clinics were previously unable to offer abortion services. At the time the service was established, Planned Parenthood had 17 clinics in Iowa, but only six were able to provide abortion care. Not all those six had a permanent on-site doctor and were, therefore, only able to offer abortion services intermittently when a doctor visited the clinic (Grossman et al. 2011; Grossman et al. 2013)—this would present an obstacle for any patients unavailable at the time the itinerant doctor happened to be on site. By June 2010, as the TEMA service had gradually been phased in, abortion care was being provided at 15 of the affiliate's clinics (Grossman et al. 2013, 73). However, even with the improvement in accessibility, this Planned Parenthood service is still very much an example of *partial* telemedicine because patients must attend a clinic. Yes, a greater number of clinics can offer the service, but there is still a limited number of clinics. In 2010, there were 15 clinics covering the entire state of Iowa—an area of more than 145km^2 with a 2010 population of just over three million—and even they were largely clustered around the state capital of Des Moines (Grossman et al. 2013).[244] At the time of writing, there are only nine Planned Parenthood clinics in Iowa, and not all of them offer abortion. That is not to criticise Planned Parenthood, as setting up additional clinics is, for the reasons outlined in Chapter 3, far from straightforward. Rather, we wish to highlight that even with this TEMA service there remain barriers to access for many in Iowa.

This service was almost forced to close in 2013 when the Iowa Board of Medicine introduced rules requiring doctors to physically examine a patient in person before providing an abortion. Planned Parenthood filed a petition in September 2013, and the District Court stayed enforcement of the new rules pending its ruling, but later upheld the rule in August 2014.[245] Planned Parenthood appealed to the Iowa Supreme Court, which again stayed enforcement pending its ruling. Then, in June 2015, the

---

[242] Iowa Admin. Code r.653-13.10(3).

[243] See Chapter 3 for a discussion of the reasons why it is difficult for clinics to recruit enough doctors.

[244] Des Moines is positioned in the longitudinal centre of the southern half of Iowa, so areas in the (admittedly more rural) North East and North West of the state were (and remain) relatively underserved by clinics.

[245] The District Court's decision was summarised in the later appeal before the Supreme Court of Iowa: *Planned Parenthood of the Heartland and Jill Meadows v. Iowa Board of Medicine* 865 N.W.2d 252 (Iowa 2015).

Supreme Court reversed the District Court's ruling with respect to the aspects of the new rules that introduced the in-person physical examination requirement.[246] This outcome is significant because, had the Court sided with the Iowa Board of Medicine, 'it could have served as a springboard for increased state action in creating carve-outs and exceptions to telemedicine services' (Yang and Kozhimannil 2016, 315). Whilst some US states have continued to try and stand in the way of TEMA (see Chapter 9), it may have happened more had the Iowa Supreme Court reached a different conclusion.

6.1.2   TelAbortion

Building on the earlier example of Planned Parenthood in Iowa, more recent TEMA models have sought to further improve access to services. Most notably, there have been moves to direct-to-patient dispensing, whereby there is no requirement to attend a clinic to obtain the drugs. An example of this is the TelAbortion Study in the US.[247]

The TelAbortion Study began in March 2016, shortly after the FDA approved an updated label for Mifeprex (a brand of mifepristone), which increased the gestational limit for EMA from 49 days to 70 (United States Food and Drug Administration 2016). The study allows patients to access EMA without first undergoing a face-to-face consultation with a doctor. It is sponsored by the nonprofit reproductive health organisation Gynuity Health Projects, and services are provided by several collaborating clinics throughout the participating states. TelAbortion had to be established as a research study because mifepristone distribution regulations imposed by the FDA are interpreted as prohibiting postal provision (Mifeprex REMS Study Group 2017).[248] As such, participation in the study is required if a patient wants to access the service. Further, even though TelAbortion is a study, patients are still required to pay for treatment—the price varies depending on location, preabortion tests required, and insurance coverage, and could be more or less than the cost of in-person EMA.

We will focus on the original design of the TelAbortion service because a second study was setup to run alongside it in response to the COVID-19 pandemic, and that second study was closer to 'full telemedicine' in nature. Patients participating in the original study first have a consultation via videoconferencing with a doctor from the abortion provider. At this point, it is determined which preabortion tests are required. Whereas certain tests, such as pelvic exams, are required only if indicated, all patients are required to obtain an ultrasound as per the FDA-approved study protocol. However, rather than attend the abortion provider's own clinic for an ultrasound and any other required tests, patients can undergo them at a facility that is local to them and have the results sent to the abortion provider (Raymond et al. 2019, 174). Following a remote consultation and required testing, eligible patients are sent a package by post that contains the drugs themselves (both mifepristone and misoprostol) as well as

---

[246] Ibid.

[247] Much of the information provided in this section is from the TelAbortion website, which can be accessed here: https://telabortion.org/. It should be noted, however, that the website is not clear on the distinctions between the original and revised studies, and we obtained some of this information through correspondence with the study team.

[248] See Chapter 3 for details of these FDA regulations.

instructions. The TelAbortion website does note that prescriptions may also be sent to a local pharmacy rather than posted directly to the patient, which is for reasons of financial bureaucracy that necessitate some providers only making mifepristone available by collection from a pharmacy despite the FDA having permitted the posting of the medication for the purposes of the study. Following the procedure, patients undergo additional follow-up tests to verify abortion completeness, such as ultrasounds, pelvic exams, and urine pregnancy tests.

At the time of writing, TelAbortion operates in 17 states: Colorado, Georgia, Hawaii, Illinois, Iowa, Maine, Maryland & Washington D.C., Massachusetts, Minnesota, Montana, Nevada, New Jersey, New Mexico, New York, Oregon, Virginia, and Washington. Across these states, the study has several collaborating clinics that provide abortion services. These collaborators are largely Planned Parenthood affiliates (covering seven of the participating states) and carafem clinics (covering five of the participating states). As these clinics are *collaborating* with the study, some have additional rules—such as minimum age requirements—which are not consistent across TelAbortion (Raymond et al. 2019, 174).

Whilst the model used by TelAbortion (ignoring temporary alterations during the COVID-19 pandemic) certainly reduces in-person requirements relative to that of Planned Parenthood in Iowa, it should still be considered an example of partial telemedicine. Users of the service are required to undergo ultrasounds and, in some cases, other tests to confirm both pregnancy and abortion completeness. The ability to be tested locally rather than at an abortion clinic (which may be a significant distance away) certainly benefits many patients by removing (or at least reducing) geographical barriers to access, but it is inevitably still challenging for some to access care in this way as distance is not the only barrier (see Chapter 3). This further highlights the importance of several care pathways being available—whereas some patients will want to attend a clinic and will appreciate being able to do so locally, in-person clinic attendance will be unsuitable for some patients regardless of the distance.

Further, TelAbortion is a study, and the participating abortion clinics are not providing remote services as standard care. According to the US National Institutes of Health clinical trials registry, the TelAbortion Study is due to end in June 2022. Ideally, the results of the study will result in the service being routinely available and, indeed, expanding to the remaining states. However, should this not happen, it is possible that the previous system will return, whereby patients must attend a clinic to be provided with the necessary drugs for EMA. This seems to be the most likely conclusion, at least in the short term, as the FDA has refused to remove barriers to TEMA even during the COVID-19 pandemic (see Chapter 9).

It is worth briefly highlighting that Gynuity Health Projects has also, since 2019, been running the TeleAborto Study in Mexico.[249] This project is largely similar to its US counterpart, though differs as required by Mexican law. Further, a similar model was launched in Australia prior to both TelAbortion and TeleAborto, in 2015, by the Tabbot Foundation. This service has been successful in serving patients in parts of Australia where access to abortion services is limited (Hyland et al. 2018).

---

[249] Further information about the TeleAborto Study can be found on the study website: https://teleaborto.org/.

Earlier, we noted that there were changes to the TelAbortion Study because of the COVID-19 pandemic. Given the need to reduce in-person contact during the pandemic, some of the abortion providers involved in TelAbortion began considering the omission of ultrasound scans in cases where it protected patient welfare. This was justified on the basis of pandemic research guidelines issued by the FDA that allowed for deviations from study protocols if necessary to protect the health of participants (2020a). Unsurprisingly, this proved to be a significant proportion of patients (roughly half, according to our correspondence with the study team). Then, in October 2020, a secondary TelAbortion Study started in which ultrasound scans were not required. The second, however, has since been closed following legal proceedings.

Early in the pandemic the FDA and the Department of Health and Human Services waived the requirement for various drugs to be collected in person by the patient (United States Food and Drug Administration 2020b).[250] Mifepristone was excluded from this action, meaning providers remained unable to post the drug directly to patients. Calling this out as an 'undue burden'[251] on those seeking abortion services, the American College of Obstetricians and Gynecologists filed a civil action against the FDA to waive the in-person requirement on mifepristone.[252] The District Court in Maryland enjoined the FDA rule in July 2020, allowing mifepristone to be posted to patients. It was because of this ruling that the second TelAbortion Study was established, as the need for specific FDA approval for the posting of mifepristone was no longer required. Whilst new participants were thereafter assigned to the second study, the initial TelAbortion Study remained open as something of a backup in case of a successful appeal by the FDA. Unfortunately, this backup became necessary when, in January 2021, the Supreme Court granted the FDA's application to stay the earlier injunction.[253] This judgment will be revisited in greater detail in Chapter 9—we note it here merely to explain why the TelAbortion Study briefly established a secondary study.

The initial TelAbortion Study is still able to operate and send mifepristone to patients by post, in line with its approval from the FDA as a research study. It is nonetheless concerning that the in-person requirement on mifepristone now remains in a time of uncertainty when the Supreme Court could not even offer a suitable justification, thereby preventing abortion providers outside of a select few studies from providing a service encompassing direct-to-patient dispensing.

6.2 Full telemedicine

Now to look to examples of 'full telemedicine'. These services enable a patient to access care without leaving their home at all.

---

[250] See Chapter 9 for further detail as to how this determination was made.
[251] See Chapter 2 for a discussion of the undue burden test originating in *Casey*.
[252] *American College of Obstetricians and Gynecologists v. U.S. Food and Drug Administration*, Civil Action No. TDC-20-1320 (D. Md. Jul. 13, 2020).
[253] *Food and Drug Administration v. American College of Obstetricians and Gynecologists*, 592 U.S. ___ (2021).

6.2.1 Women on Web

The first fully telemedical service to consider is that of Women on Web. Setup in 2005, it built on the work of the earlier established Women on Waves. Indeed, both were founded by Dr Rebecca Gomperts. Women on Waves—which continues to offer its services since the setup of Women on Web—operates aboard a ship, which stations itself off the coast (in international waters) of countries in which abortion is illegal.[254] Women on Web, however, operates (unsurprisingly) as a direct-to-patient, web-based service. It is a widely recognised name in the TEMA literature. Indeed, many of the studies concerning the safety, effectiveness, and acceptability of TEMA that we looked to in Chapter 5 used Women on Web's service as the subject of their assessments (Gomperts et al. 2008; Gomperts et al. 2012; Gomperts et al. 2014; Aiken et al. 2017; Les et al. 2017).

Those accessing Women on Web's service initially undergo an online, question-based consultation. The questions cover things such as relevant allergies, ability to reach emergency medical assistance within an hour, and confirmation of the patient's[255] eligibility for EMA (in the case of Women on Web, a patient must be less than 10 weeks pregnant). Whilst it is encouraged, patients are not required to evidence their pregnancy by way of a pregnancy test or ultrasound scan. Further, patients estimate their gestation by their last menstrual period (which, as explained in Chapter 5, is reliable). Upon completing the consultation, the patient's responses are reviewed by a doctor, and, assuming there is no cause for concern, the drugs are prescribed and posted directly to the patient. Rather than instructions on how to carry out EMA being posted with the drugs, they are emailed to the user. Instructions are also available on the website in both written and video form.[256] In sum, the Women on Web service enables patients to access care in a straightforward manner from the comfort of their own home. There is also the added benefit of patients being able to complete their consultation at a time that is convenient for them due to it being asynchronous.

Women on Web is often described as offering services only to those in countries where access to abortion is illegal. This is not strictly true. On the organisation's website, it notes that they offer their services to help those who 'live in a country where access to safe abortion is restricted'—restricted, but not necessarily illegal. Further, with some exceptions—including the US[257]—a patient seeking Women on Web's services in a country which the organisation deems as providing access to safe abortion services can complete the consultation and have their request reviewed. As such, Women

---

[254] Further information about Women on Waves can be found on the organisation's website: www.womenonwaves.org/en/.

[255] We have chosen to continue with the language of 'patient' when referring to Women on Web, even though the service is not a formal, regulated healthcare provider.

[256] The website provides a wealth of information for patients undergoing EMA, available in up to 22 languages. It can, then, prove a useful resource for those accessing care through other providers.

[257] Whilst Women on Web is unable to provide its service in the US, the website does redirect would-be patients to the alternative service Aid Access. Aid Access is very similar to Women on Web, and was also established by Dr Rebecca Gomperts. In the US, Aid Access provides its services in Alaska, Idaho, New York, New Jersey, Nevada, Vermont, and Washington, with prescriptions provided by doctors in the US and an online pharmacy in the US fulfilling prescriptions by post. In other states, due to legal restrictions, European doctors provide prescriptions, and a pharmacy in India dispenses the drugs by post.

on Web might be considered the most far-reaching TEMA provider in the world—almost all other services operate in either a single jurisdiction or a small number of jurisdictions.

One aspect of the Women on Web service that may still present a barrier to access for some is the request for a financial donation towards the service's operating costs. Following the online consultation, patients are asked to donate between €70 and €120, depending on their 'location, economic circumstances [, and] shipping method' (Women on Web a). The website does note that patients in a particularly difficult economic situation can contact the organisation for assistance, but it is feasible that some would-be patients could feel ashamed or embarassed to make such a request. This might be the case especially for those of low economic means residing in high-income countries if they feel that it is inappropriate for them to ask for assistance, comparing themselves to someone in far worse a financial situation than them in a lower-income country. This is by no means a criticism of the service offered by Women on Web. The service provides care for those with unwanted pregnancies and no access to abortion services around the world and does so as a nonprofit organisation. Provided this service entails certain costs which must be covered. The work of Women on Web is hugely important, but it remains that being asked for a financial donation may discourage some of the most vulnerable would-be patients. What is preferable is that such services are provided nationally, within the regulated healthcare system, as the regulation of healthcare providers ultimately exists to protect patients. Ideally, this will be with little to no direct cost to the patient.[258]

6.2.2 British Pregnancy Advisory Service

Early in the COVID-19 pandemic, approval orders were issued throughout Great Britain that permitted home use of the first abortion medication, mifepristone (Parsons and Romanis 2020). We will not dwell on the changes that came about as a result of the pandemic because we will examine them in Chapter 8. For now, it is enough to note that home use of both abortion medications has been lawful in Great Britain since March 2020. This change in regulation allowed BPAS—one of the leading providers of abortion services in Great Britain—to establish its so-called 'Pills by Post' service,[259] which it did on 8 April 2020.

Using the Pills by Post service, a patient first calls a central line to book a remote consultation. This remote consultation takes place with a nurse or midwife and is an opportunity for the patient to discuss their options. As part of this consultation, gestational age is assessed by last menstrual period to confirm (legal) eligibility for EMA. It is also determined whether there is a need for an ultrasound, as the service operates a

---

[258] We acknowledge that we are viewing things through the rose-tinted glasses of residing in a country with a healthcare service that is free at the point of use, and that in many countries regulated abortion services do entail out-of-pocket costs for patients. That does not, however, change the sentiment that financial barriers to abortion care are inappropriate—we similarly consider financial barriers to any essential healthcare to be inappropriate.

[259] Further details of the Pills by Post service, including its background, are detailed in a document published by BPAS in September 2020 (2020a).

'scan as indicated' model in line with clinical guidance provided by the Royal College of Obstetricians and Gynaecologists (2020) in conjunction with the Royal College of Midwives, the Faculty of Sexual and Reproductive Healthcare, and the British Society of Abortion Care Providers. Under this model, it is only in a small number of specific circumstances that the patient is required to undergo a scan (see Chapter 1).

With consultations not being conducted by doctors (but by nurses and midwives), it remains necessary for the patient notes from these consultations to be reviewed by two doctors and for both to approve treatment—as noted in Chapter 2, this is a requirement for lawful abortion in Great Britain by way of the AA 1967. Once two doctors have approved treatment—and, of course, *if*, because some will not be approved—the patient is sent a treatment pack directly to their home address. In addition to the two drugs themselves, these packs contain painkillers and information about how to carry out the abortion and what to expect as the pregnancy passes—information that is also available on BPAS' website in both written and video formats.

The treatment pack also contains a self-assessment pregnancy test for use three weeks after treatment to confirm abortion completeness, alongside a self-assessment checklist for patients to complete. This is because, unlike some of the other services discussed, patients using Pills by Post do not automatically have a follow-up appointment. Aftercare as part of this service is available, but at the patient's instigation—a helpline is available 24 hours a day, seven days a week. Assuming the abortion was successful, and the patient has no unexpected adverse reaction to treatment, they do not need to interact with BPAS again.

Importantly, BPAS' Pills by Post service is optional. Patients are still able to access care in person either partially or entirely—partially meaning the collection of the treatment pack following a telemedical consultation, an option that may be preferred by patients who, for example, do not want someone they live with to see the pack arriving. In that sense, then, BPAS offers both a full telemedicine and partial telemedicine service. We will return to this shortly in discussing the importance of choice of care pathway.

Assessment of some aspects of BPAS' new care pathways was always going to be challenging given the nature of the circumstances in which they were introduced. Nonetheless, early data from the organisation suggest the service has successfully reduced waiting times, increased service capacity, and lowered the average gestation at the time of receiving care (2020, 4–5). Further research into patient preferences after the COVID-19 pandemic, when it could become feasible for patients to choose between TEMA and in-person care,[260] will prove interesting.

The service established by BPAS was, as noted above, in response to the impact of the COVID-19 pandemic and a resulting change in regulations. Around the same time, very similar services were setup by two other providers in Great Britain. The National Unplanned Pregnancy Advisory Service launched its own 'Pills by Post' service[261] and MSI Reproductive Choices established its 'At Home Abortion Pills' option.[262]

---

[260] This depends on whether TEMA remains lawful in Great Britain. See Chapter 8.
[261] Further information about the National Unplanned Pregnancy Advisory Service can be found on the organisation's website: www.nupas.co.uk/abortion-pill-by-post/.
[262] Further information about the MSI Reproductive Choices service can be found on the organisation's website: www.msichoices.org.uk/abortion-services/online-medical-abortion/.

Similarities between these three services are such that they pooled data to report on the effectiveness, safety, and acceptability of TEMA compared with in-person delivery (Aiken et al. 2021a).

6.3 Charting a continuum

The four models outlined illustrate how TEMA can be introduced in various ways. There is a clear continuum, whereby some utilise telemedicine for only one/some element(s) of the care pathway, and others entail no in-person contact. We map this continuum in Figure 6.1. In Figure 6.1, we also detail a possible next step that *could* be considered telemedical. It *could* be considered telemedical in the sense that the lack of registered medical professional (depending on how one defines that) in the process might cause some to classify it differently. Such a pathway would entail over-the-counter availability of both mifepristone and misoprostol, accessible via an online pharmacy. A full discussion of such a model is beyond the scope of this chapter, but we will briefly revisit it in Chapter 10.

6.4 COVID-19

As noted above, the key factor behind the establishment of BPAS' Pills by Post service (and, indeed, temporary changes to the TelAbortion service) was the COVID-19 pandemic. The impact of the pandemic on access to abortion care was—eventually—widely acknowledged. Great Britain was not the only place where adjustments to service provision were made, with *somewhat* similar actions having taken place globally (Romanis and Parsons 2020a). This is not the place to focus on the impact of the pandemic on abortion services, as we will do this in later chapters. Here, we instead want to touch on some of the models of telemedical abortion that arose in response to the pandemic beyond the already discussed Pills by Post service in Great Britain. The approaches of the two countries which we will highlight—Germany and South Africa—provide interesting additional examples of how TEMA exists on a continuum.

Germany has a relatively restrictive law concerning abortion which is often criticised for that reason (Halliday 2016). Indeed, when Women on Web began providing its service to people in Germany in 2019 there was an immediate and drastic increase in people accessing the service in the first nine months alone (Killinger et al. 2020). Per Section 219 of the German Criminal Code, a person seeking abortion services must undergo counselling. This counselling 'serves to protect the unborn life' and 'must be guided by efforts to encourage the woman to carry the child to term'.[263] Further, there is a mandatory three-day waiting period between this counselling session and the abortion itself. Aside from the fact that this counselling is quite explicitly partial rather than objective, it increases the burden on the person wanting to end an unwanted pregnancy.[264] Nonetheless, whilst the requirement that the abortion be

---

[263] German Criminal Code, s.219(1).
[264] There are clear similarities here to the barriers to abortion imposed by the law in many US states. See Chapter 3.

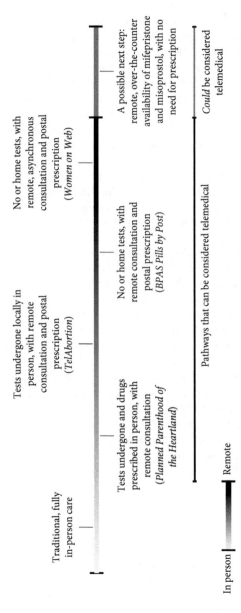

Traditional, fully
in-person care

Tests undergone and drugs
prescribed in person, with
remote consultation
(*Planned Parenthood of
the Heartland*)

Tests undergone locally in
person, with remote
consultation and postal
prescription
(*TelAbortion*)

No or home tests, with
remote consultation and
postal prescription
(*BPAS Pills by Post*)

No or home tests, with
remote, asynchronous
consultation and postal
prescription
(*Women on Web*)

A possible next step:
remote, over-the-counter
availability of mifepristone
and misoprostol, with no
need for prescription

Pathways that can be considered telemedical

Could be considered
telemedical

In person | Remote

Figure 6.1 The TEMA continuum

carried out in a clinic has remained in Germany throughout the pandemic thus far, there was a change to permit the use of telemedicine for the purposes of the mandatory counselling (European Parliamentary Forum for Sexual and Reproductive Rights and International Planned Parenthood Federation European Network 2020, 9). This example of partial telemedicine has, at least temporarily, reduced the number of clinic visits required to procure an abortion in Germany. Germany's approach is interesting as it is an example of one of the several countries with mandatory counselling—generally an indication of largely anti-abortion policy—moving to improve access. Whilst some countries with mandatory counselling instead went in the other direction by restricting access—such as Slovakia (Romanis and Parsons 2020a)—Germany moved in the direction of somewhat recognising abortion as essential healthcare. The removal of mandatory pro-life counselling is, we suggest, preferable, but where it exists there is at least the option of permitting it to be conducted remotely even if the abortion itself requires an in-person appointment.

In South Africa, a somewhat smaller, but nonetheless important, change was introduced. Previously, there was a requirement that 'routine' consultations by telemedicine should be 'restricted to situations in which a previously existing healthcare-patient relationship' exists (Health Professions Council of South Africa 2014, s.4.8.1(a)). On 26 March 2020, the Health Professions Council of South Africa issued COVID-19 guidelines, which noted that this restriction concerning the patient-provider relationship was applicable in the COVID-19 context (except for psychology and psychiatry) without the flexible specificity of 'routine' consultations (Health Professions Council of South Africa 2020a). This was, however, updated on 3 April 2020 to highlight a *preference* for an existing relationship, but, nonetheless, to permit the use of telemedicine in the absence of an existing relationship 'provided that such consultations are done in the best clinical interest of patients' (Health Professions Council of South Africa 2020b). This guidance is broadly applicable, meaning the use of telemedicine in abortion care was simplified. Such small details in regulations have the potential to act as significant barriers to accessing healthcare, and the South African example shows that often it is the smallest of changes that can enable some manner of TEMA service.

The examples discussed here are just a selection to illustrate the phenomenon. More detailed explorations of some of the partial telemedicine options implemented in response to the COVID-19 pandemic can be found elsewhere (Romanis and Parsons 2020a; Moreau et al. 2020).

6.5 The importance of choice

Thus far in this book, we have demonstrated that the traditional, fully in person, care pathway that often exists for EMA is not suitable for many patients seeking to access such care. It presents significant barriers to access that can ultimately result in some patients either having to endure more invasive methods of abortion or continue their unwanted pregnancy to term. That being said, TEMA is also not suitable for all patients. Further, even if TEMA is broadly appropriate, a *fully* remote care pathway may not be. As such, it is important that the continuum detailed above is viewed not purely as descriptive but as a normative argument; we are not only demonstrating that there *is* a continuum, but also that there *should be* one.[265] However, this continuum should be *intra*-service rather than *inter*-service in nature. Rather than some providers offering fully remote pathways and others offering partially telemedical pathways, this range should be offered by *each* provider. Providers should, in addition to fully in-person care, offer a range of telemedical services, some of which should entail in-person *elements*. We argue that the need for this intra-service range of TEMA care pathways is rooted in respect for patient autonomy and the importance of patient-centred care.

On encountering the range of TEMA models that have been established, it is understandable that one of the 'full telemedicine' options might intuitively be thought preferable. Given the access barriers that we have already outlined as (to an extent) addressed by removing the need to attend a clinic, it seems logical that we should want to *entirely* remove in-person elements from TEMA care pathways. Doing so would, prima facie, result in the most significant improvement in access to services when introducing TEMA. Such a position would favour models such as Women on Web and BPAS' Pills by Post, whilst indicating that those of Planned Parenthood in Iowa and TelAbortion are in some sense substandard. This, however, stems from a narrow view of the space TEMA fills. On the surface, TEMA is about enabling pregnant people to access services without facing the procedural barriers to in-person care. At a deeper level, however, TEMA is about patient-centred care and respecting the individual values and preferences of patients as both important to informed consent. We touched on this in Chapter 5 in arguing that TEMA should be introduced as an additional service because it is problematic for in-person provisions to be reduced by progress towards remote care. A similar line of argument, we propose, should apply *within* what is categorised as TEMA—it is problematic (if slightly less so) for 'TEMA' to be a strictly defined single option, introducing a simple either/or decision for patients.

First, let us establish the importance of patient-centred care and respect for patient autonomy. Patient-centred care is very much in vogue when it comes to health policy (Richards et al. 2015). In England, for example, the NHS is working towards its Long Term Plan (National Health Service 2019), which has patient-centricity at its heart. Incidentally, given that we are discussing the Plan in the context of telemedicine, when published in 2019, it boldly predicted that '[d]igitally-enabled care will go mainstream across the NHS' (National Health Service 2019, 91). Furthering this goal is the decentralisation of healthcare through so-called 'integrated care systems'. The purpose of these new systems is to integrate what is currently provided by several bodies (NHS organisations, local councils, etc.), resulting in fewer (42) organisations with overall responsibility for population health in a given area (National Health Service 2020).[266] Integrated care systems ultimately rest on the belief that local providers are best placed to understand the needs of their own populations, demonstrating the patient-centred focus.

---

[265] Readers of a philosophical inclination may immediately envisage an 'is-ought' problem arising here. This is not the case, as we have outlined existing models purely for the purposes of illustrating how this continuum might be realised—in this section we will make the normative case independently. Our thanks to Harleen Kaur Johal for highlighting this.

[266] Whilst the small number of integrated care systems that already exist operate on voluntary arrangements, the Government intends to establish them as statutory bodies by April 2022 (Department of Health and Social Care 2021).

In law, *Montgomery*, a UK case concerning appropriate risk disclosure, charted the social and legal developments that collectively 'point away from a model of the relationship between the doctor and the patient based upon medical paternalism'.[267] The Supreme Court noted the significance of *Pearce v United Bristol Healthcare NHS Trust*[268] in which the idea of the 'reasonable patient' was influential.[269] In the context of informed consent to treatment, *Montgomery* was clear that we have moved away from what the reasonable doctor would consider appropriate to share with a patient to a standard of risk disclosure that is what the reasonable patient would consider appropriate to have shared with them—a test of materiality.[270] It is then for the patient to make a decision about their treatment, having all of the relevant information, based on their values and preferences. Farrell and Brazier acknowledge that *Montgomery* really just endorses a reasonable patient test that had been the reality of UK healthcare practice and consent for more than a decade (2016, 85). Nonetheless, this confirmation by the Supreme Court strengthens the claim of paternalism's erosion.

This discernible shift to patient-centred care is concerned with the autonomy of patients. Whereas HCPs (not just doctors) have important specialist knowledge that plays an important role in treatment decisions, it is patients themselves that, once provided with appropriate information, are best placed to decide what the best decision is for them (Cave and Milo 2020). Individuals all have different values and preferences that will guide these decisions, and what a HCP might consider 'objectively' the best option may be entirely inappropriate for some patients. It is an important principle that a patient's right to make a decision should not be brought into question based only on the content of that decision. As already noted, the right to choose 'exists notwithstanding that the reasons for marking the choice are rational or irrational, unknown or even non-existent'.[271] It is the role of the HCP to advise the patient as to what the clinically appropriate options are, alongside a reporting of the benefits and drawbacks of each in as objective terms as possible. In the context of abortion, for example, it would be appropriate to explain what the patient will experience depending on the method chosen, allowing a patient with a serious aversion to blood, for example, to make an informed decision that may well result in them opting for a surgical rather than medical method. As discussed in Chapter 5, the information provided might also extend to acceptability, including what previous patients have reported regarding their experience of different care pathways—though, of course, in an objective manner. For example, the patient may be informed that patients who have taken both mifepristone and misoprostol in a clinic have had distressing journeys home as the drugs take effect (Women's Equality Party 2018),[272] which may cause the patient who initially had a preference for undergoing the treatment in a clinical setting to take the misoprostol at home and avoid the risk of such an experience. It remains the responsibility of HCPs

---

[267] *Montgomery* (n8), at para 81.
[268] Ibid, at para 64.
[269] [1999] PIQR P53, at para 21 per Lord Woolf MR.
[270] *Montgomery* (n8), at para 87.
[271] *Re T* (n52), at 102 per Lord Donaldson. For a discussion of autonomy in the context of mental (in)capacity, see Kong (2017).
[272] See Chapter 4 for further discussion of the issues associated with taking both drugs in a clinic before returning home.

to only provide clinically appropriate care, and sometimes there will only be one such option. However, in many cases—abortion care being one—there are usually several clinically appropriate options.

Having outlined the importance of, and wider shift towards, respect for patient autonomy, it remains to justify why this respect entails the provision of an intra-service continuum of TEMA options. Autonomy might ordinarily be considered as the patient having a choice between available options. The ruling in *Montgomery* requires that patients be made aware of 'any reasonable alternative or variant treatments'.[273] This, understandably, can only be considered to extend to treatment options that are actually available—a patient cannot demand, for example, a surgery that the hospital does not provide.[274] As such, we need to widen our understanding of autonomy here.

Beauchamp and Childress, in their widely recognised account, consider it a necessary condition of autonomy that the agent be free of limitations that 'prevent meaningful choice' (2013, 101). This procedural account[275]—or at least this particular condition—presents a conception of autonomy as a negative right on the part of the agent. Applied to the healthcare context, provided there are no active barriers preventing the patient from making a choice about their treatment in line with their own values and preferences, that choice will be considered autonomous. We will not dwell here on questions of the constitution of the patient's values and preferences, and how they may have been historically and/or socially shaped, but assume that the values and preferences a patient employs in making a treatment decision worthy of respect (Khader 2020) and instead focus on the question of tangible limitations at the time of the decision.

Consider a scenario in which no TEMA care pathway is offered and EMA is only accessible in person. As outlined in Chapter 5, the patient seeking to terminate an unwanted pregnancy in this scenario cannot be considered as having any real choice about *how* they access care. The patient is faced with a choice between attending a clinic or continuing an unwanted pregnancy, which, for someone who has decided that they need an abortion, is not a choice—it is fair to say that such a patient would choose to attend a clinic, unless they were to instead pursue clandestine options, which we do not treat as a reasonable option.[276] In this scenario, the extent to which the patient can be said to have made an autonomous choice in response to their options can be considered limited. Put in terms of Beauchamp and Childress' condition, a binary choice—by which we mean a yes/no choice regarding a single treatment option—is, we suggest, a limitation that prevents meaningful choice. Specifically, we would characterise this binary choice as a 'false choice'. To remedy this, we posit that

---

[273] *Montgomery* (n8), at para 87.

[274] *R (Burke) v General Medical Council* [2005] EWCA Civ 1003.

[275] We recognise that there are more accounts of autonomy, many of which actively disagree with the importance of procedural elements. However, given that we are here concerned more about *what* a patient *could* choose rather than *how* a patient *would* choose, many of the primary distinctions between accounts of autonomy (i.e. procedural versus substantive and individualist versus relational) are not relevant. On the particular point with which we are concerned—external constraints as in some way negatively affecting autonomy—most theories would somewhat agree.

[276] This is not to say that people who choose to use services such as Women on Web are not making reasonable decisions. Rather, we believe that there is a need for locally established TEMA services through lawful channels.

the introduction of additional choices of care pathway is appropriate and effective, and, in many settings, may prove rather simple to achieve.

In Chapter 5, we set out our case for the introduction of TEMA. Enhanced autonomy was mentioned as a benefit of telemedicine, forming part of the underlying justification of the telemedical imperative that we applied. The logic outlined above has, then, to an extent, been utilised in arguing for the availability of TEMA alongside in-person provision of EMA—indeed, we quite firmly opposed the characterisation of TEMA as removing the need for in-person services. Here we look at the specifics of the TEMA pathway in more detail. Rather than taking EMA as the service in need of additional choices of care pathway, we are looking specifically at TEMA as (potentially) in need of additional choices.

There is no escaping that this position—that additional choices are necessary to avoid false choices—requires that the meaningful choice condition of autonomy be characterised slightly differently. The negative right to be free of autonomy-compromising interference must be framed to entail a *positive* obligation on another party to *enable* (or, depending on how one perceives the situation, *enhance*) the patient's autonomy. Whether the provision of additional choices enables or enhances autonomy is, we suggest, a simple matter of numbers. In the scenario in which care is only available in person, the addition of TEMA as an option is enabling autonomy by preventing a false choice. If TEMA is available alongside in-person care, but there is only one TEMA care pathway, then the patient can still be considered autonomous in whatever choice they make; the patient is not presented with a simple binary, but now has the choice between no care and care delivered in one of two ways. In this latter scenario, then, additional choices would be a matter of enhancing the patient's autonomy. The patient is already able to make an autonomous choice but would be able to make a *more autonomous* choice—meaning one that better reflects their subjective preferences—if several TEMA care pathways were offered. Thus, if respect for autonomy is truly valued, the provision of additional choices is an appropriate actioning of this normative position.[277]

To illustrate this, consider a patient—Mary—who needs an abortion but is worried about people she knows finding out. She lives a busy lifestyle and so usually attends remote general practice appointments when she needs one. As such, Mary wants to make use of her local abortion provider's TEMA service but is still concerned about people in her household seeing the pill pack if it is posted to her—particularly as she is often out when other members of her household are at home.[278] The ideal for Mary would be to attend a remote consultation so that she can easily fit it around her busy

---

[277] Oshana's formulation of personal autonomy contains four conditions, one of which is '[a]ccess to a range of relevant options' (1998, 94). She argues that these options cannot all be dictated by duress or by bodily needs, as an assortment is inadequate 'if a person can only choose nonautonomy' (1998, 94). This condition can be considered to form the basis of the necessity of additional choices to *enable* autonomy in the event of a false choice. However, additional choices to *enhance* autonomy where the patient is already able to make an autonomous choice go beyond this minimum standard. The normative significance of additional choices to *enhance* autonomy, then, rests specifically on a broad understanding of *respect for* autonomy rather than autonomy itself.

[278] We recognise that these packs are posted discreetly so that it is not apparent what they are without opening them. However, I think many of us can sympathise with having nosy flatmates and/or family members and not wanting to appear as though we are hiding something.

lifestyle, briefly visit her local clinic the following day to collect the drugs so that no other person in her household sees them,[279] and then return home to terminate the pregnancy in her own time and with the privacy she values. However, if only a fully remote TEMA service is available, Mary is forced to choose between scheduling a full in-person consultation and risking a member of her household seeing the pill pack when it arrives. This scenario, whilst fictional, does reflect the concerns that many people have about how to access abortion, as we illustrated in Chapter 3.

One might argue that it is unrealistic for a patient to expect an array of options inclusive of one that perfectly fits their preferences and lifestyle. Certainly, it is unrealistic to expect every healthcare provider to offer a catalogue of care pathways for each and every treatment. Here, the distinction between autonomy being enabled and enhanced is relevant. There is a moral imperative to respond where autonomy is being enabled by the addition of a single telemedical option—the telemedical imperative, as applied in the previous chapter. On the other hand, when the patient's autonomy is already enabled and additional options act to enhance it, a moral *imperative* cannot be said to arise. In the latter scenario, additional options are ideal but not necessary. However, where rather simple service adjustments can be made to provide for the preferences of a larger number of patients—thereby enhancing their autonomy—it is appropriate to do so. In the context of abortion, one must also consider that these preferences may be formed in response to stigma surrounding the choice to terminate an unwanted pregnancy—the imperative might, then, be said to be greater if the desire for more private options is, at least in part, systemically created.

The issue arises here as to whether this approach may result in *too many* choices, to the point that the patient's autonomy is compromised. Certainly, there is something to be said for being overwhelmed with choice. Levy, for example, questions whether autonomy might be better enhanced by constraining it, arguing that 'we cannot expect patients to take on so much of the burden of making choices' (2014, 293). Whilst Levy discusses this in the context of informed consent and the amount of information patients should be provided with, similar logic might suggest that *fewer* choices could improve the ability of individuals to exercise autonomy. However, this approach necessitates value judgements in deciding which options to provide, which faces the same obstacle that we have already discussed of denying the range of subjective values and preferences held by patients. Limiting choices under the guise of enhancing autonomy is, then, misguided. Further, we are not advocating that an overwhelmingly vast number of options be made available. Rather, we are suggesting that a choice between in-person and telemedical care (or, of course, no care), whilst it does enable an autonomous choice, is unnecessarily restrictive in the context of EMA. As the TEMA models outlined earlier in this chapter illustrate, there are small differences that can appeal to different patients.

One must account for constraints such as resources to some extent. Where additional options could only be introduced at great cost, it may be that, on balance, it is not appropriate to divert significant resources to enhance autonomy when autonomous

---

[279] Incidentally, this could be achieved by the patient being able to collect the prescription from a local pharmacy. Whilst we would certainly support the introduction of such an option, a comprehensive defence of such a change is beyond the scope of this book. We will, however, revisit it briefly in Chapter 10.

choice is already possible. However, where nothing of comparable moral significance is compromised by the introduction of additional choices, they should be made available out of respect for patient autonomy.

In sum, choice in abortion care is important: the choice to have an abortion at all, choice of abortion method, choice between in-person and telemedical care pathways, and choice *within* in-person and telemedical care pathways. There will be instances where certain options are not clinically appropriate for a particular patient, but even in these situations it will usually be possible to offer that patient several choices. With the availability of TEMA, even if a range of care pathways are available, it is reasonable to assume that many will prefer the fully remote option. The myriad barriers to accessing in-person abortion care that we have discussed in previous chapters mean that many people simply cannot attend a clinic in person. However, others will find partial telemedicine options preferable for a variety of reasons. Given the gestational limits imposed on certain abortion methods, additional options are perhaps more important in this context than in many other areas of healthcare; a partial telemedicine care pathway might enable a person to access care within the first 10 weeks of pregnancy when they might otherwise have exceeded that limit.

Given the importance of additional options to enhance the autonomy of patients seeking abortion services, it seems that the model operated by BPAS may act as a useful foundation. As detailed earlier in this chapter, BPAS' Pills by Post service is primarily designed as a fully telemedical service—the patient undergoes a remote consultation, is posted mifepristone and misoprostol with instructions for home use, and only undergoes in-person care in the event of an unsuccessful termination or complications requiring medical attention. However, patients do have the option of collecting their medications in person if preferred. Whilst during the pandemic few patients are opting to collect pill packs in person, going forward it may be that a significant proportion of patients prefer this option. Additional options would enhance the service further, such as the ability to undergo testing through other healthcare providers if desired, but at least having a partial telemedicine option means that BPAS' service model is something of an example. That being said, the exact nature of additional choices that would best enhance patient autonomy would depend on the regulatory framework surrounding abortion care in each jurisdiction. In Germany, for example, the partial telemedicine pathway introduced in response to the pandemic entailed remote counselling prior to in-person abortion care.

6.6 Summary

We have demonstrated in this chapter that the phrase 'using telemedicine in the delivery of abortion care' is very broad indeed. It would be fair to say that, when thinking of TEMA, most envisage something not too dissimilar to the Pills by Post service offered by BPAS, with this common perception inevitably having been shaped by the events of 2020. However, the reality is that there is huge variation in the ways telemedicine can be employed to improve abortion services (see Figure 6.2).

In discussing some of these variations, we grouped models into 'partial telemedicine' and 'full telemedicine'. This is certainly a useful way to think about TEMA from an

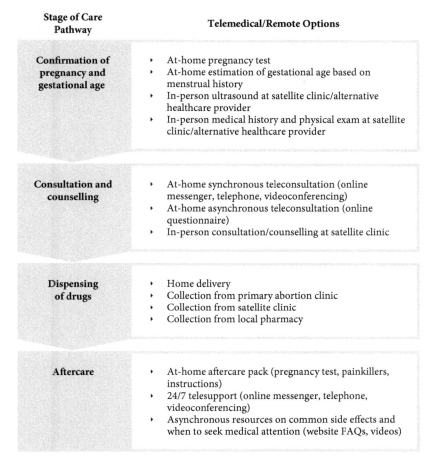

Stage of Care Pathway	Telemedical/Remote Options
Confirmation of pregnancy and gestational age	‣ At-home pregnancy test ‣ At-home estimation of gestational age based on menstrual history ‣ In-person ultrasound at satellite clinic/alternative healthcare provider ‣ In-person medical history and physical exam at satellite clinic/alternative healthcare provider
Consultation and counselling	‣ At-home synchronous teleconsultation (online messenger, telephone, videoconferencing) ‣ At-home asynchronous teleconsultation (online questionnaire) ‣ In-person consultation/counselling at satellite clinic
Dispensing of drugs	‣ Home delivery ‣ Collection from primary abortion clinic ‣ Collection from satellite clinic ‣ Collection from local pharmacy
Aftercare	‣ At-home aftercare pack (pregnancy test, painkillers, instructions) ‣ 24/7 telesupport (online messenger, telephone, videoconferencing) ‣ Asynchronous resources on common side effects and when to seek medical attention (website FAQs, videos)

Figure 6.2 Telemedical/remote options for abortion care pathways

historical perspective, as services are largely moving in the direction of full telemedicine. However, recent introductions of TEMA have retained some level of compulsory in-person contact—for example, in Germany during the COVID-19 pandemic.

Even with this general shift towards full telemedicine when it comes to TEMA services, it must be remembered that a full telemedicine care pathway is not suitable for all. Setting aside those who must access abortion care in person due to the local regulatory framework, we have discussed several examples of the kinds of patients who might simply feel more comfortable attending a clinic. In keeping with the telemedical imperative as proposed in Chapter 5, full telemedicine should not be the only, or even the default, model of care when TEMA is introduced—patients should be offered both options at first contact. Rather than shifting the access burden, it is of the utmost importance that at least some of the range within the TEMA continuum is encapsulated by all services. BPAS' offering—and, indeed, those of a similar nature—may be considered a strong example of this. The options detailed in Figure 6.2 would ideally be offered in tandem, but where this is not feasible, they can act as a *menu of options* for providers to implement where possible. At its core, the normative importance of the TEMA continuum is about respect for patient autonomy and enhancing this through choice.

In the remainder of this book, we consider how the COVID-19 pandemic intensified the need for TEMA, and the responses to this need in both the UK and US.

7

The necessity of telemedical abortion during a pandemic

In March 2020, in response to the emerging threat of COVID-19, governments across the world quickly took action and 'normal' life ceased to exist. Various government-mandated policies, such as social distancing measures and national lockdowns, prevented people from freely leaving their homes. Further, healthcare resources were swiftly redirected towards the increasing needs of those infected with the virus. Whilst the reasoning behind such policies was evident, concerns arose about the implications for access to routine healthcare—including abortion.

In the US and UK, both the rising prevalence of the virus itself, and the restrictions that were brought in to manage its transmission, had a substantial impact on people who needed an abortion. There was a clear exacerbation of the many existing socio-legal barriers to access in these jurisdictions (Romanis et al. 2020a; Nandigiri et al. 2020) (see Chapter 3). In this chapter, we argue that demand for abortion remained—and potentially increased—during the COVID-19 crisis, whilst pandemic response measures restricted patients' ability to attend abortion clinics. As a result, two problematic scenarios became reality for some people. First, a total inability to access a clinic resulting in a forced continuation of an unwanted pregnancy. Second, a delay in accessing abortion resulting in a later-term abortion. Both scenarios presented—and continue to present—health implications for those affected (Romanis et al. 2020a).

Abortion is a time-critical and essential procedure that must continue to be facilitated, even during a global health emergency. To fail to do so is to perpetuate sex-based inequality in deprioritising the health and well-being of females during the crisis. This is especially important in that there are a multitude of other ways in which females and other marginalised groups are 'likely to carry a heavier burden of what will be the devastating downstream economic and social consequences of this pandemic' (Hall et al. 2020, 1175). Abortion access is essential 'because deciding whether and when to bear a child is central to women's self-determination and equal participation in society. During the COVID-19 pandemic, such access is even more important' (Bayefsky et al. 2020, 3) as a result of the other structural disadvantages many females are facing—often along gendered lines—including, but not limited to, increased caring responsibilities at home, being more likely to be a frontline care worker (for example, nurse, midwife, or community health worker) (United Nations 2020, 10), being more likely to lose non-caring employment (Madgavkar et al. 2020), and an increase in gender-based violence (United Nations 2020). The burdens associated with unwanted reproduction are always great, but they are potentially magnified in the present circumstances.

Early Medical Abortion, Equality of Access, and the Telemedical Imperative. Jordan A. Parsons and Elizabeth Chloe Romanis, Oxford University Press. © Oxford University Press 2021. DOI: 10.1093/oso/9780192896155.003.0007

The introduction of TEMA, we argue, must be considered a necessity to ensure access to abortion during a crisis that minimises individual movement. The argument we raise here *is* specific to COVID-19, but our reasoning does apply in broader, non-emergency circumstances. Ultimately, our contention throughout this book is that TEMA is necessary to improve access in all circumstances. Our turning to the exacerbation of access issues during the pandemic serves the purpose of highlighting that the telemedical imperative in the context of abortion can no longer be ignored by lawmakers.

7.1 COVID-19 and the demand for abortion

Unwanted pregnancies will always occur, and thus demand for abortion will always exist. As the director for the United Nations Population Fund described it, 'pregnancies don't stop for pandemics, or any crisis' (Oppenheim 2021). Demand for abortion may decrease in some groups during the COVID-19 pandemic, such as amongst single people not socialising with others, but there are substantial reasons to believe that demand might increase in other groups (for example, couples living together) as a result of government 'lockdown' policies.

First, the crisis could have resulted in an increase in unplanned pregnancies. The lack of freedom of movement in many places has limited some people's ability to access contraceptives. Many contraceptive clinics in the UK were closed in the first acute wave of the pandemic (MSI Reproductive Choices 2020). Where they remained open, not everyone was in a position to easily travel to sexual health clinics, such as if they were isolating, shielding at home, or unable to travel the required distance because of 'lockdown' restrictions. This is worsened by the fact that many (safe) forms of birth control are not available without prescription. Further, many contraceptive clinics have had to halt, delay, or restrict outpatient appointments, including those for the placement of contraceptive devices (Bayefsky et al. 2020, 2). In a survey conducted by the Guttmacher Institute between April and May 2020 in the US, one in three women reported that, as a result of the pandemic and resulting restrictions, they had difficulty accessing their usual contraceptive (Lindberg et al. 2020b, 4). Notably, a reduction in access to contraceptives was more prevalent among minorities; 45% of Hispanic women and 38% of black women reported limited access compared to 29% of white women, and 48% of queer women reported limited access compared to 31% of heterosexual women (Lindberg et al. 2020b, 4). In the US, where people are reliant on their personal funds or healthcare insurance to access various contraceptives, access also appears to have been more limited as a result of the economic consequences of COVID-19 restrictions. Many people, particularly in lower-paying work, lost their jobs, which also meant they either lost health insurance or were no longer able to pay out-of-pocket (Lindberg et al. 2020b, 4). Such concerns might have been more prevalent amongst younger people because 'loss of their own or parents' earnings or health insurance creates economic barriers to accessing care and paying for' contraception (Lindberg et al. 2020a, 77). Whilst contraception is provided free of charge by the NHS in the UK, there have still been concerns about access during COVID-19. One study reported, in September 2020, that 36% of women were unsure of how to access contraception during the pandemic, with one in seven reporting that they were unable to get an appointment at a local clinic (MSI Reproductive Choices 2020).

Against a backdrop of a decline in access to some contraceptives, there could be an increase in unwanted conception as a result of 'isolation sex' (Romanis et al. 2020b) as more time at home might result in an increase in some couples' sexual activity (Beyefsky et al. 2020, 2). There is also the concern that an increase in intimate-partner violence that often occurs in times of emergency, to which COVID-19 is no exception (Peterman et al. 2020), can sometimes include 'sexual coercion and assault that may result in unplanned pregnancies' (Bayefsky et al. 2020, 3).

Second, the crisis might have resulted in an increase in *unwanted* pregnancies. With the social consequences of COVID-19, ranging from rising unemployment to the mental health crisis, many people are facing significant personal difficulty. It would be unsurprising if many (potentially unplanned) pregnancies were also unwanted pregnancies. For many people, they may feel (even more so) that they do not want to reproduce at this time, and will seek abortion.[280] In one study conducted in the US, more than one in three women reported that, as a direct result of the pandemic, they either wanted to 'delay having a child or limit future births' (Lindberg et al. 2020b, 8). There is a greater degree of economic uncertainty for the average person, even including those who have remained employed. COVID-19 has 'brought about substantial financial hardship for many families, and not having the money to support a child (or an additional child) is a leading reason that women choose to have an abortion' (Bayefsky et al. 2020, 2). Aiken and colleagues also suggest that '[t]he decision to end a pregnancy could be due to the perception of risk posed by COVID-19, reduced access to prenatal care or limited social support during lockdowns' (2021b, 6). In the UK, there have been substantial difficulties placed on pregnant people during the crisis, including conflicting advice about whether to shield, being required to go to prenatal appointments alone, potentially being denied a birth partner in hospital, and/or being denied a choice about place of birth (Romanis and Nelson 2020). The conditions for pregnant people are such that this might make many feel that carrying a pregnancy and birthing is not something they feel able to do. The absence of the usual social support networks that people have in their friends and family, and from broader services, are not available, and this can make the process of continuing a pregnancy daunting. The gravity of these factors and others combined mean that many people will feel abortion is right for them at this time. The decision to abort for such reasons is characterised as social, but this does not mean that it is not essential. People 'who choose abortion for social and emotional reasons often state that they have no choice at all—that the notion of continuing this particular pregnancy is absolutely out of the question for them' (Janiak and Goldberg 2016, 91).

---

[280] We do not mean to imply that people only want to end pregnancies *because of* the pandemic. This could be the case in many instances, but others would consider pregnancy unwanted and seek abortion irrespective of COVID-19.

7.2 Socio-legal barriers exacerbated by COVID-19

With the potential rise in unplanned—and specifically unwanted—pregnancies, it is important that access to abortion continues to be available. However, Aiken and colleagues observe that, unfortunately, this potential rise in demand is a result of the same set of circumstances that make the clinic setting even more difficult to access (2021b). The barriers that we explore here have not resulted from COVID-19 (see Chapter 3), but it is important to stress how COVID-19 has *exacerbated* structural barriers to care (Nandigiri et al. 2020; Romanis et al. 2020a).

The distance that many must travel to their nearest clinic has only increased because of pandemic-related clinic closures (Romanis and Parsons 2020a). In March 2020, the largest abortion provider in England and Wales announced that it had been forced to close 23% of its clinics due to staff shortages (British Pregnancy Advisory Service 2020b). In the US, executive orders were issued in some states forcing the closure of all 'non-essential' healthcare facilities, defined in such a way that included abortion clinics.[281] As a result, many people found themselves in a position whereby the distance they had to travel for in-person care was increased. This particularly affected those living in rural areas in the UK, and those living in states with already disparate abortion access in the US (because of a limited number of clinics in the first place). In addition, travelling became more difficult in practical terms for people during the crisis, and especially those who did not have any access to private means of transportation. Many forms of public transportation were limited in the first acute wave of the virus in March 2020 (as a response to the fact that fewer people were making use of such services), and these limitations hindered the ability of many to make necessary journeys. Further, even if such journeys were possible, them being longer in duration increased the likelihood of contracting the virus.

Difficulties in travelling only become an obstacle if someone can leave their home to access care in the first place. However, for people who have contracted the virus or are living with someone who has, leaving the home to attend a clinic is not an option. These people faced the possibility, because of an isolation period, of missing the time window for EMA. Second, there are many people who, whilst not infected, are shielding at home for other health-related reasons. These people, unable to attend a clinic, face the possibility of continuing an unwanted pregnancy. Third, there are many people who, whilst not specifically advised to shield, prefer to take a cautious approach and choose not to leave the home even to access healthcare, either for fear of their own safety or that of the people they live with (Romanis and Parsons 2020a). Whilst those in this third group are technically able to make a longer journey, they could feel very uncomfortable doing so—potentially to the extent that it interferes with their perception of the standard of care they receive. Finally, leaving the home has become increasingly difficult for those with caring responsibilities, including any existing children and/or other relatives (including, but not limited to, relatives with complex health needs). It has been noted that school closures 'might have a differential effect on women, who provide most of the informal care within families, with the

---

[281] We will discuss these changes in Chapter 9. We raise this here to highlight that these orders did result in people having to travel further to access abortion.

consequence of limiting their work and economic opportunities' (Wenham et al. 2020, 846). Arranging childcare (even within a family support network) to attend a clinic has become impossible for most due to restrictions, presenting the choice between making that (potentially longer) journey with children and not making it at all. For many, this will not feel like a choice, and access is, in every practical sense, impossible.

Further, many people reported difficulty leaving the home to access a clinic before the pandemic because of intimate partner or family violence (Aiken et al. 2018), which is likely to have escalated as a concern. There is significant evidence that such violence at home has increased as a result of the pandemic and people being confined to their homes (United Nations 2020). Those in such situations will find it harder to leave the home because of the even greater ability of a coercive partner to control their movements.

The barriers outlined are likely to disproportionately impact on individuals who are already structurally disadvantaged. Whilst not every person who will need abortion will identify as a woman, the majority do, and, as already outlined, gender inequality has been exacerbated by the pandemic. Concerns that we outlined about leaving the home related to the fear of contracting the virus could be more prominent amongst some particular groups. For example, persons with chronic illnesses, mental health issues, or other disabilities. This might also be a greater source of concern for some people from ethnic minority backgrounds, as there is evidence that (because of structural factors)[282] these groups are disproportionately dying from COVID-19 (APM Research Lab 2021; Office for National Statistics 2020). It is less likely that young people will be able to access clinics in person, because travelling longer distances 'may not be as feasible [for them] as it is for older women, owing to lack of transportation or financial resources, and lack of autonomy and privacy' (Lindberg et al. 2020a, 77).

Where people can access clinics, there is likely to have been a considerable delay in them being able to do so, as they had to overcome many or all the highlighted barriers. As a result, they may have their abortion much later than they otherwise would have, thereby increasing the risk of complications and side effects (see Chapter 1). In some instances, this might also result in the gestational limit for (early) medical abortion being exceeded, leaving the individual with fewer choices of abortion method (Romanis et al. 2020a), which either may not include their first preference or, in the US, could increase out-of-pocket costs. Further, in-person clinic visits increase the risk of exposure to COVID-19 for both staff and patients. There are, then, not only concerns about *access* to in-person care during a pandemic, but also about safety when such access is possible. When a safe, effective, and acceptable alternative exists in the form of TEMA, to keep these barriers and risks in place is unnecessary and, in line with the telemedical imperative that we explored in Chapter 5, ethically indefensible.

---

[282] This results from broader structural factors, including socioeconomics, geography, and demography. People from ethnic minorities are more likely to live in deprived areas and be employed in key worker roles (Office for National Statistics 2020).

7.3 Abortion is an *essential, time-sensitive* procedure

During a pandemic, difficult decisions inevitably must be made about what health services can continue to be made available, as resources are redeployed to immediately manage those infected and needing treatment in hospital and governments want to encourage people to stay at home. Kumar and colleagues explain that, when making these difficult decisions about what can or should remain available, 'rationales such as "essential" versus "non-essential" and "life-saving" are being used as guideposts for these decisions. Yet these terms are subjective, open to interpretation and highly influenced by personal values and social norms' (2020, 1–2). The long-standing stigma surrounding abortion, and the perception that it is a choice, has rendered it 'particularly vulnerable to marginalisation or deprioritisation, especially during emergencies' (Kumar et al. 2020, 1–2). However, it is important that abortion remains designated as an essential procedure during emergencies and that due attention is paid to the fact that it is time sensitive.

Abortion is not an elective procedure, and describing it as such is not reflective of the subjective experiences of those who experience unwanted pregnancy (Janiak and Goldberg 2016). For people who access abortion, they rarely consider it to be a matter of choice, even in those circumstances in which others refer to their decisions as being for 'social or emotional reasons', and instead they feel that they have no option but to end their pregnancy (Janiak and Goldberg 2016, 91). Delays in the provision of abortion services only lead to unsafe abortions as individuals potentially turn to other means to end their pregnancies (Todd-Gher and Shah 2020). Unwanted pregnancy risks not only damage to a person's short- and long-term physical health, but also to their mental health (Todd-Gher and Shah 2020), and potentially, therefore, their life. Unwanted pregnancy also threatens a person's future conception of their life and their ability to make decisions about their future (Cornell 1995). Many of the reasons why individuals may feel the need to end their pregnancy (some of which may be related to the pandemic) amplify quite how important abortion is as a form of healthcare that is necessary for the preservation of female equality.

Abortion is time sensitive because of the gestational limits that are placed on different methods both clinically and by law, and because of the increased risks involved when abortion is performed later in a pregnancy. Further, a person experiencing an unwanted pregnancy often wants access to abortion as soon as possible both for peace of mind and to avoid the physical symptoms of pregnancy. We emphasise that abortion is time sensitive to demonstrate that it is not a service which should be considered capable of being suspended, or one in which delays should be considered acceptable, because of inevitable changes that have to be made with regard to the organisation of services during a pandemic.[283] Permitting individuals to access care at home using

---

[283] Some might argue that there could be a tipping point at which a healthcare system is under such strain that only emergency or life-saving (narrowly construed) abortions can be provided. However, this is a point that countries such as the UK and US are unlikely to ever reach, and they certainly have not reached in the COVID-19 pandemic. Further, in many countries, abortion is provided by independent providers that do not use the resources of the broader health service, so the suggestion that abortion services might need to cease to divert resources is not in line with the reality of their provision.

TEMA during the pandemic (and even beyond) 'is not simply about harm reduction; it is a human rights imperative' (Todd-Gher and Shah 2020, 30).

7.4 An appeal to human rights for reform in the United Kingdom

There is no legal right to abortion in the UK (see Chapter 2), nor is there any right to abortion contained in the European Convention on Human Rights (hereafter, the Convention), to which the UK is a signatory.[284] This has one important caveat: that abortion must be available in those circumstances where pregnancy threatens the life (narrowly understood) of the pregnant person.[285] There has, however, been acknowledgement that restrictions on access to abortion constitute an interference with a person's right to private life (Article 8 of the Convention).[286] The right to private life is not absolute, however, which means that a signatory state can interfere with the right (and thus prevent access to abortion) where they do so in line with stipulations in Article 8(2). Interference is permissible where: 'in accordance with the law'; 'necessary in a democratic society' for, amongst other reasons, the protection of health or morals; or for the protection of the rights and freedoms of others.

Our argument here is not an attempt to claim that Article 8 does in fact encompass a positive right to abortion, because such an exercise is likely futile given the past decisions of the European Court of Human Rights, and the wide margin of appreciation they afford to signatory states to make law about the permissibility of abortion (Fenwick 2012; Scott 2016). It is instead that, in pandemic circumstances, TEMA must be lawfully facilitated as a matter of the protection of the right to private life, because a failure to do so is 'the government unnecessarily delaying access to lawful treatment, ultimately meaning that a person has to incur more risk in that treatment, or potentially entirely denying access to lawful treatment altogether' (Romanis et al. 2020a, 15). Whilst the European Court of Human Rights has refused to find for any claim that access to abortion is itself guaranteed under the Convention (Fenwick 2012), it has stressed that 'once a legislature decides to allow abortion, it must not structure its legal framework in a way which would limit real possibilities to obtain it'.[287] Decisions of the European Court of Human Rights have illustrated that there exists a positive obligation to organise the provision of health services in such a way that persons can access abortion services to which they are legally entitled[288] (Romanis et al. 2020a). As Scott explains, it 'is that once a state has said that abortion is lawful on certain grounds, it must protect or guarantee the availability of abortion on those grounds, since its margin of appreciation in relation to abortion will have been significantly reduced' as they have already recognised, in domestic law, that it is permissible in certain circumstances (2016, 4–5).

---

[284] *A, B and C v. Ireland* [2010] ECHR 2032, at para 7 per Judge Geoghegan.
[285] Ibid.
[286] *A, B and C v Ireland* (n284); *Tysiąc v Poland* [2007] ECHR 212; *RR v Poland* [2011] ECHR 828.
[287] *Tysiąc v Poland* (n286), at 288.
[288] *RR v Poland* (n286).

The requirement for in-person clinic attendance for lawful EMA that existed in Great Britain prior to 2020 (see Chapters 3 and 4), for the reasons already explored, effectively made care inaccessible to many during the pandemic. Prima facie, abortion appears lawful on broad socio-medical grounds in law in Great Britain and Northern Ireland, but the change in circumstances demanded a response from the governments of the UK to ensure that this service was, in actuality, available to those who needed it, and were lawfully entitled to it. In the next chapter, we discuss the extent to which the UK did make these changes. Here, we simply note that there is a human rights imperative for a response based on the fact that Article 8 rights would be violated by inaction.

We do need to consider whether there would be a justification for any substantive failure to facilitate abortion at this time (by failing to make a change in policy to allow for TEMA) by reference to the permissible circumstances for derogation from respecting the right to private life in the Convention. A claim that a failure to provide TEMA is necessary for the protection of public health or morals is unlikely to be successful in the circumstances because, not only is TEMA safe for service users, but during a pandemic it is *safer* for both the individual and the community because it minimises COVID-19 transmission. It is not only 'in fact' necessary for TEMA to be provided during such an emergency, but also a matter of law (Romanis et al. 2020a).

7.5 An appeal to the Constitution for reform in the United States

In the US, abortion is recognised as part of the constitutional right to privacy, though it is only a negative right. The possibility of a positive obligation on states to ensure people have *access* to abortion (similar to that observable in the European jurisprudence) has been precluded. In *Casey*,[289] the Supreme Court stipulated only that states must refrain from introducing any regulations that constitute an undue burden on access. Whilst no laws that effectively ban or limit abortion access can be considered constitutional, there is equally no constitutional obligation on states to pass laws or regulation that *improve* access to care. We argue, however, that laws or regulations that might not have been considered an undue burden on access prior to the pandemic are *now* having this effect, and it is important to ensure that the undue burden test, examining the extent to which state measures constitute undue interference with the abortion right, is considered in context. Any federal or state laws that specifically ban TEMA, or that make in-person clinic attendance mandatory for abortion (because of a requirement that mifepristone be dispensed in a clinic, or that a doctor conduct a physical examination and/or supervise the administration of the medication in person) must be understood, in the context of a pandemic, to be an undue burden. This must be the case even if these measures were not considered to be an undue burden outside the COVID-19 context. These measures are an interference with a pregnant person's right to privacy because they effectively ban abortion in the circumstances, especially in states where there are few clinics (Romanis et al. 2020a).

---

[289] *Casey* (n22).

In Chapter 9, we will consider the extent to which appropriate action has been taken at both the federal and state level to ensure access during the pandemic. Our observation here is that the removal of these barriers is necessary to protect the (negative) right to abortion. The intersection of COVID-19 (and the response to it) and principles of constitutional law mean that action is necessary to ensure even noninterference with the constitutional right to privacy.

7.6 Summary

COVID-19 has exacerbated the problems that many have in accessing abortion because of how much more difficult it has made attending clinics for people in both the UK and US. Simultaneously, the demand for abortion, which is essential and time-sensitive healthcare, has not decreased—and there is reason to believe it may have increased. The data that have been collected thus far in the pandemic demonstrate the necessity of making complete 'service model changes to make medication abortion more accessibly during and beyond the COVID-19 pandemic', which, 'in line with the [WHO] recommendations would help to meet the demand [...] observed for remote provision and would truly ensure patient-centred care' (Aiken et al. 2021b, 6). The pandemic 'presents an opportunity for rapid regulatory change and programme innovation', but the extent to which this can be achieved may be limited by 'shortcomings of political will, regulation, finances, and weak infrastructure' (Church et al. 2020, 523). In the next two chapters, we consider the extent to which the UK and the US stepped up to the challenge of ensuring access to abortion during the crisis.

8

The legal and policy response to abortion care in the United Kingdom during COVID-19

In this chapter, we consider the changes to abortion regulation that occurred in Great Britain in 2020 because of the COVID-19 pandemic. As outlined, the circumstances that surrounded the pandemic and responsive actions taken by UK governments to limit the transmission of COVID-19 meant that access to abortion care became increasingly difficult for people across the UK, and particularly for those for whom access was already difficult. With the existing 'fractures and fissures in abortion access and provision' becoming more pressing in light of COVID-19 (Nandagiri et al. 2020, 83), the impetus for UK governments to act grew. The need was so pressing that such change came in March 2020—the same month that the first national lockdown commenced.

8.1 Uncertainty in March 2020

As the gravity of the pandemic was emerging in March 2020 and the UK went into its first national lockdown to attempt to control the spread of the virus, the problems lockdown was causing for people needing abortions became quickly apparent to health professionals and researchers in sexual and reproductive health (Romanis and Parsons 2020b). It was estimated by BPAS, based on abortion statistics from the previous year, that in the 13 weeks following 25 March 2020 (so between March and June 2020) around 44,000 people would need access to care in England and Wales (2020b).[290] With the law requiring that these persons attend clinics to receive care, and with clinics closing because of staffing shortages related to the virus and virus response (British Pregnancy Advisory Service 2020b), there were real concerns that these 44,000 people would experience severe delays, or surpass the gestational limit on abortion and, in extreme cases, be forced to endure an unwanted pregnancy.

On 23 March 2020, a temporary change to the law in England to allow home use of mifepristone, and therefore enable TEMA provision, appeared on the Department of Health and Social Care's website. The published approval order, within the parameters of the powers afforded to the Secretary of State for Health under sections 1(3) and (3A) of the AA 1967, explicitly named the home as an appropriate place of the

---

[290] Statistics now available reveal that between March and June 2020, 60,584 abortions took place (Department of Health and Social Care 2020c). This does not map onto the same period exactly because the records our calculation here is based on encompass all of March and June 2020—but this does demonstrate the number of people affected by decisions regarding how abortion would be accessible during this time.

Early Medical Abortion, Equality of Access, and the Telemedical Imperative. Jordan A. Parsons and Elizabeth Chloe Romanis, Oxford University Press. © Oxford University Press 2021. DOI: 10.1093/oso/9780192896155.003.0008

administration of *both* abortion medications. The approval order set out that a person could administer both medications to procure abortion in their home provided that:

- They had consulted with a clinic via video link, telephone conference, or any other electronic means;
- They had consulted with a registered medical practitioner via video link, telephone conference, or other electronic means;
- They were prescribed the abortion medications for the induction of miscarriage;
- Their pregnancy had not exceeded nine weeks and six days; and
- They administer the medications in the place where they are 'ordinarily resident'.[291]

However, within hours of the initial online publication of the approval order, it was withdrawn from the website, meaning that its terms were revoked, and the law lapsed back to allowing home use of misoprostol only. No explanation was given. The Secretary of State for Health and Social Care, Matt Hancock, was questioned on the matter in the House of Commons the next day (24 March 2020). Jonathan Ashworth MP raised the issue, asking: 'will the Secretary of State quickly update the House on an issue that has emerged overnight about access to abortion care, as a result of some of the implications of the Coronavirus Bill? Will he assure the House that women who want access to abortion care will continue to be able to get it?'.[292] Hancock answered only: 'we have no proposals to change any abortion rules as part of the covid-19 response'.[293] On being further pressed by Members of Parliament, including questions highlighting the sheer volume of people that were likely affected by the requirement to attend a clinic, and asking for an explanation as to why there was a change in the law only for it to be reversed within a matter of hours, he further answered only: 'all I can do is repeat the clarity that there are no proposals to change abortion law'.[294] In a witness statement given by Andrea Duncan, policy head for Sexual and Reproductive Health at the Department of Health and Social Care, to a divisional court in a dispute regarding home use of mifepristone later in 2020,[295] it was explained that the order was withdrawn because Matt Hancock had personally objected to it. The reason for the personal objection was not given.

Following this U-turn in Government policy (a running theme of the pandemic response in the UK), there was a great deal of frustration, panic, and uncertainty amongst providers and those attempting to access abortion services. On 25 March 2020, Baronesses Bennett and Barker both attempted to introduce temporary amendments to the AA 1967 in order to allow home use of mifepristone and to permit

---

[291] The text of this approval order is no longer available from any official government source. For a blog post summarising the detail of the order that was published the same day as the order was made, see Romanis and colleagues (2020c).

[292] HC Deb 24 March, vol 674, col 243.

[293] Ibid, col 244.

[294] Ibid, col 250.

[295] *R (on the application of Christian Concern) v Secretary of State for Health and Social Care* [2020] EWCA Civ 1239.

nurses and midwives to certify abortions. Baroness Bennett stressed that 'taking the pill [mifepristone] at a clinic is not a medical necessity; the provision is in the 1967 Abortion Act – an Act that was passed 25 years before medical abortions were even introduced'.[296] The Baronesses both stated their cases with references to the concerns that people accessing abortion in person (despite this not being clinically necessary) would undermine efforts to contain the spread of the virus and disadvantage people who were shielding, and that clinic closures were reducing the availability of in-clinic care. The Government strongly opposed the amendment. Lord Bethell, Parliamentary Under Secretary of State at the Department of Health and Social Care, made clear that the Government's position was still that there should be no change in abortion regulation. He stated:

> we do not agree that women should be able to take both treatments for medical abortion at home. We believe that it is an essential safeguard that a woman attends a clinic, to ensure that she has an opportunity to be seen alone and to ensure that there are no issues. Do we really want to support an amendment that could remove the only opportunity many women have, often at a most vulnerable stage, to speak confidentially and one-to-one with a doctor about their concerns on abortion and about what the alternatives might be? The bottom line is that, if there is an abusive relationship and no legal requirement for a doctor's involvement, it is far more likely that a vulnerable woman could be pressured into have an abortion by an abusive partner.[297]

Following some debate, the amendment was ultimately withdrawn. Also, on 25 March 2020, a collective of 50 experts in reproductive and public health published an open letter requesting that the Government act urgently to preserve abortion services in the circumstances. It warned that '[a]bortion services are at risk of collapse if the Prime Minister does not act swiftly' (Open letter 2020) and recommended that TEMA could eliminate the risks associated with travel to abortion clinics, or people being forced to endure unwanted pregnancies where unable to access services. They noted that vulnerable people were already turning to online sources 'outside the regulated healthcare system' to access abortion, thus 'breaking the law and foregoing the inbuilt safeguarding and support provided by regulated services' (Open letter 2020). A spokesperson for Women on Web called on the UK Government to act, noting that their organisation was increasingly being contacted by people in the UK asking for assistance (British Pregnancy Advisory Service 2020b). The Government's insistence that abortion not be provided remotely was inconsistent with the approach they had already taken to other aspects of healthcare, whereby they claimed to be moving to a principle of 'digital first'.[298]

---

[296] HL Deb 25 March 2020, vol 802, col 1759.
[297] Ibid, col 1762. We summarised our response to such objections in Chapter 5. Our reasoning—particularly regarding ensuring access to time-critical and essential healthcare—is even more pertinent in context.
[298] HC Deb 11 March 2020, vol 673, col 383.

8.2 Changes in March 2020

With public pressure mounting, the open letter from health professionals providing a clear case, and further evidence demonstrating the extent to which remote services were necessary, the Secretary of State for Health and Social Care took the decision to relax abortion regulations in England on a temporary basis on 30 March 2020. Following this, changes were then made in Wales and Scotland on 31 March 2020. This section outlines the changes that were made. Before this, there are two preliminary observations to make.

First, the actions of individuals within government in making changes, reversing them, and then again implementing them in England brought about significant distress and confusion for providers and people seeking abortions. For providers, the uncertainty created real problems for those attempting to draw up protocols to best manage and organise service provision in pandemic conditions (with the ever-present dangers of virus transmission for those providing and receiving care and with depleting staff numbers due to sickness etc.). It was inappropriate for the Government to have shrouded their planning in so much uncertainty about the extent to which they could adapt their services (like many other providers of healthcare were doing without interference from the law) (Romanis et al. 2020b). As a consequence of the change in regulations, there was also a great deal of misreporting from various media outlets about how abortion care was accessible in each jurisdiction, which further contributed to the confusion and anxiety of people who were seeking abortion at the time. We estimated that, based on previous abortion statistics, approximately 14,000 women in England and Wales would have been pregnant at this time and seeking abortion (Romanis et al. 2020c). Government statistics have since revealed that there were, in fact, 14,072 abortions that took place in March 2020 (6,842 of which involved both medications being administered in a hospital or clinic, and 7,230 of which had only misoprostol administered at home) (Department of Health and Social Care 2020b).[299] It is hard to state the degree of distress that the actions of the Government, in an already difficult time in which people were dealing with other pandemic-related disruption with a near moratorium on access to social support networks, caused to individuals.

Second, whilst the approval orders that were introduced across Great Britain at the end of March 2020 did make significant changes to abortion law, they made no substantive changes to the *criteria* under which abortion is lawful. The changes were procedural in nature—changing where and how abortion could be provided, but not the *why*. Abortion can still only lawfully be provided based on one of the grounds contained in sections 1(1)(a)–(d) of the AA 1967. The abortions that we discuss will likely be provided under the social ground in section 1(1)(a), and thus two doctors still need to certify that the continuance of the pregnancy would involve risk greater than if pregnancy were aborted to the physical or mental health of the pregnant person or any existing children of their family, taking into account the person's actual or reasonably

---

[299] Note that these statistics only include those abortions that were obtained through lawful channels.

foreseeable environment. Failure to justify abortion in these terms remains a criminal offence in Great Britain (see Chapter 2).

8.2.1   England

The 30 March 2020 approval order, superseding the previous approval order allowing home use of misoprostol only, stipulates both that the home of a pregnant person is an approved suitable place for the administration of both abortion medications, and that the home of a registered medical practitioner is an approved place for the prescribing of abortion medications (Department of Health and Social Care 2020c). The approval order specifies that treatment provided remotely (involving home administration of both medications) *must* be undertaken in the following manner:

- The pregnant person must have had a consultation with an approved place via video link, telephone conference, or other electronic means, or had a consultation with a registered medical practitioner by electronic means;
- The pregnant person must be prescribed mifepristone and misoprostol for the purposes of pregnancy termination; and
- The pregnancy must not have exceeded nine weeks and six days duration at the point mifepristone is administered. (Department of Health and Social Care 2020c)

The approval 'expires on the day on which the temporary provisions of the Coronavirus Act 2020 expire, or the end of the period of 2 years beginning with the day on which it is made, whichever is earlier' (Department of Health and Social Care 2020c). The order being temporary is the key difference between it and the order that was issued and revoked on 23 March 2020. The approval order automatically lapses on 30 March 2022, or earlier if the Coronavirus Act 2020 is repealed before this date, which means that the changes are not permanent. As such, the law will, without further government action, revert to requiring pregnant people to attend clinics, and to administer the first of the medications in a clinic. The provision made in this order for the automatic revocation of home use means that 'regressive and *unnecessary* rules regarding the place of medical abortion will come back into effect without the Government having to act' (Romanis et al. 2020a, 8). That the Government does not have to actively revoke the approval in the future allows the avoidance of scrutiny in taking that specific action at that time. It might be argued that, because this order was issued in response to a temporary situation, it was appropriate (or at least not inappropriate) that it was made explicitly temporary. However, because there was already considerable evidence on the safety of TEMA prior to the necessity of these changes during the pandemic (see Chapter 1), introducing regulation with the presupposition that it will revert is not an evidence-based approach. It would have been more reflective of the evidence for the Government to introduce the changes without a sunset clause and commit to reviewing the changes as life returns to 'normal', and data collected during this time could be reviewed without automatic revocation imposing a deadline. Further, including a sunset clause introduces the possibility that, if life does not return to 'normal' within the two-year period, the access issues we outlined in Chapter 7 specifically related to the pandemic will be reinstated. At the time of writing, we are one year on from the first national lockdown, and we are still in a national lockdown (albeit a different one). A sunset clause is innately dangerous in an unpredictable emergency situation because—if COVID-19 has taught us anything—it is not possible for us to predict how long we will need to adjust our lifestyles, and how we organise critical and essential services, in response to such an emergency.

Despite this approval order finally allowing home administration of *both* medications, it still embodies some restrictions on *where* abortion medications can be administered, including providing a strict definition of home.[300] As we noted in Chapter 3, defining the home in this way means that, to ensure that treatment is strictly compliant with the law, people must administer EMA in less appropriate or less (personally) acceptable environments (Lohr et al. 2020; Romanis 2020c). These concerns are particularly acute in the circumstances in which lockdowns continue to limit the social support that people have access to, and there may be some vulnerable people living alone who would, for example, prefer to have their abortion in the home of a person with whom they have formed a support bubble. This may have been overlooked because the changes the approval order was issued in an emergency but, given the time period over which the relaxation of the rules in England was being considered by the Department of Health and Social Care, it is unfortunate that some of the broader access issues that might result from defining the home when making an order to explicitly permit home use of EMA were not considered.

Christian Concern (a UK evangelical advocacy group), with particular objections to TEMA, launched a legal challenge against the 30 March approval order in England, which was eventually heard in the Court of Appeal in July 2020.[301] Christian Concern argued that the order was in direct contention with the legislative purpose of the AA 1967—to ensure that abortions are safely carried out in hygienic conditions and by persons with the appropriate knowledge and skill. Further, it was argued that section 1 of the AA 1967 requires abortion to be 'terminated *by* [emphasis added] a medical practitioner' and where a person administers medication at home this cannot be described as having been done *by* a medical practitioner. Ultimately, their contestation was that the approval order was beyond the powers afforded to the Secretary of State in the law. Davies LJ, giving the judgment in the Court of Appeal in September 2020, dismissed the challenge, thereby upholding the approval order.

There was found to be no evidence to support Christian Concern's submission that the home was an unsafe place for the administration of EMA. The judgment made substantial reference to medical evidence that the risks associated with a continued requirement for in-clinic administration of mifepristone, including the increased risk of COVID-19 infection to patients and providers, with people increasingly having later-term abortions as a result of having to waiting longer, and with people opting for unlawful abortions, outweighed any risks associated with TEMA.[302] It was noted

---

[300] The 'home' is defined as 'the place in England where a pregnant woman has her permanent address or usually resides' (Department of Health and Social Care 2020b).
[301] *R (on the application of Christian Concern)* (n295).
[302] Ibid, at para 19.

that the only material difference in terms of the treatment procedure between this approval order and its 2018 predecessor was that the administration of both medications, rather than just the second, occurs at home. Pregnant people in England have been safely terminating pregnancies at home since 2018, as it is misoprostol that actually causes the miscarriage (see Chapter 1), and thus there was 'no good evidence before this court upon which to begin to find that the nature and effect of the first pill is such as to render the same unsafe to be taken in a home and thus provide the basis for the appellant's argument that the taking of the first and second pill can properly be distinguished'.[303]

Christian Concern suggested that TEMA was unsafe because of the risk of coerced abortion and an inability to properly obtain proper consent would raise problems. The court referred to evidence provided by an independent expert, who noted that teleconsultation is a longstanding feature of abortion, and effective systems are, and can be, implemented to ensure that any potential issues with consent or safeguarding can be appropriately identified.[304] Further, the court referred to the Royal College of Obstetricians and Gynaecologists guidance for abortion care during COVID-19 which acknowledged that consent can still be appropriately obtained for abortion remotely and that, whilst safeguarding remained important, 'there is no automatic need to have to do this in person if adequate assessment is possible via remote consultation' (2020, 24).

On the issue of whether a pregnancy can be described as terminated *by* a medical practitioner where medications are administered at home, Davies LJ drew on a body of legal authorities already clear on this point. In stipulating that treatment must be terminated *by* a medical practitioner, what the AA 1967 requires is that a 'registered medical practitioner accepts responsibility for all stages of the treatment for termination of pregnancy', but this need not mean that the doctor perform all aspects of the treatment; the requirements of the AA 1967 are met 'when the treatment for termination of a pregnancy is one prescribed by a registered medical practitioner carried out in accordance with his directions and of which a registered medical practitioner remains in charge throughout'.[305]

In the SPUC Scotland challenge to home use of misoprostol outlined in Chapter 4,[306] the Court of Session concluded that the term 'treatment' in the AA 1967 is to be interpreted widely, because it is so dependent on context. Not all acts involved in the termination of a pregnancy need be carried out personally by a registered medical professional.[307] A registered medical practitioner does not cease to be responsible for treatment merely by virtue of the fact that it is not administered physically by them, or in front of them.[308] Davies LJ approved this statement of the law in her judgment, affirming that any suggestion that every step in terminating a pregnancy must be carried out personally by a registered medical practitioner is clearly not a matter of law. Davies

---

[303] Ibid, at para 47.
[304] Ibid, at para 23.
[305] *Royal College of Nursing v Department of Health and Social Security* [1981] AC 800, at 828F-829A per Lord Diplock.
[306] *SPUC v Scottish Ministers* (n99).
[307] Ibid, at 31.
[308] Ibid, at 30.

LJ cited with approval the earlier decision of the Divisional Court in the Christian Concern challenge, that had concluded: "The doctor does not cease to be 'in charge' of treatment merely because the medication is to be taken by the patient herself at home, because it is inevitable that the method of taking the medicine will have formed part of the discussion during the required consultation between doctor and patient."[309]

This is the only possible interpretation of the AA 1967 that does not result in an absurd conclusion. Where medicines are prescribed by doctors, in whatever context, they are responsible for that prescription and for overseeing the course of treatment in its entirety. It is routine for a doctor to prescribe a whole range of medications to treat a variety of ailments that the patient is then responsible for managing the administration of themselves over a period of time. Just because the course of treatment is not, in its entirety, witnessed by the doctor, it does not follow that the treatment was not determined by them, directed by them, and that they are responsible for the outcomes of the medication's use where administered in line with their instructions. To suggest that doctors only perform treatment (or that treatment is performed *by* them) when they physically administer it is not only out-of-step with most medical practice but would enable doctors to avoid liability for the consequences of their prescriptions which, again, is counter-intuitive. In *R (on the application of Christian Concern)*, Davies LJ also observed that there was no material difference between the at-home administration of misoprostol and of both mifepristone and misoprostol[310] regarding the conclusion that the treatment was still supervised by doctors because of their role in consultation and prescription.

Finally, the Court of Appeal also dismissed the claim that the approval order was beyond the powers afforded to government ministers in sections 1(3) and (3A) of the AA 1967. Davies LJ described the AA 1967 as conferring:

> a broad discretion on ministers to approve a place or class of places where termination of pregnancy can take place. Parliament in using the word "place" did not stipulate where abortions must be carried out. It conferred on the Secretary of State the function of deciding whether a place or class of places was suitable. Any implied requirement that the class of place be safe and suitable will be for the permitted specified purpose, namely the taking of medication. For the reasons given, a woman's home is suitable as such a "place".[311]

The power afforded by the AA 1967 is not only clear in terms of its effect, but is of particular importance in enabling the Government 'to react to changes in medical science' and to enable changes that 'reflect a change in circumstances which could at any time arise. That is exactly what happened in 2020, a decision was made in the context of a public health emergency'.[312] This power allows changes to quickly be made to the regulation of abortion that can implement medical best practice, without substantive

---

[309] *R (on the application of Christian Concern) v Secretary of State for Health and Social Care* [2020] EWHC 1546 (Admin), at para 43.
[310] Ibid.
[311] *R (on the application of Christian Concern)* (n295), at para 55.
[312] Ibid, at para 48.

changes to the law that could be difficult to achieve through primary legislative channels. We have seen in recent years that substantive (evidence supported) attempts to
liberalise abortion law in the UK, including many attempts to decriminalise it,[313] are
often shut down in the democratic process. What must be noted, however, is that the
extent to which this power is utilised in practice to bring abortion regulation in line
with modern developments and medical best practice has been rather limited. It is
unfortunate that the discretion that the Act affords is dependent on the political and
personal opinions of individuals. The result is often that, where the sympathies of the
Secretary of State for Health and Social Care are not with pregnant people needing
access to abortion, there is often a delay in implementing necessary change. We saw
the unfortunate consequences of this power being dependent on the inclinations of
one individual play out in the delay in bringing home use of misoprostol to fruition
in England (see Chapter 4). For almost a year after people in Scotland were accessing
more comfortable care, people in England were unnecessarily miscarrying on public
transport on their way home from clinics. The same can also be said of the week in
March 2020 between approval orders when many people and providers were uncertain as to how they might receive or provide care, respectively.

The 2020 approval order places a gestational time limit on home use of EMA; the
pregnancy must not have exceeded nine weeks and six days (Department of Health
and Social Care 2020c). This limit is the same as that imposed on the home use of
misoprostol by the earlier December 2018 approval order in England, and the same
observation might be made that this time limit could be thought of as conservative
considering WHO recommendations (see Chapter 1). The fact that the time limit was
not adjusted in 2020 illustrates that abortion policy in this jurisdiction cannot be accurately described as evidence led. It is pertinent that the inevitable lifestyle changes
that we have all been forced to make in response to the pandemic, including being
less physically active, in combination with increased levels of stress and anxiety, have
resulted in significant changes to many people's menstrual cycles. There is significant
anecdotal evidence for this (Rosenbloom 2020) and at least one, yet to be peer reviewed, study has concluded that over 55.6% of female people in a sample of 749 participants saw a change in their menstrual cycle during lockdown (Bruinvels et al. 2021).
Consequently, there is an increased likelihood that more people are having difficulty
identifying that they have become pregnant and need access to abortion. Thus, a gestational limit that increased the amount of time in which people can access home use
might have better reflected not only the increasing medical evidence, but also the realities of discovering a pregnancy during lockdown.

On the matter of whether the UK Government has responded sufficiently (in line
with their human rights obligations outlined in Chapter 7) in the circumstances to
allow remote care in England, it can clearly be argued that their approach—with
the uncertainty that resulted from the way in which changes were made (including
the sunset clause), the failure to address issues in the definition of home that will affect some vulnerable people, and the gestational limit imposed—leaves much to be

---

[313] At the time of writing, the most recent attempt to decriminalise abortion in the UK was in the form of
amendments to the 2020 Domestic Violence Bill, suggested by Diana Johnson MP, but these were tabled: see
HC Deb 6 July 2020, vol 678, cols 693–770.

desired. There was a particularly significant increase in abortions performed in April 2020—from 11,284 in April 2019 to 17,911 in April 2020 (Department of Health and Social Care 2020b). This seems likely to be the result of some people who realised they were pregnant towards the end of March 2020 being delayed in accessing services because of the confusion.

8.2.2   Wales

On 31 March 2020, the Welsh Minister for Health and Social Services, Vaughan Gething, issued an approval order permitting home use of both abortion medications after teleconsultation that was almost identical to the English order issued the day before. The Welsh order has the same sunset clause, meaning that it expires at the point that the Coronavirus Act 2020 ceases to apply in the UK, or 31 March 2020— whichever is sooner (Welsh Government 2020). The order has similar issues as outlined regarding the English order in the sense that it is temporary, and that the home is defined restrictively. Therefore, it may still result in access issues. In Wales, the issuing of the approval order was a far more straightforward process. Although there was no news about whether action would be taken until the approval was issued (and after England), for people in Wales there was not the distress that resulted from an approval being introduced and subsequently revoked. Of course, the same concerns about access, and the anxieties about whether there would be government action to allow TEMA at this time, were prevalent for both people in Wales needing access to abortion and for providers. It is still possible, however, to describe the process by which the change was made as more compassionate because anxieties existing because of the current situation were not exacerbated by government action.

There has been less legal and political controversy surrounding the Welsh approval order, as it has not been legally challenged. However, this is only because a challenge was launched in England, and thus the outcome of that dispute would be determinative. Any legal question about whether the Welsh Minister for Health and Social Services has the power to make changes to allow home use of both medications are found in the same provision of the AA 1967, and, as such, the answer is the same as any decision made about the power of the Secretary of State for Health and Social Care in England. Challenges based on the proper construction of the AA 1967 were also answered in R (on the application of Christian Concern). A challenge in Wales is likely not considered a good use of resources by campaign groups opposed to TEMA.

The Welsh order has been subject to far less scrutiny in the Welsh Assembly. Following media reporting in England suggesting that TEMA had enabled a rise in later-term abortions at home, Darren Millar MS, on 8 August 2020, questioned Vaughan Gething directly about the safety of TEMA. He argued that thought must be given to reversing the temporary changes considering 'adverse consequences for some women's health'[314] resulting from TEMA. In response, Vaughan Gething noted

---

[314] Senedd WQ 12 August 2020, WQ80926(e).

there had only been a very small number of cases in England in which pregnant people had administered abortion medications past the imposed gestational limit. He stated that:

> Whilst each case is tragic, they represent a tiny percentage of the home abortions that have taken place since the regulations were changed. There have been no such incidents in Wales although we accept that there is a risk this could happen. To mitigate that risk, we have ensured the guidance provided to clinicians undertaking early medical abortions at home clearly states they must arrange for the woman to attend a clinic if there is any concern about the accuracy of the gestation age. Termination of pregnancy remains an essential service [....] The protocol used to deliver early medical abortion services via teleconference was developed by clinicians and supported by guidelines by [both the NICE and the Royal College of Obstetricians and Gynaecologists]. [...] I am confident that all clinical and safeguarding risks are being considered and managed appropriately including the assessment of gestation.[315]

This response, which explicitly affirms abortion as essential healthcare, demonstrates that Vaughan Gething perhaps has a more progressive attitude towards abortion than his English counterpart. However, we cannot describe Welsh policy on this matter as being evidence based given the failings we discussed in Chapter 4 and the delay in acting to ensure abortion access during COVID-19.

8.2.3   Scotland

Scotland also issued an approval order to allow home use of both abortion medications after teleconsultation on 31 March 2020 (Scottish Government Chief Medical Officer Directorate 2020). There are, however, three differences between the approval orders issued in England and Wales and that issued in Scotland by then Scottish Minister for Public Health and Sport and Wellbeing, Joe Fitzpatrick.

In Scotland, the only conditions on lawful at-home administration of mifepristone are that the pregnant person has consulted with a registered medical practitioner or nurse by video link or telephone and has been prescribed both abortion medications for the purposes of ending their pregnancy, that home is the place where the person is ordinarily resident in Scotland, and that the pregnant person wants to undergo their treatment (the taking of the medications) at home (Scottish Government Chief Medical Officer Directorate 2020). The order is specific that communication must be by video link or telephone. In the orders in England and Wales, however, these two forms of communication are specified (perhaps indicating that they are preferable or likely to be more commonplace), but the orders also stipulate that 'any other electronic means' would be sufficient (Department of Health and Social Care 2020c; Welsh Government 2020). There is no doubt that for the purposes of satisfactory 'consultation' that the means of communication must be instantaneous and involve a two-way

---

[315] Ibid.

exchange between the consulting professional and the patient. But it is perhaps interesting that in England and Wales the approval orders do not directly exclude this consultation taking place, for example, on an instant messaging platform. In Scotland, however, this possibility is excluded.

The second difference is that the Scottish order does not contain a gestational limit on the provision of TEMA. In the conditions outlined above, there is no limitation placed on the lawfulness of home use of mifepristone based on gestational age. Instead, it is *recommended* in the explanatory note provided by then Scottish Chief Medical Officer, Dr Catherine Calderwood, that TEMA be utilised only up to 12 weeks' gestation. She explains that 'while there will still be some patients needing face to face treatment, this approval should minimise the number of patients at under 12 weeks gestation needing to travel to a clinic' (Scottish Government Chief Medical Officer Directorate 2020, para 4). She also notes that clinicians are encouraged to start offering teleconsultations as soon as possible where judged appropriate in line with Scottish Abortion Care Providers guidance attached to the order as Annex B. This guidance is clear that patients should be enabled to access TEMA at or before 11 weeks and six days' gestation (Scottish Government Chief Medical Officer Directorate 2020; Parsons and Romanis 2020).

This difference is important for several reasons. In not stipulating a gestational limit, and instead allowing clinicians to decide on the appropriateness of home use based on their clinical expertise, the approval order *explicitly* affords more discretion to medical practitioners to determine the parameters of treatment, and they are able to do so in line with medical best practice. WHO (2012) guidance does recommend medical abortion as an appropriate method up to 12 weeks' gestation, at which point the approach of the Scottish Government in deferring to the clinical recommendations for safe abortion on this point means that the Scottish order can be considered more compatible with medical best practice. The additional time in which people in Scotland can (based on the guidance) access abortion at home (the two-week period between nine weeks six days and 11 weeks six days) might seem like a small window of time, especially as people try to access abortion care as early as possible. However, in the circumstances this additional time might mean the difference for many between being able to access TEMA and having to attend a clinic. Given emerging evidence that EMA is safe up to 12 weeks, and that it is safe for care to be undertaken at home in this time window (see Chapter 1), it seems unnecessary that the English and Welsh orders place their limits lower than Scotland. This could have impactful consequences for people seeking care in England and Wales, even if only for a very small minority, compared to their counterparts in Scotland.

Thirdly, the Scottish approval order does not contain a sunset clause (Romanis et al. 2020). This was a deliberate decision on the part of the Scottish Executive, as explained in Dr Calderwood's explanatory note: 'this approval does not have an expiry date, but we intend that it will have effect for a limited period and so would revoke it and replace it with the terms of the previous approval (dated October 2017) at an appropriate time when it is judged that it is no longer necessary in relation to the pandemic response' (Scottish Government Chief Medical Officer Directorate 2020, para 2). There was the same intention, at the time it was passed, (as in England and Wales) that this order made as part of the COVID-19 response not be a permanent change. However, in *not* having the order automatically expire this seems to better symbolise an intention to continually review the appropriateness of the change. Within this decision, a conversation about TEMA being made permanently available is easier. A return to the situation in which people must be supervised administering mifepristone in a clinic before being allowed to administer misoprostol at home in Scotland requires government action. This means that—even if only triggered by a government suggestion about when to repeal the approval—there can be open scrutiny of that *active* decision. This contrasts with the sunset clauses in the English and Welsh orders that automatically restrict mifepristone again as a passive process. Further, the Scottish approach, in allowing more flexibility in how long the order is in force, is a more appropriate response to the circumstances given that it is unknown (at the time of writing) how long restrictions in response to the pandemic conditions will need to remain in force. It is certainly possible that some level of restrictions will remain in place past the two-year mark, which would result in access in England and Wales returning to square one unless action is taken to extend the approvals. That Scotland approached the issue in this way dispels the argument that might be raised that England and Wales did the obvious thing in making a temporary order in response to a temporary situation.

Whilst the Scottish order is comparatively more progressive than those made in England and Wales because there is no gestational limit or sunset clause contained within it, it still has the issue of a restrictive definition of home that could result in some ongoing access issues for some vulnerable people in Scotland. In addition, that other electronic means of communication are excluded (unlike in England and Wales) is something that should be revisited.

8.2.4 Northern Ireland

Northern Ireland is a different story to the rest of Great Britain, as no action was taken to allow TEMA in response to the pandemic. The regulations brought into force to regulate abortion in 2020, much like the AA 1967 in Great Britain, stipulate the places where treatment for the termination of pregnancy can be lawfully performed. Termination must be performed in a health and social care trust hospital, clinic, or general practitioners' premises. The home[316] is a suitable place only for the administration of *misoprostol*. This is subject to the limitation that the person has been lawfully prescribed EMA, and mifepristone was first administered in a hospital, clinic, or general practitioners' surgery.[317] As McGuiness and Rooney (2020) have explained, TEMA is effectively precluded by the regulations' mandatory clinic requirement and failure to authorise the home as a suitable place for the administration of *mifepristone*. The regulations afford the Department of Health the power to approve further places for abortion care where in writing and published appropriately. This includes a power to specify how the administration of abortion medications must be carried out in any approved places.[318]

---

[316] The given definition of 'home' is similar to that in England, Scotland, and Wales, and, therefore, the problems outlined in the context of those jurisdictions also apply to Northern Ireland.
[317] The Abortion (Northern Ireland) (No. 2) Regulations 2020, regulation 8.
[318] Ibid, regulation 8(4).

Despite this power being readily available to the Northern Irish Health Minister, Robin Swann, and the action taken by the other three UK nations to approve the home as an appropriate place for EMA, Swann has consistently refused to act. As such, local service provision of TEMA could not (and still cannot) be lawfully established in Northern Ireland. The consequences of this were such that people in Northern Ireland in need of lawful access to care were having to do so outside of their homes. Local service provision remains limited in Northern Ireland on account of being only recently lawful and because the Executive has yet to commission any services (Kirk et al. 2021). Where services have been established locally, the effect of Robin Swann's failure to make TEMA lawful in the circumstances means that people must attend the clinic *in person* for care. In Northern Ireland, this is particularly concerning because, as noted by the Royal College of Obstetricians and Gynaecologists in October 2020, towards the end of 2020, Northern Ireland was among the areas in the UK with the highest rates of COVID-19 infection, and, therefore, 'asking women to travel further than necessary to access care needlessly risks exposure to, and transmission of, the virus' (Oppenheim 2020). Further, there is extreme inequality in that people in Northern Ireland are the only people who must risk exposure to the virus to obtain a lawful abortion in the UK. For many people in Northern Ireland, access to abortion *still* means travel to other jurisdictions (most commonly England), and the burden of this journey for socioeconomic reasons, as well as COVID-specific reasons, will be a major barrier (see Chapter 3). In some instances, travel options are extremely limited—at one point there were no flights available from Northern Ireland to England, meaning people had to take an eight-hour ferry to access care (British Pregnancy Advisory Service 2020c). In addition, since the TEMA services in Great Britain are limited by law to those who have a permanent home address in the nation in which care is provided, these people must have their whole abortion in a healthcare facility, rather than a place that they might feel more comfortable.

As a result of the almost nonexistent lawful routes to access domestically in Northern Ireland, it was thought that people were likely to continue turning to online providers like Women on Web. One study has observed a 28% increase in requests for assistance from Women on Web by people living in Northern Ireland, in contrast to Great Britain where these requests decreased by 87.6% (Aiken et al. 2021b, 4). This illustrates the inequality in access resulting from the failures of the Northern Ireland Executive, and that abortion is still being undertaken—just outside of the medical model established by the 2020 regulations. Whilst self-managed medical abortion obtained through these means is generally safe (Gomperts et al. 2008; Gomperts et al. 2012; Gomperts et al. 2014; Aiken et al. 2017; Les et al. 2017), and pregnant people in Northern Ireland are no longer subject to criminal penalty for abortion even if procured outside of the regulations (see Chapter 2), this is not a sustainable alternative to local service provision and associated aftercare. There remains the risk that many people in Northern Ireland may still fear legal repercussions for having obtained abortion medications online and be afraid to seek help in the rare event it becomes necessary.

The limited availability of abortion in Northern Ireland at this time has had catastrophic consequences for many people. In October 2020, the Royal College of Obstetricians and Gynaecologists criticised Robin Swann's failure to act, noting that, as a consequence, 'there have already been at least two cases of attempted suicide by women in Northern Ireland unable to access care. We are also aware of a substantial increase (plus 28 per cent) in women turning to unregulated methods of abortion during the pandemic, which demonstrates access to regulated services remains an issue, and places these women at risk' (Oppenheim 2020). A spokesperson for Amnesty UK stated:

> as a direct consequence of [Robin Swann's] failings, we are seeing health services becoming increasingly more fragile, especially as they are already feeling the strain of operating under the pressure of the Covid-19 pandemic. The Northern Ireland Office must also step up by providing telemedicine services if the Department of Health continue to fail, and by ensuring women do not have to go online to purchase pills or travel during a pandemic which, for many, is neither a safe nor a viable option (Oppenheim 2020).[319]

In response to the dire situation, BPAS launched emergency TEMA provision to people in Northern Ireland in limited circumstances on 9 April 2020. BPAS stated that it believed the service was lawfully provided under regulation 11(2)(b) of the 2020 regulations as this allows clinicians to provide abortion for the purpose of preventing grave, permanent injury to a pregnant person's physical or mental health (British Pregnancy Advisory Service 2020c). This must encompass abortion provided as TEMA because these are emergency circumstances, and the service will be provided in such a way that ensures that those receiving care are receiving it lawfully by virtue of regulation 11. The BPAS website now states that the service remains available for people in Northern Ireland who are less than 10 weeks pregnant and 'cannot leave home because they are shielding or self-isolating because they or someone in their household has COVID-19 symptoms' (British Pregnancy Advisory Service 2021). As a result, the service is—for legal reasons—not available to all people who need access to abortion in Northern Ireland.

With the matter still unresolved, on 14 January 2021, Paula Bradshaw MLA questioned Robin Swann on access to abortion in a committee meeting about the COVID-19 response. She noted that:

> There are a lot of very vulnerable, isolated young women out there who are looking for leadership and access to services. Minister, I do not want the response that this is a contentious issue on which it is up to the Executive to decide. Can you explain to women out there why you have not brought forward abortion services and why you have not introduced telemedicine when you have done that for other branches of the health service?[320]

In response, Swann simply stated: '[m]y answer may not be the one that you want me to give, but it is the realistic answer: because abortion in Northern Ireland is a

---

[319] This suggestion might be of great concern to UK constitutional lawyers.
[320] Northern Ireland Assembly Official Report Committee for Health 14 January 2021, 'COVID-19 Response: Mr Robin Swann MLA, Minister of Health; Dr Michael McBride, Chief Medical Officer'.

contentious issue. It is with the Executive at this time'.[321] He continued to note that while these services have not been directly commissioned by the Executive, some services have been established and do operate, and that people needing access to TEMA can have this facilitated by BPAS. It is almost beyond comprehension that the Minister has defended the status quo on the grounds that there is sufficient provision in the limited service that has been offered as an *emergency* by a *charitable provider* that operates in a different jurisdiction that has stepped up to ensure at least some people in Northern Ireland have access. This is clearly insufficient and is a very clear illustration of people's health being side-lined because of the political and personal opinions of politicians.

8.3 Long-term changes: consultations

The temporary changes in Great Britain are to be welcomed for how they have helped ensure access in difficult circumstances. However, TEMA is necessary beyond pandemic circumstances for reasons we have given throughout this book. As such, we argue that the changes to the law must be made permanent. From the implementation of TEMA during this time we have seen that the major concerns about TEMA appear unfounded, as initial data from service provision in England (Aiken et al. 2021a) and Scotland (Reynolds-Wright et al. 2021) have demonstrated that it has been safe, effective, and acceptable to patients. At the time of writing, the changes to the law in England and Wales remain temporary, and there has been no indication from the Scottish Government about their intentions regarding the long-term status of the changes. However, throughout Great Britain there is an open conversation about whether these changes to the law should become (or, in the case of Scotland, remain) permanent.

Public consultations were launched in Scotland, England, and Wales in autumn 2020 and closed in January and February 2021, the purposes of which were explicitly to consider whether the arrangements should be made permanent. The Scottish Government stated in their consultation paper the reasons why they were gathering evidence in this way:

> [We] recognise that there are a range of strongly held views on this issue, with many people welcoming the current arrangements, but others raising concerns about the physical or mental health risks of not seeing women in person. This is why we wish to consult on this issue to allow abortion providers and other health professionals, women who have accessed abortion services and the general public the opportunity to comment and submit evidence. The responses and any evidence provided will help to inform the Scottish Government's decisions on whether the current arrangements should be allowed to continue once there is no longer a significant risk of COVID-19 transmission. (2020, 3)

[321] Ibid.

Whilst the questions asked by the devolved administrations differed, the scope of the consultations is similar. It is arguable, however, that the questions asked by the Scottish Government seem more sympathetic to the continuation of remote provision. The questions asked specifically for comments on a number of issues that are (empirically) known benefits of TEMA—for example—how the changes have impacted on accessibility and convenience of service access, waiting times, how the changes might have impacted on equalities groups, the potential impact on socioeconomic equality, and the potential impact for those living in rural areas or the island communities, and, finally, they explicitly asked the question of whether the changes should remain permanent (Scottish Government 2020, 10–3). In places, the Welsh consultation was also framed in a way that indicates the Government is interested in hearing evidence that the change has been positive. Many of the questions asked: 'do you consider that the temporary measure has had a positive impact on', for example, safety, accessibility, and convenience of services in one question, and on those delivering services in another (Welsh Government 2020).

The English consultation, however, was framed slightly differently. First, in that it encouraged binary answers by giving multiple choice options to every question along the lines of this has been positive, negative, or neutral. There might be concerns that if the resulting data are considered quantitatively there may be insufficient nuance regarding the reasoning—including the lived experiences that underlie it—that people might give for their answer. The English consultation also asked many questions that directly speak to the objections often raised by opponents of TEMA. For example, whilst it asks questions about accessibility and privacy, it explicitly asked for opinions about whether there are disadvantages associated with safeguarding and pregnant people's safety (Department of Health and Social Care 2020d).

The Welsh consultation also asked for evidence on these points explicitly, but the questions were qualified by asking those who said a clinic visit is important for safety or safeguarding to explain what the benefit of the clinic visit is explicitly ('please outline these benefits') (Welsh Government 2020). The English consultation did not ask for the same explanation for such claims. Further, the Welsh consultation frequently asked—in places where some of the potential issues with TEMA could be raised—whether these are risks that can be mitigated, and ways in which this might be done. The English consultation did not ask such questions. The English consultation appeared to be interested in obtaining information about what some of the potential issues might be, without necessarily also obtaining information about the management of potential risks.

We are not criticising governments for asking for information about some of the potential issues that are raised about TEMA, such as safety or safeguarding. Although we do not agree that there is an empirical basis for many of these objections, it is important that they are addressed. This includes offering those who have looked at the evidence an opportunity to explain why many of these objections are ill-founded. We make the observation here as a matter of interest about the kinds of evidence different governments are trying to source.

Further, in the English consultation, in asking the question about the future of home use of both medications, it not only offered options for respondents to indicate that they believe that this should be a permanent or temporary measure, but also that the service 'be ended immediately' (Department of Health and Social Care 2020d). It was the only consultation to ask this—in Wales and Scotland this was not provided as an option for respondents. There seems to be some more political resistance to home use as a permanent feature of abortion care within Westminster that can be seen in how the English consultation was framed.

At the time of writing, the outcomes of these consultations have not been published, and it is not clear what will happen with TEMA in the longer-term in Great Britain. There is, at present, no indication of when decisions will be made. The consultations are obviously no guarantee that positive change will result, but we are hopeful that permanent approvals of home use of mifepristone will be made. The evidence is certainly there to support the change, especially with the data that have been collected during this period of temporarily lawful TEMA. The Scottish Government has the most promising history of the UK nations in terms of being responsive to clinical evidence about best practice in abortion care, and it closed its consultation first so is likely to respond first. We are cautiously optimistic that Scotland will make the right decision to approve TEMA permanently. As a result of the political peer-pressure relating to the evolution of abortion services that exists between the nations of the UK to some extent (see Chapter 4), Scotland making a positive change could put considerable pressure on Wales and England to do the same. Since devolution, England has the most complex history with making changes to abortion regulations and tends to drag its feet. We hope that this will not be the case here.

On a final note, the fact that UK governments (except for Northern Ireland) decided to consult on this issue is interesting in itself. They have decided to make this a matter of public consultation, as opposed to following the empirical evidence that has been generated by researchers and clinicians and listening to the recommendations of reproductive and public health professionals. We suspect that this decision was made because abortion is still a contentious issue for many in the UK, and there has been some vocal opposition (by small groups) to TEMA in the UK.

8.4 Summary

The changes made at the end of March 2020 across Great Britain to allow TEMA are to be welcomed. We have raised some issues surrounding the process (in England) and in the substance of the orders (the strict definition of home in all three nations, and sunset clauses and gestational limits in England and Wales), but despite these reservations it must be recognised that these changes have made a monumental difference to people's lives in ensuring access remained in place during the most significant public health emergency in living memory. Early reporting on abortion during the pandemic in England and Wales clearly demonstrates not only that access was ultimately preserved, but it appeared to improve in many ways. The data suggest that, following the introduction of TEMA, abortions were increasingly performed earlier in gestation (50% before seven weeks' gestation, compared to 40% in the same period in 2019) (Department of Health and Social Care 2020b). Demand for abortion through unlawful channels also decreased (Aiken et al. 2021b). There was a 4% increase in abortion incidence in January to June 2020 compared to the same period in 2019

(Department of Health and Social Care 2020b). This might reflect either increasing demand for abortion because of the pandemic context (see Chapter 7) or the fact that it is easier for many to access abortion through lawful channels since the introduction of TEMA. Thus, the increase may be attributable not to the number of abortions increasing overall, but the number performed through lawful channels (and thus appearing in reporting) increasing. This is better for pregnant people as it ensures they have the care they need without fear of criminal sanction.

Changes, however, have not been made in Northern Ireland. As such, access through lawful channels for people there remains almost impossible. This is nothing short of a human rights violation that requires urgent rectification (see Chapter 7).

Public consultations have been conducted in Great Britain about whether changes to the law should be made permanent. There is a strong case, made throughout this book, that these changes must be made permanent. We suggest that in the process of making TEMA permanently lawful the issues that we have raised in this chapter (how to define the home, removing gestational limits) should be afforded due attention. Action must also be taken to ensure TEMA is brought to Northern Ireland *locally* (rather than people in Northern Ireland having to rely on unlawful channels or overseas services) to prevent abortion remaining practically inaccessible for many, despite being lawful.

9

Legal and policy restrictions on telemedical early medical abortion in the United States during COVID-19

Abortion access during COVID-19 is a drastically different story in the US compared to Great Britain. Whilst the legal and policy changes made in Great Britain—described in the previous chapter—are not without criticism, changes to enable the establishment of TEMA services have better guaranteed access to care during a global crisis. In Great Britain, the number of reported abortions increased (Department of Health and Social Care 2020b), and the number of requests through unlawful channels to providers like Women on Web substantially decreased (Aiken et al. 2021b), suggesting that TEMA is a success. There is no such success story to be told in the US.

There has been a substantive failure at federal level, by the FDA, to remove barriers to TEMA embodied in the mifepristone REMS protocol. The protocol mandates the drug only be dispensed at a clinic, thereby making clinic attendance compulsory for care. Many state governments have also taken no action to preserve access to abortion. Of greater concern, some state executives have utilised the situation to effectively ban abortion (Donley et al. 2020). Access has thus been made *more* difficult in much of the US. People are being forced to look to unlawful online abortion providers. Requests to Aid Access[322] increased by 27% between March and April 2020 (Aiken et al. 2020, 835). Rates of increase varied across states, some of which were particularly startling. For example, there was a 93.6% increase in Texas (Aiken et al. 2020, 836). This is no coincidence, as Texas was one of the states to take aggressive steps to limit abortion early in the pandemic.

In this chapter, we outline and critique the legal and policy approach taken to abortion access during the COVID-19 pandemic in the US. First, we consider the extent to which the federal REMS requirements have constituted an absolute barrier to TEMA provision, and the harm this has caused. Second, we consider existing state barriers to TEMA provision that do, or would, prevent the establishment of services even if the federal REMS requirements were to be suspended or revisited. Finally, we consider the pandemic-specific response of state executives to abortion access.

We concur with Rebouché that 'expanding access to medication abortion – not restricting access – is the right policy to protect public health and reduce the burden of COVID-19 for pregnant individuals, healthcare workers and medical systems' (2020, 9). However, the picture that has emerged in the US remains one of (even more)

---

[322] See Chapter 6 for an explanation of the Aid Access service.

Early Medical Abortion, Equality of Access, and the Telemedical Imperative. Jordan A. Parsons and Elizabeth Chloe Romanis, Oxford University Press. © Oxford University Press 2021. DOI: 10.1093/oso/9780192896155.003.0009

restricted access to EMA—a failure for pregnant people's autonomy and privacy, for equality, and for public health.

9.1 REMS in pandemic context

As noted in Chapter 3, mifepristone is subject to a REMS programme limiting how the drug can be prescribed—it must be dispensed to patients only in certain healthcare settings (United States Food and Drug Administration 2019), meaning patients cannot have mifepristone posted to them, nor can they collect it from a pharmacy. This has proved to be a significant legal barrier to the provision of abortion care during COVID-19 because the FDA has continued to enforce the in-person requirement,[323] thereby prohibiting the establishment of *fully* telemedical services across the country. Whilst providers can (where state law does not prohibit it) determine EMA eligibility and counsel about abortion through telephone or videoconferencing, the patient must travel to the clinic to collect mifepristone and sign the REMS-mandated patient agreement form.[324] As such, the barriers to care resulting from travel, which are exacerbated by pandemic circumstances (see Chapter 7), cannot be mitigated by providers. Where an HCP does not comply with the in-person requirements, they may lose their status as a certified prescriber and/or the FDA may interfere to prevent EMA medications being shipped to them—there may even be criminal penalties.[325]

The REMS' in-person requirement has long been criticised (i.e. before COVID-19) on the grounds that the now accumulated body of 'knowledge about mifepristone strongly suggests that the current restricted distribution system is not aligned with the limited risks that are known to be posed by the drug' (Henney and Gayle 2019, 597). The in-person dispensing requirement is considered medically unnecessary because of the safety of the medication (see Chapter 1), and because teleconsultation can safely be used to determine eligibility for treatment. On 20 March 2020, attorneys general from 21 states[326] wrote to the FDA requesting that:

> In light of the unprecedented COVID-19 crisis, we request you remove the FDA's restrictive REMS designation for Mifepristone thereby removing these unnecessary, undue burdens in accessing safe and time-sensitive, essential medical care. Alternatively, at a minimum, we request that you use your enforcement discretion to allow certified prescribers to use telehealth for mifepristone. (State of California Office of the Attorney General 2020, 4)

The request highlighted how FDA requirements were causing people to put themselves and their families at risk to 'seek out healthcare that they need, and the federal

---

[323] The drug must be dispensed to patients only in certain healthcare settings: 1 U.S.C. §355-1(f)(3)(c). Readers should note the update to the enforcement of the REMS in the preface to this book.
[324] As noted in Chapter 6, some studies are permitted exceptions to this—for example, TelAbortion.
[325] 21 U.S.C. §333(a).
[326] California, Colorado, Connecticut, Delaware, District of Columbia, Hawaii, Illinois, Iowa, Maine, Maryland, Massachusetts, Minnesota, Nevada, New Mexico, New York, North Carolina, Oregon, Pennsylvania, Rhode Island, Vermont, and Virginia.

government must act to ensure that no matter where they live, they can continue to receive necessary, safe, and legal abortion care' (State of California Office of the Attorney General 2020, 4). As Ahmed notes, 'if COVID moves the [FDA] in this direction, it would set a positive path forward for access to abortion via telehealth' (2020, 4). The request, however, went unanswered.

On 27 May 2020, the American College of Obstetricians and Gynecologists and others filed a complaint against the FDA and Department of Health and Human Services in the District Court of Maryland for an injunction staying the enforcement of the in-person elements of the REMS during the COVID-19 pandemic. The challenge was not against the general validity of the REMS mifepristone scheme (though such a challenge has been underway since 2017[327]) but instead that the scheme is constitutionally invalid because *in the particular circumstances of COVID-19* its enforcement deprives individuals of their constitutionally protected right to abortion.

In the decision issued on 13 July 2020,[328] District Judge Chuang found that, following the precedent established in the US Supreme Court,[329] his judgment would examine the burdens the in-person requirement imposes on abortion access together with the benefits it is intended to confer.[330] Precedent requires that there must be no '[u]ncritical deference' to the benefits that are asserted by lawmakers when considering if a law is an undue burden.[331] Further, in determining whether the in-person requirement constitutes an undue burden it need not be demonstrated that it places a substantial obstacle in the path of *every* person seeking abortion,[332] but that it places a substantial obstacle in the path of a 'large fraction' of those people for whom the requirement 'is an actual rather than irrelevant restriction'.[333] The operative question, then, in making a determination about whether to grant the preliminary injunction, was whether the in-person requirement creates an obstacle for a significant number of people who are seeking EMA but do not require an in-person visit to be appropriately assessed and counselled.[334]

9.1.1 District Court: recognising the burdens and questioning the benefits of REMS in context

The primary burden of mandatory in-clinic attendance during a pandemic is risk of infection. It is undeniable that 'any time that abortion patients venture out of their

---

[327] *Chelius v. Azar* (filed in the District Court for Hawaii in October 2017).

[328] *American College of Obstetricians and Gynecologists v. U.S. Food and Drug Administration* (n252).

[329] The judgment goes into considerable detail about how the *Hellerstedt* (n81) formulation of the undue burden test standard remains the correct standard following *June Medical* (n86). Roberts J's obiter suggestion that there is actually no need to assess state motivations in passing TRAP laws (which would be a shift in the jurisprudence that we discussed was a potential cause for concern in Chapter 2) was not approved by the necessary plurality of the Supreme Court.

[330] *American College of Obstetricians and Gynecologists v. U.S. Food and Drug Administration* (n252), at 38.

[331] *Hellerstedt* (n81), at 2310.

[332] *June Medical* (n86), at 21.

[333] *Casey* (n22), at 895.

[334] *American College of Obstetricians and Gynecologists v. U.S. Food and Drug Administration* (n252), at 40–1

residence, including to fulfill the In-Person Requirements, they risk contracting a highly dangerous disease'.[335] It was observed that this risk was also more likely to affect vulnerable groups, including minorities. The judgment cited evidence that 60% of people accessing abortion in 2016 were people of colour, and 75% were low-income.[336] The health risks for these groups are amplified, and evidence suggesting higher rates of serious illness and death from COVID-19 in communities of colour in the US was cited.[337] It was also noted that these groups of people are far less likely to have adequate access to suitable medical care generally.[338] It is, then, understandable that high levels of anxiety might prevent individuals from travelling to access care.

The FDA and Department of Health and Human Services attempted to argue that the actual risk to any one person travelling to a medical clinic for abortion is low and that the difficulty of undertaking such travel will not, for the broader population, impose a substantial obstacle. The judge remarked that such claims by the defendants were 'belied by their own actions'[339] because the FDA suspended its REMS requirements for other medications. In (nonbinding) guidance issued in March 2020, the FDA explained that it would not enforce REMS requirements for laboratory testing or imaging studies before prescription of certain drugs during the COVID-19 emergency where accommodations (to not undertake such testing) were made 'based on the judgment of a health care professional' (United States Food and Drug Administration 2020b, 7).[340] The reasons for doing so were clearly explained—requiring people to attend clinics for tests and imaging because of REMS 'can put patients and others at risk for transmission of the coronavirus' (United States Food and Drug Administration 2020b, 7). The Department of Health and Human Services had also taken multiple (legal and policy) steps to promote telemedicine during the pandemic.[341] That these federal departments acknowledged elsewhere that travel *is a substantial obstacle for many people* who might need healthcare, but not in its regulation of abortion, is a clear inconsistency. It further speaks to the deep-rooted abortion exceptionalism we detailed in Chapter 2.

The judgment then referenced further access burdens arising at the intersection of the pandemic and the REMS requirements for mifepristone, including clinic closures, reduced capacity at clinics,[342] and difficulties arranging transportation[343] and adequate childcare.[344] It was concluded:

[335] Ibid, at 42.
[336] Ibid, at 46.
[337] Ibid.
[338] Ibid.
[339] Ibid, at 14.
[340] A footnote to this recommendation is explicit that 'this guidance is limited to our enforcement policy with respect to laboratory testing and imaging study requirements and does not address other REMS requirements' (United States Food and Drug Administration 2020b, 7).
[341] In March 2020, the federal 'telemedicine exception' power was introduced to allow doctors to use telemedicine to satisfy otherwise compulsory in-person evaluation requirements before prescribing controlled substances: 21 U.S.C. §802(54)(D).
[342] *American College of Obstetricians and Gynecologists v. U.S. Food and Drug Administration* (n252), at 45.
[343] Again, more likely to affect minorities as they are less likely to own a car. Ibid, at 47.
[344] Ibid, at 48.

In light of the convergence of all of these factors stemming from the COVID-19 pandemic, the Court finds that the In-Person Requirements impose a substantial obstacle to abortion patients seeking medication abortion care [because] these barriers, in combination, delay abortion patients from receiving a medication abortion, which can either increase the health risk to them or, in light of the ten-week limit on the Mifepristone-Misoprostol Regimen, prevent them from receiving a medication abortion at all.[345]

In the specific context of COVID-19, therefore, the REMS' in-person requirement constitutes an undue burden.

The Court reviewed the evidence regarding the safety of TEMA (see Chapter 5) and concurred that there are comparable health outcomes to more 'traditional' methods of abortion. The judgment also placed emphasis on the fact that because 'there is no requirement for in-person administration of the drug and patients may take it at home, in-person dispensing does nothing to provide for monitoring of the patient for complications'.[346] The medical evidence that the FDA attempted to rely on was the submission that in having to attend the clinic to receive the drug and sign the paperwork it is better ensured that there is an adequate consultation about the risks of mifepristone and how to use it, and that patients pick up the mifepristone for administration in a timely manner for proper use. The Administration submitted that its finding on this matter 'should not be subject to second-guessing by an unelected federal judiciary'[347] because the FDA is afforded the power to make such determinations based on their special expertise.

However, Justice Chuang noted that the FDA's formal determinations on the necessity of the in-person requirements were made some time prior to 2020, and were of limited utility since COVID-19 had so drastically changed the context against which the benefits of the in-person requirement must be considered.[348] He concluded that timely administration cannot be conceptualised as a benefit of the in-person requirement because this requirement makes no reference to (or controls in any way) the timing of the *administration* of mifepristone. Moreover, because of the additional burdens in the pandemic context, the in-person requirement would not better ensure that the medication was taken in a timely manner but instead *actively delay* its administration. It is possible for providers to ensure patients receive the medication in a timely manner when they are sent by courier. Therefore, it was found that 'the evidence does not support a finding that the In-Person Dispensing Requirement provides any significant health-related benefit relating to an alleged elimination of delay in the taking of mifepristone'.[349] Suitable consultation can and does occur through telemedicine, even with these requirements in place.

In conclusion, the Court emphasised that in the unique circumstances of a public health emergency and the impact that the in-person requirements had in this context,

---

[345] Ibid, at 49.
[346] Ibid, at 51.
[347] Ibid, at 54.
[348] Ibid, at 55.
[349] Ibid, at 59.

patients faced several substantial obstacles to exercising their constitutional right to abortion. Further, *even if* the barriers were not thought to be substantial obstacles, the alleged benefits of the in-person requirements were nonexistent in the context. Properly comparing the in-person requirements 'with no significant health-related benefit' against the 'serious burdens' they impose in the COVID-19 context 'further establishes that the In-Person Requirements are likely imposing a substantial obstacle to a woman's choice during the pandemic'.[350] Further, the substantial obstacle these requirements impose will affect a significant number of people for whom it is an 'actual rather than an irrelevant restriction'[351] because the nature of the pandemic and the difficulties that it results in for individuals affect the population generally—and across the whole country. In denying the realisation of a constitutional right, or causing substantial physical or emotional distress in exercising that right, the requirements thereby constitute an irreparable harm such that the Court granted a preliminary injunction to enjoin enforcement of the in-person requirements of the mifepristone REMS nationwide (without geographic limitation) until 30 days beyond the expiration of 'the public health emergency based on COVID-19 declared by the Secretary of HHS pursuant to the Public Health Service Act'.[352]

The effect of the preliminary injunction was to allow the mailing of mifepristone to patients at home—where this was permissible under state law. Other REMS requirements, including that there must be a consultation with a certified prescriber and that the patient must sign the agreement form, would remain in place, but satisfied by telemedical means. However, the FDA appealed to the Supreme Court to stay this injunction, so that the in-person requirement of the mifepristone REMS could be enforced.

9.1.2 Supreme Court decision

The Supreme Court handed down its decision, staying the injunction, on 21 January 2021.[353] Most concerning in this decision is the relative lack of explanation in the Supreme Court's judgment, compared to the District Court's thorough evaluation of the contextual impact of the intersection of the pandemic and the in-person requirement for mifepristone on people seeking abortion. Justice Roberts merely stated that the question before the Court was not one about whether the requirements constituted an undue burden on a person's constitutional right to abortion, but whether the District Court should have ordered the FDA to lift established requirements, noting his view that 'courts owe significant deference to the politically accountable entities' that have the expertise to assess public health.[354] The majority decision given by Justice Roberts is fewer than 200 words, simply stating that there is not a 'sufficient basis here for the District Court to compel the FDA to alter the regimen for medical abortion'.[355] The

---

[350] Ibid, at 62.
[351] As necessary per *Casey* (n22), at 895.
[352] *American College of Obsetricians and Gynecologists v. U.S. Food and Drug Administration* (n252), at 78.
[353] *Food and Drug Administration v. American College of Obstetricians and Gynecologists* (n253).
[354] Ibid, at 1–2.
[355] Ibid, at 2.

Court therefore refused to engage with the facts at issue and the question of whether FDA requirements were preventing people from realising their right to abortion in the circumstances.

There was, however, a considered dissent—given by Justice Sotomayor with Justice Kagan in agreement. In the dissent, Justice Sotomayor explains that she considers the in-person requirements to be an undue burden, noting the situation whereby 'Government policy now permits patients to receive prescriptions for powerful opioids without leaving home, yet still requires women to travel to a doctor's office to pick up mifepristone, only to turn around, go home, and ingest it without supervision'.[356] The dissent also places emphasis, much like the District Court, on the willingness of the FDA and Department of Health and Human Services to waive many in-person requirements for other drugs subject to REMS because of COVID-19, 'yet the Government has refused to extend that same grace to women seeking medication abortions'.[357] Justice Sotomayor also explicitly endorses the District Court's conclusions of facts about the extent to which the in-person requirements, in the context of COVID-19 pandemic, place a substantial obstacle in the way of people seeking EMA. That the Government denies this 'provides little insight'.[358] Justice Sotomayor powerfully states:

> What rejoinder does the Government have to the possibility that refusing to suspend the FDA's in-person requirements for mifepristone during the COVID–19 pandemic will cause some women to miss the 10-week window altogether? No cause for concern, the Government assures this Court, because even if the FDA's in-person requirements cause women to lose the opportunity for a medication abortion, they can still seek out a surgical abortion. What a callous response.[359]

This is because there are reasons why, for some patients, EMA may be preferable to surgical abortion (see Chapter 1). In the COVID-19 context, the fear of virus transmission is added to the existing concerns about physically attending clinics, such as the time, expense, and difficulty that travel entails. In closing her dissent, she finally reiterates the important point that the decision of the Government on this issue is ultimately one rooted in abortion exceptionalism:

> This country's laws have long singled out abortions for more onerous treatment than other medical procedures that carry similar or greater risks.[360]

The Supreme Court's decision is a wholly unsatisfactory result for people needing access to abortion. Further, as was well put in the District Court's decision, it is devastating for particular groups of vulnerable people. There were concerns even before COVID-19 that people are increasingly turning to internet sources to access

---

[356] Ibid.
[357] Ibid, at 3–4.
[358] Ibid, at 9.
[359] Ibid, at 8.
[360] Ibid, at 9.

mifepristone because fewer clinics can satisfy FDA restrictions. Because the FDA cannot effectively control these medications purchased online it may be, ironically, that the FDA, by virtue of its own restrictions called 'elements for safe use', make abortion *less* safe. Henney and Gayle argue that FDA policy should be amended to ensure that people have 'access to FDA-approved products whose safety and effectiveness are confirmed' (2019, 598).

These concerns are only heightened by the current situation. Early data—before the FDA requirements were enjoined—demonstrate that people were turning to extralegal sources of abortion medication (Aiken et al. 2020). With the FDA in-person requirements back in place, and being enforced by the FDA, it is likely that the number of people doing so is once again increasing. The decision of the Supreme Court is misconceived—the argument we presented in Chapter 7, and the reasoning given by the District Court, clearly demonstrates that the context means that in-person requirements are, at the very least *contextually*,[361] an unconstitutional interference with the right to privacy, and one in which the injury is likely to be exacerbated along the lines of socioeconomics and race.

9.2 State prohibitions on TEMA

Even if the FDA were to relax the REMS' requirements on mifepristone, it would still not be feasible for TEMA to be provided in a large part of the US because of state-level regulation (Upadhyay 2017), as was explicitly observed by Justice Chuang.[362] In eight states, there are explicit prohibitions on TEMA (see Table 9.1). There was also a state legislative prohibition on TEMA in a ninth state, however this has been permanently enjoined by the Iowa Supreme Court since 2015.[363] In most of the states with this ban on TEMA it is absolute. In West Virginia, however, there is an exception for an emergency, or where there is a pre-existing relationship between the patient and doctor that has involved previous in-person encounters.[364]

It is not only explicit TEMA bans that pose an obstacle to the establishment of TEMA. There are several different state laws which, whilst not *explicit* that TEMA is prohibited, have this effect (see Table 9.1) (Romanis et al. 2020a). There is significant variation across these laws—many of which prevent TEMA entirely by limiting the use of telecommunications (in any form) in abortion provision. In many ways, state requirements on *how* abortion can be provided are far stricter than those implemented at federal level by the FDA.

Some states require that consultation prior to abortion take place in person. Other states require that an examination (or specifically an ultrasound) take place in person before abortion medications are prescribed. Such provisions have the effect of prohibiting TEMA by making it mandatory that certain interactions take place in person. The

---

[361] We would argue they could also be considered unconstitutional in broader circumstances, but this is not the point here.

[362] *American College of Obstetricians and Gynecologists v. U.S. Food and Drug Administration* (n252).

[363] *Planned Parenthood of the Heartland v. Iowa Board of Medicine* (n245).

[364] WV Code §30-14-12d. This compares with the prepandemic situation in South Africa, as considered in Chapter 6.

Table 9.1 State barriers to TEMA in the United States[1]

Barrier to TEMA	States implementing
Express prohibition of TEMA	Arizona, Arkansas, Indiana, Kentucky, Ohio, South Carolina, Texas, and West Virginia
Consultation must take place in person	Alabama, Arizona, Arkansas, Indiana, Florida, Louisiana, Missouri, Mississippi, Ohio, South Dakota, Tennessee, Texas, Utah, and Wisconsin
Examination (either physical or in person) must be performed before medications can be prescribed	Arizona, Alabama, Arkansas, Alaska, Idaho, Indiana, Mississippi, Oklahoma, South Dakota, Texas, and Wisconsin
Ultrasound must be performed before medications can be prescribed	Alabama, Arizona, Florida, Iowa, Kentucky, Louisiana, Mississippi, North Carolina, Oklahoma, and South Carolina
A doctor must be present during the administration of mifepristone	Arkansas, Kansas, Kentucky, Louisiana, Mississippi, Missouri, Nebraska, North Carolina, North Dakota, Oklahoma, Tennessee, and Wisconsin
Mifepristone must be administered in a hospital, doctor's office, or clinic	Idaho, Minnesota, North Carolina, and Utah
A follow-up visit must be scheduled for after abortion	Arizona, Arkansas, Idaho, Iowa, Kansas, Mississippi, Missouri, Oklahoma, Texas, and Wisconsin

[1] The sources of these state laws are detailed in Appendix 7.

mandatory nature of the clinic visit goes further than that mandated by the FDA since these state requirements prevent the establishment of a clinic 'pick-up' service (discussed in Chapter 6) in which consultation takes place by telecommunication, with no physical examination necessary, and then patients can attend the clinic just to collect medications. These requirements, whilst limiting TEMA, do not prevent home use of abortion medications in themselves, since if only these requirements were in place the patient could attend the clinic for their consultation or examination, and then take the medications home for self-administration. These laws all go above and beyond the federal requirements and thus constitute additional barriers to TEMA (for example, two clinic visits rather than one). Some states—Arizona, Alaska, Michigan, Ohio, South Dakota, and Texas—have introduced provisions requiring contact between patient and doctor before abortion, but not that limit *where* mifepristone can be administered.

There are 15 states that, whilst making no explicit reference to prohibiting TEMA, have prohibited it by introducing a requirement that a doctor be physically present *when* mifepristone is administered. These laws are explicit that the drug inducing abortion must be administered in the *same room as* and in the *physical presence of* the prescribing doctor to be lawful. In some states with such a law, the legislature explicitly acknowledged that the requirement would effectively prohibit TEMA. For example, the requirement in Arkansas that mifepristone be administered in the same room as and in the physical presence of a doctor specifies that the requirement 'does not affect telemedicine practice that does not involve the use of mifepristone or another drug or chemical to induce abortion'.[365] In 2015, the Supreme Court of Iowa permanently enjoined a requirement that a doctor be physically present when mifepristone is administered. In this case, Justice Wiggins observed that 'it is not disputed that this rule would have the effect of prohibiting telemedicine abortions'.[366]

Some state legislatures have codified their justification for rules requiring the doctor's physical presence. The Alabama State Code specifies that because 'abortion and reproductive health centers do not currently provide the level of personal contact found in many physician/patient relationships and in other medical care settings, it is necessary for the Legislature to mandate the personal presence and participation of the physician in the process'.[367] The evidence we evaluated in Chapter 5, however, is clear that supervision in this way is not medically necessary to ensure the safety of EMA.

In an additional five states, where there is not a requirement that the doctor be physically present, there is a specific requirement that mifepristone must be administered in a doctor's office, clinic, or hospital. This has the same effect in terms of prohibiting TEMA and has the same connotations in terms of requiring some level of supervision of the abortion, even if not phrased in such explicit terms. These requirements are reminiscent of the regulation of mifepristone administration in Great Britain— prohibition of home use—prior to the (temporary) 2020 changes (Romanis et al. 2020a; see Chapter 8).

There are also some states with an additional requirement that a doctor recommend or, in some cases, make 'reasonable efforts to ensure'[368] that a patient return to the facility in person for a follow-up within a specified period after the administration of abortion medications to confirm abortion completeness and/or the patient's condition. Most of these states have a requirement that mifepristone be administered in the clinic. There is one notable exception—Arizona—where there is no requirement prohibiting home use of mifepristone, but the law instructs that aftercare, where possible, be provided in person. The law requires that preabortion counselling must take place in person[369] and that 'a medication abortion includes a follow-up visit, scheduled between seven and 21 days after the initial dose of a substance used to induce abortion'.[370]

The purpose of outlining these restrictions is to demonstrate that, even if the Supreme Court had ruled that the FDA's mifepristone REMS was unconstitutional in pandemic circumstances, there remain substantial barriers to TEMA enforced by state legislatures. Further, states have also failed to acknowledge the undue burdens that these laws place on access in the pandemic context (see Chapter 7). No action has been taken in states that ban telemedicine to remove these provisions, even temporarily, from their state codes in response to the pandemic. In fact, Ohio's TEMA

---

[365] AR Code §20-16-603(c) (2019).
[366] *Planned Parenthood of the Heartland v. Iowa Board of Medicine* (n245), at 254.
[367] AL Code §26-23E-2 (2019).
[368] For example, in Idaho: ID Code §18-617(3) (2019).
[369] AZ Rev Stat §36-2153(A)(1) (2019).
[370] Ariz. Admin. Code §R9-10-1509.

ban was only signed into law on 9 January 2021. The Ohio Senate Bill 260, specifically banning the use of telemedicine to prescribe abortion medication, was passed in the Ohio Senate on 4 March 2020 despite there already being an emerging sense of the pandemic and the circumstances it might create (Romanis et al. 2020a). It then proceeded to be passed in the Ohio House of Representatives in December 2020, before being signed by the Ohio Governor in January 2021. The hostility towards TEMA in some state legislatures remains throughout, and continues to grow in response to, the pandemic. This is in stark contrast to the action taken in Great Britain to relax regulation and enable TEMA provision in response to the circumstances (see Chapter 8).

In some states with alternative in-person requirements, action has been taken to minimise the restrictions on access in the COVID-19 context. For example, the Governor of Virginia repealed the legal requirements for ultrasound and a mandatory 24-hour waiting period, meaning a pregnant person would only have to make one trip to a clinic (and only because of the FDA requirements remaining intact). In a statement, the Governor said: 'No more will legislators in Richmond—most of whom are men—be telling women what they should and should not be doing with their bodies' (Gillett 2020). Such action, however, is an exception.

In Chapter 7, we made the case that the enforcement of legislative bans on TEMA, and other requirements that effectively preclude TEMA, should be considered—at the very least in the context of COVID-19—an unconstitutional undue burden on the right to privacy (encompassing the right to an abortion). Such provisions, however, remain in force. TEMA bans and requirements for a doctor to be present during mifepristone administration have been upheld by State Courts of Appeal in the past (pre-COVID-19) on the grounds that in-person care is 'more effective'[371] and that this did not constitute an undue burden for a significant number of people seeking access to abortion.[372] We have argued elsewhere that 'neither of these grounds for justifying bans can apply in the current emergency, as we have demonstrated that in-person care is unlikely to be as safe for patients or providers and that these restrictions are likely to prevent a significant number of people from accessing care or from accessing timely and safe care' (Romanis et al. 2020a, 20). It is likely that state legislatures, however, will attempt to rely on the reasoning of the Supreme Court in several cases that reiterate the abortion right as a negative right. For example, in *Harris v. McRae*,[373] the majority reiterated that the right to privacy does not equate to a state obligation to 'remove barriers that are not of its own creation'.[374] States hostile to abortion access are likely to emphasise that the impact COVID-19 has had on the ability or willingness of pregnant people to travel or to afford travel, for example, are beyond their control. Such framing, however, is inadequate because in many cases (though not all) state measures—rather than the virus itself—are what prevent people from accessing clinics.

In any event, with the Supreme Court having upheld mifepristone REMS in the COVID-19 context,[375] there is now a persuasive authority for states to rely on to

[371] *Planned Parenthood Arizona Incorporated v. Association of Pro-Life Obstetricians & Gynecologists* 27 Ariz. 262, 257 P.3d 181 (Ct. App 2011).
[372] *Planned Parenthood of Arkansas v. Jegley* 64 F.3d 953 (8th Cir 2017).
[373] *Harris v. McRae* (n159).
[374] Ibid, at 316.
[375] *Food and Drug Administration v. American College of Obstetricians and Gynecologists* (n253).

mandate the enforcement of in-person requirements during the pandemic. However, this case was very quickly dismissed, and the reasoning of both the dissent and the District Court's earlier judgment[376] were both compelling and well-evidenced. As such, it is hoped that other district courts might make better decisions about state requirements.

9.3 Pandemic-specific response: executive orders

As well as measures *not* being taken to make EMA *more* accessible at both federal and state level by enabling even the temporary provision of TEMA, in many states the executive exercised considerable power to erect even more barriers to care during the COVID-19 crisis. In many cases, this resulted in a near total ban on abortion.

In all 50 states in March and April 2020, executive orders were issued by state governors to declare a state of emergency and place limitations on activity in response to the crisis, including a requirement that any nonessential healthcare be halted. No state *explicitly* said within their executive order itself that abortion was nonessential healthcare or decreed that abortion care be halted. However, eight states interpreted this to 'cover at least some types of abortion and have attempted to enforce them against abortion providers' (Donley et al. 2020, 2). The Texas Attorney General, for example, was clear that abortions not medically necessary to preserve the person's life or health must be postponed (Attorney General of Texas 2020). In Ohio, similar statements were made, and the Deputy Attorney General wrote to clinics directly ordering them to close as 'a necessary measure amid a public health crisis' (Knowles 2020). The effect of these orders, their interpretation, and the actions of state officials to enforce them, was that abortion became de facto unlawful and impossible to access as HCPs were ordered to cease providing these services.

As Ahmed explains, against the backdrop of COVID-19 'abortion is being conceptualized as a procedure that can be delayed' (Ahmed 2020, 3). That states were able to seamlessly adopt provisions within their COVID-19 response that explicitly target abortion on the grounds that it is 'nonessential' in an emergency demonstrates how entrenched abortion exceptionalism is (see Chapter 2). Whilst these restrictions are not explicitly about TEMA, they demonstrate general hostility towards abortion care. That these orders mandate clinic closures means that TEMA becomes even more imperative. There being fewer (or even no) open clinics makes for a more compelling argument that both federal and state barriers to TEMA are an unconstitutional interference, at the very least *contextually*, with people's right to privacy.

At the time of writing, none of the orders interpreted as meaning abortion should be postponed are still in force. They have all either been lifted by state executives, effectively legally challenged and enjoined,[377] or expired.[378] Even though these orders eventually ceased to have effect, they had a significant impact during the first wave of the pandemic, against the backdrop of broader panic and uncertainty. As the extreme

---

[376] *American College of Obstetricians and Gynecologists v. U.S. Food and Drug Administration* (n252).
[377] For example, in Alabama, Ohio, Oklahoma, and Tennessee.
[378] For example, in Texas.

example, abortion was effectively banned in Texas for a four-week period. Dr Amna Dermish, Regional Director of Planned Parenthood in Texas, explained that 'the brutality of it was terrible to experience' and that at one point in the crisis, as a result of the executive order and the surrounding legal action, HCPs were 'regularly telling patients in the waiting room who were there for their medication abortions, 'Actually, sorry – turns out an hour ago we could have done your medication abortion, but now we can't'" (Littlefield 2021). There were also inevitably delays experienced by many people in the eight states where abortion had been deemed nonessential in the circumstances. One study in Texas reported an increase in abortions at 12 weeks and beyond after the executive order impacting abortion clinics ceased in April 2020, which it was suggested was attributable to the inevitable delays the order caused (White et al. 2021). Delays had the effect of increasing the existing logistical and economic challenges associated with accessing abortion in the US (see Chapter 3), and specifically during the pandemic (see Chapter 7) (Lindberg et al. 2020). Importantly, these laws will, consequently, have had a disproportionate impact on low-income people because they would have been less able to mitigate the impact of these bans at the time by, for example, attending a clinic in a neighbouring state (Donley et al. 2020). The data also suggest that there were larger increases in people seeking abortion care through online providers in states with the most restrictive measures—Texas in particular (Aiken et al. 2020).

There were three justifications often provided in the orders, or by executives, when explaining the necessity of suspending 'nonessential' procedures: to preserve hospital capacity for COVID-19 patients, to preserve personal protective equipment, and to reduce community transmission of the virus (Hill 2020). However, it has been argued that '[f]rom a medical services standpoint, abortion could easily remain accessible throughout the pandemic without using precious hospital resources' (Senderowicz and Higgins 2020, 81). Further, as Rebouché highlights, EMA requires 'no gown, mask, eyewear, shoe covers, or gloves; in other words, no PPE' (2020, 6). Also, given the safety of EMA (see Chapter 1), it is implausible that abortion-related complications would impact a hospital's capacity to divert resources to COVID-19 patients. Consequently, 'rather than being about preservation of PPE, the abortion restrictions imposed in recent weeks are the latest round in a long-running debate about whether abortion is a legitimate health care service' (Beyefsky et al. 2020, 2).

The most striking thing to highlight here is the direct tension in the positions advanced by the federal and state governments. The FDA and Department of Health and Human Services continue to insist that the in-person REMS requirements in federal law (that prevent TEMA) do not increase the risk in virus transmission, whilst some states have simultaneously attempted to close clinics on the grounds that it is necessary to contain community transmission. These positions appear mutually exclusive and can, in their totality, be explained only by the fact that neither position is developed out of concern for anything other than limiting abortion access. The concerns that states have raised about abortion need not be issues at all were it not for the federal requirements (and some of their own requirements) that abortion care involve an in-person element. TEMA is safe and is unlikely to impact hospitals, and TEMA would reduce the risk of virus transmission that might exist from people travelling to access care.

9.6 Summary

It is, unfortunately, clear that 'the COVID-19 pandemic has put on full display the physical and doctrinal isolation of abortion from healthcare more generally' (Hill 2020, 99). Unlike in Great Britain, where the pandemic has improved access to EMA because of legal and policy shifts to enable TEMA, federal and state requirements continue to limit TEMA across the US. The impact is that TEMA provision has not been established, and people remain in a situation of having to make long journeys that they may struggle to afford or organise, or risk not having an abortion at all. This is no doubt having the greatest effect on those structurally disadvantaged by socioeconomics and race.

The Supreme Court failed to uphold the constitutional right to abortion, threatened as it is in the circumstances, when asked to evaluate the extent to which federal requirements preventing TEMA were an undue burden on abortion access in the circumstances. Not only was this decision wrong, but it illustrates the tone of this (now majority conservative) Supreme Court's positionality on abortion, which will likely further problematise abortion access in the US going forward.

Conclusion

We began this book with some ambitious goals. Our overarching purpose has been to demonstrate the importance of TEMA, and to consider how TEMA has been and can be implemented effectively. In doing so, we have covered a lot of ground. Let us revisit some of the key points.

Even though EMA is a common method of abortion that is widely recognised to be safe and effective, access in both the UK and US is often challenging because of a whole host of socio-legal barriers. The regulation of EMA—and, indeed, of abortion more broadly—is such that it being legal and available does not come close to equating with it being accessible. In the UK, the law is constructed such that all pregnancies before 24 weeks can lawfully be terminated, but there remain legal restrictions on these abortions because of who can provide them and where. There is evidence that some people still feel that they have no choice but to access care through unlawful channels because of access barriers (Aiken et al. 2018). In the US, abortion is legal in every state because it is recognised as part of a person's constitutional right to privacy. However, because this right to abortion is constructed as negative and requiring only that states refrain from legislating in ways that unduly burden access, states have been emboldened to pass myriad different laws that create an environment hostile to the realisation of the abortion right. In both jurisdictions, legal barriers construct, reinforce, or exacerbate social conditions that limit access. There is, then, a real need for change that adequately addresses socio-legal barriers to ensure access to essential, time-sensitive healthcare.

As important as this change is, the realities of politics are such that progress is slow. Given how controversial abortion is treated as a policy point, lawmakers are often reluctant to make significant regulatory leaps. Instead, progression is piecemeal, as was demonstrated by the glacial pace at which the FDA updated its REMS protocol for mifepristone, and by the introduction of home use of misoprostol in the UK. Over a period of just under four years, the UK went from a strict in-person requirement on the administering of both misoprostol (or, in the case of Northern Ireland, a complete lack of lawful access) to permitting patients to self-administer the drug in the comfort of their own homes.

In this gradual progression of abortion regulation, the natural next step is TEMA. Indeed, this change came in Great Britain (albeit temporarily) in 2020. TEMA is certainly nothing novel, though all too often it is available only outside of the regulated healthcare system—through charitable organisations, such as Women on Web, operating extra-legally. To remove barriers to access, and to improve the safety of care, it is vital that TEMA is available within jurisdictions, through regulated (and suitably accessible) providers.

Early Medical Abortion, Equality of Access, and the Telemedical Imperative. Jordan A. Parsons and Elizabeth Chloe Romanis, Oxford University Press. © Oxford University Press 2021. DOI: 10.1093/oso/9780192896155.003.0010

The case for TEMA can be framed around the telemedical imperative (Parsons 2021a). Overwhelmingly, the evidence is that TEMA is safe, effective, and acceptable to patients. Further, the most commonly raised issues in opposition to TEMA—clinic closures, inadequate safeguarding, and an inability to accurately date pregnancies—are empirically unfounded. Given the wealth of evidence that satisfies these criteria, there is a moral imperative for TEMA to be introduced, retained, or reinstated (as applicable).

In implementing TEMA, there are various existing service models that can be looked to for inspiration. Ranging from the simple addition of videoconferencing to allow satellite clinics to provide in-person care to an entire removal of face-to-face contact, there are several tried and tested care pathways. Perhaps the best candidate for a standard model moving forward is that of BPAS (and, indeed, other providers in Great Britain with largely similar models that were implemented in 2020). In addition to a fully remote care pathway, BPAS offers a partial telemedicine option that allows patients to collect a treatment pack from a clinic following a remote consultation. In addition to the choice between in-person and telemedical care, patients are afforded choice within the option of telemedical care. This additional choice is important to respect patient autonomy in a climate of increasing patient-centricity. Providers should, then, be looking to incorporate as much choice along the care pathway as is feasible.

The 2020 COVID-19 pandemic drastically changed the world. With people unable to safely leave the home, it acted as a catalyst for telemedicine. In some cases, this included abortion. Many people found themselves struggling to access both contraceptive and abortion care; people were confined to their homes and unable or hesitant to leave for fear of contracting the virus, they no longer had means of making the trip to the nearest clinic, and/or they had additional caring responsibilities in the home. In the UK, though there was initially a hesitancy to make any changes to abortion regulation to allow TEMA, the governments of Great Britain eventually succumbed to significant pressure from reproductive and public health professionals and organisations to make changes that enabled TEMA provision. These changes were made tentatively, and on a temporary basis (with the exception of Scotland). But they were still made, and they enabled the establishment of services that have drastically improved access to care for the better in Great Britain. In Northern Ireland, there has been no such change.

The picture of abortion access in the US during this crisis is bleak. The FDA has refused to remove federal requirements that place a barrier in the path of TEMA provision, continuing to enforce the requirement that mifepristone only be dispensed in clinics. This was temporarily enjoined by the District Court in Maryland, however, the Supreme Court, in January 2021, intervened, allowing the FDA to mandate clinic attendance. In the US and Northern Ireland, people must risk their health (and potentially their lives) to travel—potentially long distances—to attend a clinic to collect medication that they can then safely administer at home. We have argued that, in Northern Ireland, there has been substantive failure on the part of the executive to respect the right to private life of citizens as required by the European Convention on Human Rights, and in the US that FDA requirements are (at the very least contextually) an undue interference with the abortion right. Even in Great Britain, where changes have been made, they have not gone far enough—and cannot be described as evidence-based changes—because they are not, at present, permanent.

Even where TEMA is introduced, there remain service-level practical barriers to overcome—some of which we touched upon throughout this book. Of note, the success of telemedicine ultimately relies on HCPs being appropriately trained. Whilst our focus is abortion care, the need for appropriate training for remote consultation is applicable to the introduction of telemedicine in all areas of healthcare. Healthcare has traditionally been delivered in person (whether necessary or not), meaning the training of HCPs in relation to effective communication with patients has focused on in-person interaction. Given this, it is understandable that some HCPs working in abortion care might be initially resistant to change; if you have always delivered care in person, a sudden change to interacting with your patients by telephone is going to feel other. Even amongst those who embrace TEMA, appropriate training in communication will be important. No doubt the COVID-19 pandemic has provided a crash course for many clinicians in communicating using telemedicine, but a real focus on purpose-designed training is needed. It cannot be underestimated how important staff buy-in is when making significant operational changes—and this is true in all contexts—so providers who introduce TEMA must make the effort to bring staff with them to ensure a smooth transition and quality care. A certain level of responsibility must also fall to educational institutions. One would imagine that medical and nursing schools globally will, in response to the COVID-19 pandemic, make a concerted effort to factor telemedicine-appropriate communication training into their syllabi. This is important across healthcare systems – and not only in abortion care - so it will be interesting to see how universities adapt courses to align with the greater focus on telemedicine we are seeing in both policy and practice.

As important as TEMA is, it is crucial to reflect honestly on the reality of personal values and preferences in the provision of abortion care. Much of the literature on TEMA—including some of our own work—implicitly (or even explicitly, in some cases) endorses EMA as the ideal method in abortion care and suggests that an ability for patients to access it with minimal effort is a no brainer. The problematic result of the continued reiteration of this position is almost as damaging as it is improving. There is no denying that EMA is the best option for many—perhaps even the majority—of those seeking to end an unwanted pregnancy. It is also clear that there is a strong desire amongst them for care to be accessible without physically attending a clinic. However, it is vital that patients with almost the entire opposite preferences are not made new victims of a different form of lack of choice. The push for TEMA, then, should be attentive to the reality that surgical abortion better aligns with the subjective values and preferences of some patients, and ensuring access to this option is equally as important.

Looking forward with abortion care

We have argued in favour of the permanent introduction of TEMA in the UK, and the removal of federal requirements that, in effect, prohibit TEMA in the US. TEMA, however, represents just one of a range of important developments in the provision of abortion care. Some additional developments can streamline TEMA, whilst others can improve access to in-person care. Others are more about principle, and more formally recognising abortion as essential healthcare.

In Great Britain—and we are purposely excluding Northern Ireland in our discussion here for good reason—under the current (temporary) approvals, TEMA is permitted. However, the requirement for prescriptions to be signed off by doctors remains. A nurse or midwife can—as they long have—carry out the consultation and confirm the patient's eligibility, but prescriptions still require the signatures of two doctors. Northern Ireland can be looked to as an example here, as the introduction of new regulations in 2020 afforded registered nurses and registered midwives the power to prescribe mifepristone and misoprostol for the purposes of EMA. TEMA remains unlawful in Northern Ireland, but these prescribing powers have at least been extended in relation to lawful services. Similarly, in the US, the requirements of the FDA REMS protocol for mifepristone that limit who can become a certified prescriber (US Food and Drug Administration 2019) must also be revisited to ensure that more individuals, appropriately qualified to provide care, are able to do so. Here, also, better protection for abortion care providers to ensure their safety at work from protestors turning violent might also encourage more HCPs to become certified prescribers (where this remains a requirement) and begin providing care.

As well as such improvements to existing points of access, there are various opportunities for introducing additional options (in addition, of course, to TEMA) in both the UK and US. Various possibilities exist, such as through primary care and pharmacies. One of the principal barriers to in-person abortion care at designated clinics that TEMA overcomes is distance. When in-person services are only available at a small number of locations, pregnant people may have to travel significant distances to attend. TEMA removes this need for many, but, as explained throughout this book, there are various reasons why a patient may prefer in-person care to TEMA. There being more physical locations at which to access care, then, will improve access for those fitting this description. General practitioner surgeries and pharmacies are far greater in number than abortion clinics. Even many remote areas have a local pharmacy. If pregnant people were able to access EMA through these locations, it would allow in-person interaction with their care provider without having to travel a potentially significant distance. To enable this, changes would have to be made to the mifepristone REMS protocol in the US.

Of course, if EMA were accessed through a general practitioner or pharmacist, then ultrasound testing would not be possible. Such a care pathway would, much like many TEMA services, have to rely on pregnant people dating their pregnancies based on their last menstrual period. If a particular patient's desire to access care in person is for reassurance as to gestational age, visiting a general practitioner or pharmacy would not be appropriate. However, if the only reason TEMA does not appeal to a patient is because of the lack of face-to-face communication, then these additional options may be ideal.

Ultimately, making all these options available can be considered important in line with our argument advanced in Chapter 6. Pregnant people seeking to end unwanted pregnancies should not be viewed as a homogenous group with exactly the same care needs, so offering a range of options enhances their autonomy and improves access to care. As such, all these options could be available in tandem, allowing patients to access care in the way that best suits their needs.

We did not reflect on decriminalisation of abortion in Great Britain, or the need to reframe the abortion right in the US so that it is afforded better protection from hostile legislation, because neither of these larger whole-scale changes to the law are necessary to enable the availability of TEMA. Whilst we are both supportive of such changes, our primary concern is with access. Framing matters, but access matters more. As one of us has argued elsewhere, the picture of access in the US really illustrates that '[it] seems less important to have a formally declared constitutional right to services than it does to have access to them' (Romanis 2020a, 28). Even if the law does not recognise a right to abortion in the UK, it better enables access for people in the UK than their US counterparts. That said, decriminalisation would improve things further in the UK. The regulation of abortion as distinct from other aspects of healthcare in the UK (and equally in the US) prevents the natural evolution of abortion services by providers in line with best medical practice (Lohr et al. 2020). Were it not for the heavy regulation of abortion in both jurisdictions, TEMA would likely have been commonplace some time ago.

A final comment

Abortion is essential, time-sensitive healthcare that will be accessed by a significant number of people at some point in their life. However, it has been exceptionalised in law, resulting in significant socio-legal barriers to access. At root, this exceptionalism is the perpetuation of stigma—the idea that pregnancy is the norm, and that a desire to end a pregnancy must be indicative of some type of mental or moral issue. This archaic view is entirely at odds with the reality of abortion. There are myriad reasons why people choose to terminate their pregnancies, many of which are themselves a result of systemic issues—deficiencies in law and society are themselves causing a need for abortion, which law and society then go on to scrutinise in a hypocritical self-fulfilling prophecy.

These foundational issues do themselves need addressing. There is some extent to which TEMA can contribute to this in demonstrating that abortion is so routine that it can happen at home. However, in the interim, there are simple changes that can be made to at least enable access to safe and effective abortion care. Key amongst these changes is the implementation of TEMA. Against the criteria of safety, effectiveness, and acceptability, TEMA scores highly. Further, there are no other concerns that stand up to empirical scrutiny. As such, objection to TEMA boils down to value judgements and gut feelings—neither of which are sufficient to deny access to healthcare that people are lawfully (in both the UK and US) entitled to.

In this book, we advanced the case for TEMA in contexts where EMA is already, in some sense, a lawfully available treatment option. When EMA is already provided, it is more straightforward for telemedicine to be incorporated into care pathways to improve access. Where there is an entire lack of lawful options for the termination of unwanted pregnancies, however, the move to TEMA is more of leap than a step. There is still a real need for TEMA—and, we would suggest, a much greater need—in such settings, but there could be a far longer list of 'service-specific concerns' (see Chapter 5) to contend with. As such, we invite further scholarship to cement the case for TEMA beyond the parameters we set in this book.

To conclude, there is a moral imperative to begin dismantling abortion exceptionalism through the introduction, retention, or reinstating (as applicable) of TEMA. The ever-growing body of evidence in support of this position cannot be denied, and it is essential to abandon the highly political application of the precautionary approach in pursuit of equality of access to essential, time-sensitive abortion care.

United Kingdom chronology

All acts and regulations are included based on their commencement. If the date of commencement is not known, the date of enactment is used.

November 1861	Offences Against the Person Act 1861 criminalises the unlawful procurement of miscarriage, or the supply of abortifacients, punishable by life imprisonment in England and Wales.
May 1929	Infant Life (Preservation) Act 1929 criminalises child destruction—the offences of killing a fetus 'capable of being born alive'—in England and Wales.
July 1938	*R v Bourne* establishes that abortions provided by doctors where they believe it to be necessary to save a pregnant person's life are not unlawful.
December 1945	Criminal Justice (Northern Ireland) Act 1945 criminalises child destruction in Northern Ireland, much like the offence in England and Wales.
April 1968	Abortion Act 1967 introduces legal grounds for abortion.
November 1990	Human Fertilisation and Embryology Act 1990 introduces powers to approve a 'class of places' where abortion can lawfully take place.
April 1991	Abortion Regulations 1991 introduce requirements for the reporting of abortion in England and Wales.
	Abortion (Scotland) Regulations 1991 introduce requirements for the reporting of abortion in Scotland.
July 1991	Mifepristone licensed for use in the UK.
October 2007	House of Commons Science and Technology Committee issues report recommending home use of misoprostol be approved.
October 2017	Home use of misoprostol approved in Scotland.
December 2017	SPUC Scotland threatens legal challenge to the home use of misoprostol in Scotland.
February 2018	United Nations CEDAW report published.
April 2018	Intention to approve home use of misoprostol in Wales announced.
June 2018	Home use of misoprostol approved in Wales.
August 2018	SPUC Scotland legal challenge fails.
	Intention to approve home use of misoprostol in England announced.
December 2018	Home use of misoprostol approved in England.
July 2019	Northern Ireland (Executive Formation etc) Act sets deadline of 21 October 2019 for the formation of a Northern Ireland Executive, providing for the liberalisation of abortion laws if not.
October 2019	Northern Ireland Executive fails to reform, triggering a requirement to liberalise abortion laws.

March 2020	Home use of mifepristone approved in England (23 March) but revoked that same day.
	Home use of misoprostol approved in Northern Ireland by the Abortion (Northern Ireland) Regulations.
	Home use of mifepristone (temporarily) approved in England (30 March), Wales (31 March), and Scotland (31 March) in response to the COVID-19 pandemic.
April 2020	BPAS launches 'Pills by Post' service.
May 2020	Abortion (Northern Ireland) (No. 2) Regulations replace those of March 2020, but with no relevant changes.
September 2020	Consultation on home use of mifepristone/telemedicine opens in Scotland.
November 2020	Consultation on home use of mifepristone/telemedicine opens in England.
December 2020	Consultation on home use of mifepristone/telemedicine opens in Wales.
January 2021	Consultation on home use of mifepristone/telemedicine closes in Scotland.
February 2021	Consultation on home use of mifepristone/telemedicine closes in Wales.
	Consultation on home use of mifepristone/telemedicine closes in England.

United States chronology

January 1973	*Roe v. Wade* recognises a person's right to abortion as encompassed within the constitutional right to privacy.
September 1976	The Hyde Amendment bans the use of federal funds for abortion care, except where necessary to save the pregnant person's life. This comes into force in 1980.
June 1980	*Harris v. McRae* holds that a ban on federal funding for abortion is not an unconstitutional interference with the right to privacy.
June 1992	*Planned Parenthood v. Casey* introduces the undue burden test to assess whether state laws interfere with the constitutional right to privacy.
October 1993	Changes to the Hyde Amendment allow federal funding for abortions where pregnancy results from rape or incest in addition to where necessary to save life.
May 1994	Freedom of Access to Clinic Entrances Act of 1994 prohibits using force to intimidate or injure a person attempting to access an abortion clinic, physically obstructing access to a clinic, and/or damaging facilities.
September 2000	Mifeprex (a brand of mifepristone) licensed by the FDA for use in the US, subject to certain conditions.
September 2007	FDA Amendments Act of 2007 grants new powers to introduce Risk Evaluation and Mitigation Strategies (REMS). Mifepristone was then subjected to such a program.
June 2008	Planned Parenthood in Iowa launches its partial telemedicine care pathway.
March 2010	Obamacare enacted, introducing 'Health Benefit Exchanges' for health insurance comparison shopping. States are permitted to prohibit policies offered on the exchange from covering abortion.
June 2015	Supreme Court of Iowa enjoins enforcement of the requirement that doctors physically examine a patient before providing an abortion.
March 2016	Mifepristone REMS amended, allowing use of the drug up to 70 days' gestation and allowing non-doctors (who are certified prescribers) to dispense.
	TelAbortion Study begins providing fully remote, direct-to-patient prescription of early medical abortion.
June 2016	*Whole Women's Health v. Hellerstedt* rearticulates the undue burden test, allowing for greater scrutiny of legislative provisions.
April 2019	First generic form of mifepristone is licensed for use by the FDA.
March 2020	21 state attorneys general request that the FDA suspend the REMS requirement for in-person dispensing of mifepristone during the pandemic.

June 2020   *June Medical v. Russo* demonstrates the willingness of the Supreme Court to revisit long-standing precedent on abortion rights (though ultimately the decision upholds the right to abortion).

July 2020   District Court in Maryland enjoins in-person requirements of the REMS requirements for mifepristone without geographical limitation.

January 2021   *Food and Drug Administration v. American College of Obstetricians and Gynecologists* allows the FDA to resume enforcing the in-person requirements on mifepristone.

Demand-side TRAP laws in the United States

Chapter 3 features a table detailing demand-side TRAP laws in the United States. The sources of law are detailed below.

Informed consent requirements (biased materials):

Alabama	AL Code §26-23A-5 (2019).
Alaska	AK Stat §18.16.060 (2019).
Arizona	AZ Rev Stat §36-2153 (2019).
Arkansas	AR Code §20-16-1703 (2019).
Florida	FL Stat §390.0111(2) (2019).
Georgia	GA Code §31-9A-3 (2019).
Idaho	ID Code §18-609 (2019).
Indiana	IN Code §16-34-2-1.1 (2019).
Iowa	IA Code §146A.1(1)(d) (2019).
Kansas	KS Stat §65-6709 (2019).
Kentucky	KY Rev Stat §311.725 (2019).
Louisiana	LA Rev Stat §40:1061.17 (2019).
Michigan	MI Comp L §333.17015 (2019).
Minnesota	MN Stat §145.4242 (2019).
Mississippi	MS Code §41-41-33 (2019).
Missouri	MO Rev Stat §188.027 (2019).
Nebraska	NE Code §28-327 (2019).
North Carolina	NC Gen Stat §90-21.82 (2019).
North Dakota	N.D. Cent. Code §14-02.1-02-11(a) (2019).
Ohio	Ohio Rev Code §2317.56 (2019).
Oklahoma	63 OK Stat §63-1-738.2 (2019).
Pennsylvania	18 PA Cons Stat §3205 (2019).
South Carolina	SC Code §44-41-330 (2019).
South Dakota	SD Codified L §34-23A-10.1 (2019).
Tennessee	TN Code §39-15-202 (2019).
Texas	TX Health & Safety Code §171.012 (2019).
Utah	UT Code §76-7-305 (2019).
West Virginia	WV Code §16-2I-2 (2019).
Wisconsin	WI Stat §253.10(3)(c) (2019).

Mandatory waiting period:

18 hours:

Indiana	IN Code §16-34-2-1.1 (2019).

24 hours:

Arizona	AZ Rev Stat §36-2153(1) (2019).
Florida	FL Stat §390.0111(3)(a) (2019).
Georgia	GA Code §31-9A-3(1) (2019).
Idaho	ID Code §18-609(4) (2019).
Kansas	KS Stat §65-6709(a) (2019).
Kentucky	KY Rev Stat §311.725(1)(a) (2019).
Michigan	MI Comp L §333.17014(h) (2019).
Minnesota	MN Stat §145.4242(a)(1) (2019).
Mississippi	MS Code §41-41-33(1)(a) (2019).
Nebraska	NE Code §28-327(1) (2019).
North Dakota	N.D. Cent. Code §14-02.1-02-11(b) (2019).
Ohio	Ohio Rev Code §2317.56(B)(1) (2019).
Pennsylvania	18 PA Cons Stat §3205(a)(1) (2019).
South Carolina	SC Code §44-41-330(C) (2019).
Texas	TX Health & Safety Code §171.012(4) (2019).
West Virginia	WV Code §16-2I-2(a) (2019).
Wisconsin	WI Stat §253.10(3)(c) (2019).

48 hours:

Alabama	AL Code §26-23A-4(a) (2019).
Tennessee	TN Code §39-15-202(d)(1) (2019).

72 hours:

Arkansas	AR Code §20-16-1703(b)(1) (2019).
Iowa	IA Code §146A.1(1) (2019).
Louisiana	LA Rev Stat §40:1061.17(B)(3)(a) (2019).
Missouri	MO Rev Stat §188.027(1) (2019).
North Carolina	NC Gen Stat §90-21.82(1) (2019).
Oklahoma	63 OK Stat §63-1-738.2(B)1.a (2019).
Utah	UT Code §76-7-305(2) (2019).

72 + hours:

South Dakota	SD Codified L §34-23A-56 (2019).

Abortion provider restrictions in the United States

Chapter 3 features a box detailing abortion provider restrictions in the United States. The sources of law are detailed below.

Only a doctor can provide abortion care:

Alabama	AL Code §26-23E-4 (2019).
Alaska	AK Stat §18.16.010(a) (2019).
Arkansas	AR Code §5-61-101 (2019).
Connecticut	Conn. Agencies Regs. §19-13-D54(a).
Delaware	24 DE Code §1790(a) (2019).
Florida	FL Stat §390.0111(2) (2019).
Georgia	GA Code §16-12-141(e)(2) (2019).
Hawaii	HI Rev Stat §453-16(1) (2019).
Idaho	ID Code §18-608A (2019).
Indiana	IN Code §16-34-2-1 (2019).
Iowa	IA Code §707.7 (2019).
Kansas	KS Stat §65-4a10(a) (2019).
Kentucky	KY Rev Stat §311.750 (2019).
Louisiana	LA Rev Stat §40:1061.10(A)(1) (2019).
Maryland	MD Health-Gen Code §20-208 (2019).
Massachusetts	MA Gen L ch 112 §12l (2019).
Minnesota	MN Stat §145.412(1) (2019).
Mississippi	MS Code §41-41-107(1) (2019).
Missouri	MO Rev Stat §188.020 (2019).
Nebraska	NE Code §28-335(1) (2019).
Nevada	NV Rev Stat 442.250(1) (2019).
New Mexico	NM Stat §30-5-1(C) (2019).
North Carolina	NC Gen Stat §14-45.1(a) (2019).
North Dakota	N.D. Cent. Code §14-02.1-02.1-03.5 (2019).
Ohio	Ohio Rev Code §2919.123(A) (2019).
Oklahoma	63 OK Stat §63-1-731(A) (2019).
Pennsylvania	18 PA Cons Stat §3204(a) (2019).
South Carolina	SC Code §44-41-20 (2019).

South Dakota	SD Codified L §34-23A-3 (2019).
Tennessee	TN Code §39-15-201(c)(1) (2019).
Texas	TX Health & Safety Code §171.063(1) (2019).
Utah	UT Code §76-7-302(2) (2019).
Washington	WA Rev Code §9.02.110 (2019).
Wisconsin	WI Stat §940.04(5)(a) (2019).
Wyoming	WY Stat §35-6-111 (2019).
South Carolina	SC Code §44-41-20 (2019).
South Dakota	SD Codified L §34-23A-3 (2019).
Tennessee	TN Code §39-15-201(c)(1) (2019).
Texas	TX Health & Safety Code §171.063(1) (2019).
Utah	UT Code §76-7-302(2) (2019).
Washington	WA Rev Code §9.02.110 (2019).
Wisconsin	WI Stat §940.04(5)(a) (2019).
Wyoming	WY Stat §35-6-111 (2019).

State regulation of exchange health policies in the United States

Chapter 3 features a box detailing state regulation of exchange health policies regarding abortion in the United States. The sources of law are detailed below.

State health insurance exchange policies exclude abortion coverage:

Alabama	AL Code § 26-23C-3(a) (2019).
Arizona	AZ Rev Stat §20-121 (2019).
Arkansas	AR Code §23-79-156 (2019).
Florida	FL Stat §627.64995(1) (2019).
Georgia	GA Code §33-24-59.17(a) (2019).
Idaho	ID Code §41-1848(a) (2019).
Indiana	IN Code §27-8-13.4-2 (2019).
Kentucky	KY Rev Stat § 304.5-160(1) (2019).
Kansas	KS Stat §40-2,190(b) (2019).
Louisiana	LA Rev Stat §22:1014(B) (2019).
Michigan	MI Comp L §550.542 (2019).
Mississippi	MS Code §41-41-99(1) (2019).
Missouri	MO Rev Stat §376.805 (2019).
Nebraska	NE Code §44-8403(1) (2019).
North Carolina	NC Gen Stat §58-51-63(a) (2019).
North Dakota	N.D. Cent. Code §14-02.3-03 (2019).
Ohio	Ohio Rev Code §3901.87(A) (2019).
Oklahoma	63 OK Stat § 63-1-741.3(A) (2019).
Pennsylvania	40 PA Cons Stat §3302(b) (2019).
South Carolina	SC Code §38-71-238 (2019).
South Dakota	SD Codified L §58-17-147 (2019).
Tennessee	TN Code §56-26-134 (2019).
Texas	TX Ins. Code §1696.002(a) (2019).
Utah	UT Code §31A-22-726(3) (2019).
Wisconsin	WI Stat §632.8985(2) (2019).

Limitations on the use of state funds in the United States

Chapter 3 features a figure detailing limitations on the use of state funds for abortion in the United States. The sources of law are detailed below.

No public funds to be used for abortion:

Except where necessary to save the pregnant person's life:

Arizona	AZ Rev Stat §35-196.02(B) (2019).
Arkansas	Arkansas Constitution of 1874 Amendment 68, §1.
Colorado	CO Rev Stat §25.5-3-106 (2019).
Indiana	Ind. Admin. Code tit. 405, r. 5-28-7.
Kentucky	KY Rev Stat §311.715 (2019).
Louisiana	LA Rev Stat §40:1061.6(A)(1) (2019).
Michigan	MI Comp L §400.109d (2019).
Missouri	MO Rev Stat §188.205 (2019).
Nebraska	NE Code §44-1615.01 (2019).
North Dakota	N.D. Cent. Code §14-02.3-01 (2019).
South Dakota	SD Codified L §28-6-4.5 (2019).

Except where necessary to save the pregnant person's life, or pregnancy results from rape or incest:

Alabama	Ala. Admin. Code r. 560-X-6-.09(1).
Delaware	'Delaware Medical Assistance Program Practitioner Provider Specific Policy Manual'. Available at: https://www.matrc.org/wp-content/uploads/2019/08/DE-Provider-Manual.pdf?9b3fb7&9b3fb7, §2.7.
District of Columbia	'Policy and Procedure: Coverage of Medical Abortions. Transmittal #19-18'. Available at: https://dhcf.dc.gov/sites/default/files/dc/sites/dhcf/publication/attachments/Transmittal%2019-18-%20Policy%20and%20Procedure-%20Coverage%20of%20Medicaid%20Abortions.pdf.
Idaho	ID Code §56-209c (2019).
Georgia	'2019 Georgia Medicaid Provider Manual'. Available at: https://www.wellcare.com/~/media/PDFs/Georgia/Provider/Medicaid/2019/GA_CAID_Provider_Manual_ENG_2019_R.ashx, 85.
Kansas	'Kansas Medical Assistance Professional Services Provider Manual Benefits & Limitations'. Available at: https://www.kmap-state-ks.us/Documents/Content/Provider%20Manuals/Professional%20092006%206102.pdf, 8-3.

Minnesota	MN Stat §256B.0625(16) (2019).
Nevada	'Sterilization and Abortion Policy Billing Instructions'. Available at: https://www.medicaid.nv.gov/downloads/provider/nv_billing_sterilization.pdf, 6.
North Carolina	NC Gen Stat §143C-6-5.5 (2019).
Ohio	Ohio Rev Code §5101.56(B) (2019).
Oklahoma	Okla. Admin. Code §317:30-5-6(a).
Pennsylvania	18 PA Cons Stat §3215(c) (2019).
Rhode Island	210 R.I. Code R. 30-05-2.27(A)(2).
South Carolina	SC Code §1-1-1035 (2019).
Tennessee	TN Code §9-4-5116 (2019).
Wisconsin	WI Stat §20.927(1m) (2019).
Wyoming	WY Stat §35-6-117 (2019).

Except where necessary to save the pregnant person's life, or to avert a serious risk of substantial physical impairment of a major bodily function:

Alaska	AK Stat §47.07.068(a) (2019).

Except where necessary to save the pregnant person's life, or to avert a serious risk of substantial physical impairment of a major bodily function, or where pregnancy results from rape or incest:

Florida	FL Stat §627.64995 (2019).
Utah	UT Code §76-7-331(2) (2019).

Except where necessary to save the pregnant person's life, or where pregnancy results from rape or incest, or there is a serious fetal abnormality:

Iowa	Iowa Admin. Code r. 441-78.1(17).
Mississippi	MS Code §41-41-91 (2019).
Virginia	VA Code §32.1-92 (2019).

Except where necessary to save the pregnant person's life, or to avert a serious risk of substantial physical impairment of a major bodily function, or there is a serious fetal abnormality:

Texas	TX Health & Safety Code §285.202(b) (2019).

Except where necessary to save the pregnant person's life, or to avert a serious risk of substantial physical impairment of a major bodily function or where pregnancy results from rape or incest, or there is a serious fetal abnormality:

West Virginia	WV Code §9-2-11 (2019).

State barriers to TEMA in the United States

Chapter 9 features a table detailing state barriers to TEMA in the United States. The sources of law are detailed below.

Express prohibition of TEMA:

Arizona	AZ Rev Stat §36-3604(A) (2019).
Arkansas	AR Code §17-80-407(2) (2019).
Indiana	IN Code §25-1-9.5-8(a)(4) (2019).
Kentucky	KY Rev Stat §311.728 (2019).
Ohio	Senate Bill 260 (2020-2021).
South Carolina	SC Code §40-47-37(C)(6) (2019).
Texas	TX Occ Code §111.005(c) (2019).
West Virginia	WV Code §30-3-13a(5) (2019).

Consultation must take place in person:

Alabama	AL Code §26-23A-4(b) (2019).
Arizona	AZ Rev Stat §36-2153(A)(1) (2019).
Arkansas	AR Code §20-16-1703(b)(1) (2019).
Indiana	IN Code §16-34-2-1.1 (2019).
Florida	FL Stat §390.0111(3)(a)(1) (2019).
Louisiana	LA Rev Stat §40:1061.17(B)(2) (2019).
Missouri	MO Rev Stat §188.027.1(1) (2019).
Mississippi	MS Code §41-41-33(1)(a) (2019).
Ohio	Ohio Rev Code §2317.56(B)(1) (2019).
South Dakota	SD Codified L §34-23A-56 (2019).
Tennessee	TN Code §39-15-202(b) (2019).
Texas	TX Health & Safety Code §171.012(b)(1) (2019).
Utah	UT Code §76-7-305(2)(d) (2019).
Wisconsin	WI Stat §253.10(c)(2) (2019).

Examination (either physical or in person) must be performed before medications can be prescribed:

Arizona	AZ Rev Stat §36-449.03(D)(2) (2019).
Alabama	AL Code §26-23E-7 (2019).
Arkansas	AR Code §20-16-1504(b) (2019).

Alaska	AK Stat §18.16.010(a)(2) (2019).
Idaho	ID Code §18-617(2)(b) (2019).
Indiana	IN Code §16-34-2-1 (2019).
Mississippi	MS Code § 41-41-34(2) (2019).
Oklahoma	63 OK Stat §63-1-729a(F) (2019).
South Dakota	SD Codified L §34-23-56 (2019).
Texas	TX Health & Safety Code §171.063(c) (2019).
Wisconsin	WI Stat §253.105(2)(a) (2019).

Ultrasound must be performed before medications can be prescribed:

Alabama	AL Code §26-23A-6 (2019).
Arizona	AZ Rev Stat §36-449.03(D)(4) (2019).
Florida	FL Stat §390.0111(3)(1)(b) (2019).
Iowa	IA Code §146A.1(1)(A) (2019).
Kentucky	KY Rev Stat §311.727(2)(a) (2019).
Louisiana	LA Rev Stat §40:1061.10(D) (2019).
Mississippi	MS Code §41-41-34(1)(a) (2019).
North Carolina	NC Gen Stat §90-21.85(a)(1) (2019).
South Carolina	SC Code §44-41-330(A)(1) (2019).
Oklahoma	63 OK Stat §63-1-738.3d(B) (2019).

A doctor must be present during the administration of mifepristone:

Arkansas	AR Code §20-16-603 (2019).
Kansas	KS Stat §65-4a10(b)(1) (2019).
Kentucky	KY Rev Stat §311.728 (2019).
Louisiana	LA Rev Stat §40:1061.11 (2019).
Mississippi	MS Code §41-41-34(3) (2019).
Missouri	MO Rev Stat §188.021 (2019).
Nebraska	NE Code §28-335(2) (2019).
North Carolina	NC Gen Stat § 90-21.82(1)(a) (2019).
North Dakota	N.D. Cent. Code §14-02.1-03.5 (2019).
Oklahoma	63 OK Stat §63-1-729.1(G) (2019).
Tennessee	TN Code §63-6-241 (2019).
Wisconsin	WI Stat §253.105(2)(b) (2019).

Mifepristone must be administered in a hospital, doctor's office, or clinic:

Idaho	ID Code §18-608(1) (2019).
Minnesota	MN Stat §145.412(2) (2019).
North Carolina	NC Gen Stat §14-45.1(a) (2019).
Utah	UT Code §76-7-302(4) (2019).

A follow-up visit must be scheduled for after abortion:

Arizona   AZ Rev Stat §36-449.03(G)(1) (2019).

Arkansas   AR Code §20-16-1504(e)(1) (2019).

Idaho   ID Code §18-617(3) (2019).

Iowa   Iowa Admin. Code r. 653-13.10(4) (2019).

Kansas   KS Stat §65-4a10(c) (2019).

Oklahoma   63 OK Stat § 63-1-729a(A) (2019).

Missouri   MO Rev Stat §188.021 (2019).

Mississippi   MS Code §41-41-107 (2019).

Texas   TX Health & Safety Code §171.063(f) (2019).

Wisconsin   WI Stat §253.10(c)(1)(hm) (2019).

Bibliography

Ahmed, Aziza. 2020. 'How the COVID-19 response is altering the legal and regulatory landscape on abortion'. *Journal of Law and the Biosciences 7* (1): lsaa012.

Aiken, A.R.A, R. Gomperts, and J. Trussell. 2017. 'Experiences and characteristics of women seeking and completing at-home medical termination of pregnancy through online telemedicine in Ireland and Northern Ireland: a population-based analysis'. *British Journal of Obstetrics and Gynaecology 124* (8): 1208–15.

Aiken, Abigail R.A., Jennifer E. Starling, and Rebecca Gomperts. 2021. 'Factors associated with use of an online telemedicine service to access self-managed medical abortion in the US'. *JAMA Network Open 4* (5): e2111852.

Aiken, Abigail R.A., Katherine A. Guthrie, Marlies Schellekens, James Trussell, and Rebecca Gomperts. 2018. 'Barriers to accessing abortion services and perspectives on using mifepristone and misoprostol at home in Great Britain'. *Contraception 97* (2): 177–83.

Aiken, Abigail R.A., Jennifer E. Starling, Rebecca Gomperts, Mauricio Tec, James G. Scott, and Catherine E. Aiken. 2020. 'Demand for Self-Managed Online Telemedicine Abortion in the United States During the Coronavirus Disease 2019 (COVID-19) Pandemic'. *Obstetrics and Gynecology 136* (4): 835–7.

Aiken, Abigail, Patricia A. Lohr, Jonathan Lord, Nabanita Ghosh, and Jennifer Starling. 2021a. 'Effectiveness, safety and acceptability of no-test medical abortion provided via telemedicine'. *British Journal of Obstetrics and Gynaecology* [online first]: 10.1111/1471-0528.16668.

Aiken, Abigail R.A., Jennifer E. Starling, Rebecca Gomperts, James G. Scott, and Catherine E. Aiken. 2021b. 'Demand for self-managed online telemedicine abortion in eight European countries during the COVID-19 pandemic: a regression discontinuity analysis'. *BMJ Sexual & Reproductive Health* [online first]: 10.1136/bmjsrh-2020-200880.

American College of Obstetricians and Gynecologists. 2021. *ACOG applauds the FDA for its action on mifepristone access during the COVID-19 pandemic.* Available at: https://www.acog.org/news/news-releases/2021/04/acog-applauds-fda-action-on-mifepristone-access-during-covid-19-pandemic

APM Research Lab. 2021. 'The Color of Coronavirus: COVID-19 deaths by race and ethnicity in the U.S'. Available at: https://www.apmresearchlab.org/covid/deaths-by-race.

Attorney General of Texas. 2020. 'Health care professionals and facilities, including abortion providers, must immediately stop all medically unnecessary surgeries and procedures to preserve resources to fight COVID-19 pandemic'. Available at: https://www.texasattorneygeneral.gov/news/releases/health-care-professionals-and-facilities-including-abortion-providers-must-immediately-stop-all.

Austin, Nichole, and Sam Harper. 2018. 'Assessing the impact of TRAP laws on abortion and women's health in the USA: a systematic review'. *BMJ Sexual & Reproductive Health 44* (2): 128–34.

Back Off. a. 'Recorded protests outside clinics'. Available at: https://back-off.org/recorded-protests/.

Back Off. b. 'The Campaign'. Available at: https://back-off.org/the-campaign/.

Bauer, Keith A. 2001. 'Home-based telemedicine: A survey of ethical issues'. *Cambridge Quarterly in Healthcare Ethics 10* (2): 137–46.

Bayefsky, Michelle J., Deborah Bartz, and Katie L. Watson. 2020. 'Abortion during the COVID-19 Pandemic—Ensuring Access to an Essential Health Service'. *New England Journal of Medicine 382* (19): e47.

Bearak, Jonathan M., Kristen Lagasse Burke, and Rachel J. Jones. 2017. 'Disparities and change over time in distance women would need to travel to have an abortion in the USA: a spatial analysis'. *Lancet Public Health 2* (11): e493–e500.

Beauchamp, Tom L., and James F. Childress. 2013. *Principles of Biomedical Ethics*. 7th edition. New York: Oxford University Press.

Berglas, Nancy F., Heather Gould, David K. Turok, Jessica N. Saunders, Alissa C. Perrucci, and Sarah C.M. Roberts. 2017. 'State-mandated (mis)information and women's endorsement of common abortion myths'. *Women's Health Issues 27* (2): 129–35.

Blumenthal, Paul D. 2015. 'Mifepristone with buccal misoprostol for medical abortion: a systematic review'. *Obstetrics & Gynecology 126* (5): 1107.

Borgmann, Caitlin E. 2014. 'Abortion exceptionalism and undue burden preemption'. *Washington and Lee Law Review 71* (2): 1047–87.

Bracken, Hillary, Rasha Dabash, George Tsertsvadze, Svetlana Posohova, Milind Shah, Selma Hajri, Shuchita Mundle, Hela Chelli, Dhouha Zeramdini, Tamar Tsereteli, Ingrida Platais, and Berely Winikoff. 2014. 'A two-pill sublingual misoprostol outpatient regimen following mifepristone for medical abortion through 70 days' LMP: a prospective comparative open-label trial'. *Contraception 89* (3): 181–6.

Bracken, H., W. Clark, E.S. Lichtenberg, S.M. Schweikert, J. Tanenhaus, A. Barajas, L. Alpert, and B. Winikoff. 2011. 'Alternatives to routine ultrasound for eligibility assessment prior to early termination of pregnancy with mifepristone-misoprostol'. *British Journal of Obstetrics and Gynaecology 118* (1): 17–23.

Brazier, Margaret, and Emma Cave. 2016. *Medicine, Patients and the Law*. 6th edition. Manchester: Manchester University Press.

Bridges, Khiara M. 2010. 'Capturing the judiciary: *Carhart* and the undue burden standard'. *Washington and Lee Law Review 67* (3): 915–84.

British Medical Association. 2007. *First Trimester Abortion: A Briefing Paper by the BMA's Medical Ethics Committee*. London: ARM.

British Medical Association. 2019. 'The removal of criminal sanctions for abortion: BMA Position Paper'. Available at: https://www.bma.org.uk/media/1963/bma-removal-of-criminal-sanctions-for-abortion-position-paper-july-2019.pdf.

British Pregnancy Advisory Service. a. *Surgical abortion*. Available at: https://www.bpas.org/abortion-care/abortion-treatments/surgical-abortion/.

British Pregnancy Advisory Service. b. 'Medical abortion: the abortion pill up to 10 weeks'. Available at: https://www.bpas.org/abortion-care/abortion-treatments/the-abortion-pill/abortion-pill-up-to-10-weeks/.

British Pregnancy Advisory Service. 2020a. 'Pills by Post: telemedical abortion at the British Pregnancy Advisory Service (BPAS)'. Available at: https://www.bpas.org/media/3385/bpas-pills-by-post-service.pdf.

British Pregnancy Advisory Service. 2020b. 'Healthcare professionals call on Boris Johnson to intervene to protect women's health—reckless failure to listen to scientific advice is putting vulnerable women at severe risk'. Available at: https://www.bpas.org/about-our-charity/press-office/press-releases/healthcare-professionals-call-on-boris-johnson-to-intervene-to-protect-women-s-health-reckless-failure-to-listen-to-scientific-advice-is-putting-vulnerable-women-at-severe-risk/.

British Pregnancy Advisory Service. 2020c. 'BPAS launches emergency abortion pills by post for women in Northern Ireland amid shameful political gameplay with women's health during the Covid-19 pandemic'. Available at: https://www.bpas.org/about-our-charity/press-office/press-releases/bpas-launches-emergency-abortion-pills-by-post-for-women-in-northern-ireland-amid-shameful-political-gameplay-with-women-s-health-during-the-covid-19-pandemic/.

British Pregnancy Advisory Service. 2021. 'Abortion pills by post for women from Northern Ireland'. Available at: https://www.bpas.org/abortion-care/considering-abortion/northern-ireland-pills-by-post/.

Bruinvels, Georgie, Esther Goldsmith, Richard C. Blagrove, Dan Martin, Laurence Shaw, and Jessica Piasecki. 2021. 'How lifestyle changes within the COVID-19 global pandemic have affected the pattern and symptoms of the menstrual cycle'. *medXxiv* [online first]: 10.1101/2021.02.01.21250919.

Cameron, Sharon, Patricia A. Lohr, and Roger Ingham. 2017. 'Abortion terminology: views of women seeking abortion in Britain'. *BMJ Sexual & Reproductive Health 43* (4): 265–8.

Cates, Willard, David A. Grimes, and Kenneth F. Schulz. 2003. 'The public health impact of legal abortion: 30 years later'. *Perspectives on Sexual and Reproductive Health 35* (1): 25–8.

Cave, Emma, and Caterina Milo. 2020. 'Informing patients: the *Bolam* legacy'. *Medical Law International 20* (2): 103–30.

Chaet, Danielle, Ron Clearfield, James E. Sabin, and Kathryn Skimming, on behalf of the Council on Ethical and Judicial Affairs American Medical Association. 2017. 'Ethical practice in telehealth and telemedicine'. *Journal of General Internal Medicine 32* (10): 1136–40.

Chalmers, James, and Fiona Leverick, eds. 2016. *The Criminal Law of Scotland*. 4th edition, Volume 2. Edinburgh: W. Green.

Chavkin, Wendy, Liddy Leitman, and Kate Polin, for Global Doctors for Choice. 2013. 'Conscientious objection and refusal to provide reproductive healthcare: a White Paper examining prevalence, health consequences, and policy responses'. *International Journal of Gynecology & Obstetrics 123* (S3): S41–S56.

Chen, Melissa J., and Mitchell D. Creinin. 2015. 'Mifepristone with buccal misoprostol for medical abortion'. *Obstetrics & Gynecology 126* (1): 12–21.

Chong, Erica, Tara Shochet, Elizabeth Raymond, Ingrida Platais, Holly A. Anger, Shandhini Raidoo, Reni Soon, Melissa S. Grant, Susan Haskell, Kristina Tocce, Maureen K. Baldwin, Christy M. Boraas, Paula H. Bednarek, Joey Banks, Leah Coplon, Francine Thompson, Esther Priegue, and Beverly Winikoff. 2021. 'Expansion of a direct-to-patient telemedicine abortion service in the United States and experience during the COVID-19 pandemic'. *Contraception 104* (1): 43–48. https://doi.org/10.1016/j.contraception.2021.03.019Christian Concern. 2021. 'Tell the government not to extend DIY abortion policy'. Available at: https://christianconcern.com/action/tell-the-government-not-to-extend-diy-abortion-policy/.

Church, Kathryn, Jennifer Gassner, and Megan Elliott. 2020. 'Reproductive health under COVID-19—challenges of responding in a global crisis'. *Sexual and Reproductive Health Matters 28* (1): 522–4.

Collaborative Group on Hormonal Factors in Breast Cancer. 2004. 'Breast cancer and abortion: collaborative reanalysis of data from 53 epidemiological studies, including 83 000 women with breast cancer from 16 countries'. *Lancet 363* (9414): 1007–16.

Collins, K., P. Nicolson, and I. Bowns. 2000. 'Patient satisfaction in telemedicine'. *Health Informatics Journal 6* (2): 81–5.

Conley, Dalton, and Rebecca Glauber. 2008. 'Wealth Mobility and Volatility in Black and White'. Available at: https://cdn.americanprogress.org/wp-content/uploads/issues/2008/07/pdf/wealth_mobility.pdf?_ga=2.259451150.540449463.1615928659-428530588.1615928659.

Cook, Rebecca J. 2014. 'Stigmatized meanings of criminal abortion law'. In *Abortion Law in Transnational Perspective: Cases and Controversies*, edited by Rebecca J. Cook, Joanna N. Erdman, and Bernard M. Dickens, pp. 347–70. Philadelphia: University of Pennsylvania Press.

Cook, Rebecca J., and Simone Cusack. 2010. *Gender Stereotyping: Transnational Legal Perspectives*. Philadelphia: University of Pennsylvania Press.

Cornell, Drucilla. 1995. *The Imaginary Domain: Abortion, Pornography and Sexual Harassment*. Routledge: New York.

Cowles, Charlotte. 2018. 'How much does an abortion cost? Learn the facts'. *The Cut*. Available at: https://www.thecut.com/2018/11/how-much-does-an-abortion-cost.html.

Cozzarelli, Catherine, Brenda Major, Angela Karrasch, and Kathleen Fuegen. 2000. 'Women's experiences of and reactions to antiabortion picketing'. *Basic and Applied Social Psychology* 22 (4): 265–75.

Craig, Sophia A. Kimber, and Ross Kitson. 2010. 'Risks associated with anaesthesia'. *Anaesthesia & Intensive Care Medicine* 11 (11): 464–8.

Creinin, Mitchell D. 2000. 'Ramdomized comparison of efficacy, acceptability and cost of medical versus surgical abortion'. *Contraception 62* (3): 117–24.

Creinin, Mitchell D., Courtney A. Schreiber, Paula Bednarek, Hanna Lintu, Marie-Soleil Wagner, and Leslie A. Meyn, for the Medical Abortion at the Same Time (MAST) Study Trial Group. 2007. 'Mifepristone and misoprostol administered simultaneously versus 24 hours apart for abortion'. *Obstetrics & Gynecology 109* (4): 885–94.

Daniels, Cynthia R., Janna Ferguson, Grace Howard, and Amanda Roberti. 2016. 'Informed or misinformed consent? Abortion policy in the United States'. *Journal of Health Politics, Policy and Law 41* (2): 181–209.

Daniel, Sara, Jay Schulkin, and Daniel Grossman. 2021. 'Obstetrician-gynecologist willingness to provide medication abortion with removal of the in-person dispensing requirement for mifepristone'. *Contraception 104* (1): 73–76. https://doi.org/10.1016/j.contraception.2021.03.026

Department of Health. 2014. 'Guidance in relation to requirements of the Abortion Act 1967'. Available at: https://assets.publishing.service.gov.uk/government/uploads/system/uploads/attachment_data/file/313459/20140509_-_Abortion_Guidance_Document.pdf.

Department of Health and Social Care. 2018a. 'The Abortion Act 1967—approval of a class of places'. Available at: https://assets.publishing.service.gov.uk/government/uploads/system/uploads/attachment_data/file/768059/Approval_of_home_use_for_the_second_stage_of_early_medical_abortion.pdf.

Department of Health and Social Care. 2018b. 'Government confirms plans to approve the home-use of early abortion pills'. Available at: https://www.gov.uk/government/news/government-confirms-plans-to-approve-the-home-use-of-early-abortion-pills.

Department of Health and Social Care. 2020a. 'Abortion statistics, England and Wales: 2019'. Available at: https://assets.publishing.service.gov.uk/government/uploads/system/uploads/attachment_data/file/891405/abortion-statistics-commentary-2019.pdf.

Department of Health and Social Care. 2020b. 'Abortion statistics for England and Wales during the COVID-19 pandemic'. Available at: https://www.gov.uk/government/publications/abortion-statistics-during-the-coronavirus-pandemic-january-to-june-2020/abortion-statistics-for-england-and-wales-during-the-covid-19-pandemic.

Department of Health and Social Care. 2020c. 'The Abortion Act 1967—approval of a class of places'. Available at: https://assets.publishing.service.gov.uk/government/uploads/system/uploads/attachment_data/file/876740/30032020_The_Abortion_Act_1967_-_Approval_of_a_Class_of_Places.pdf.

Department of Health and Social Care. 2020d. 'Home use of both pills for early medical abortion up to 10 weeks gestation'. Available at: https://www.gov.uk/government/consultations/home-use-of-both-pills-for-early-medical-abortion.

Department of Health and Social Care. 2021. 'Integration and Innovation: working together to improve health and social care for all'. Available at: https://assets.publishing.service.gov. uk/government/uploads/system/uploads/attachment_data/file/960549/integration-and-innovation-working-together-to-improve-health-and-social-care-for-all-print-version.pdf.

Derse, Arthur R., and Tracy E. Miller. 2008. 'Net effect: professional and ethical challenges of medicine online'. *Cambridge Quarterly of Healthcare Ethics 17* (4): 453–64.

Dickens, Bernard M. 1966. *Abortion and the Law*. London: MacGibbon & Kee.

Dickens, Bernard. 2014. 'The right to conscience'. In *Abortion Law in Transnational Perspective: Cases and Controversies*, edited by Rebecca J. Cook, Joanna N. Erdman, and Bernard M. Dickens, pp. 210–38. Philadelphia: University of Pennsylvania Press.

Dolowitz, David, and David Marsh. 1996. 'Who learns what from whom: a review of the policy transfer literature'. *Political Studies 44* (2): 343–57.

Donley, Greer, Beatrice A. Chen, and Sonya Borrero. 2020. 'The legal and medical necessity of abortion care amid the COVID-19 pandemic'. *Journal of Law and the Biosciences 7* (1): lsaa013.

Donovan, Megan K. 2017. 'In real life: federal restrictions on abortion coverage and the women they impact'. *Guttmacher Policy Review 20*: 1–7.

Duffy, Sean, and Thomas H. Lee. 2018. 'In-person health care as option B'. *New England Journal of Medicine 378 (2)*: 104–06.

Electronic Medicines Compendium. 2019. 'Cervagem 1 mg essary'. Available at: https://www. medicines.org.uk/emc/product/2202/.

Elgot, Jessica, and Nicola Slawson. 2018. 'Ealing council votes for UK's first 'safe zone' around abortion clinic'. *The Guardian*. Available at: https://www.theguardian.com/world/2018/apr/10/ealing-council-vote-buffer-zone-near-marie-stopes-clinic-intimidation-anti-abortion-groups.

Endler, M., A. Lavelanet, A. Cleeve, B. Ganatra, R. Gomperts, and K. Gemzell-Danielsson. 2019. 'Telemedicine for medical abortion: a systematic review'. *British Journal of Obstetrics and Gynaecology 126*: 1094–102.

Engender. 2016. 'Our bodies, our choice: the case for a Scottish approach to abortion'. Available at: https://www.engender.org.uk/content/publications/Our-bodies-our-choice---the-case-for-a-Scottish-approach-to-abortion.pdf.

European Parliamentary Forum for Sexual and Reproductive Rights and International Planned Parenthood Federation European Network. 2020. 'Sexual and reproductive health and rights during the COVID-19 pandemic'. Available at: https://www.ippfen.org/sites/ippfen/files/2020-04/Sexual%20and%20Reproductive%20Health%20during%20the%20COVID-19%20pandemic.pdf.

Farrell, Anne Maree, and Margaret Brazier. 2016. 'Not so new directions in the law of consent? Examining *Montgomery v Lanarkshire Health Board'. Journal of Medical Ethics 42* (2): 85–8.

Fenwick, Daniel. 2012. 'The modern abortion jurisprudence under Article 8 of the European Convention on Human Rights'. *Medical Law International 12* (3–4): 249–76.

Fetrow, Kate L. 2018. 'Taking abortion rights seriously: toward a holistic undue burden jurisprudence'. *Stanford Law Review 70* (1): 319–62.

Findlay, J.K., M.L. Gear, P.J. Illingworth, S.M. Junk, G. Kay, A.H. Mackerras, A. Pope, H.S. Rothenfluh, and L. Wilton. 2007. 'Human embryo: a biological definition'. *Human Reproduction 22* (4): 905–11.

Finer, Lawrence, and Junhow Wei. 2009. 'Effect of mifepristone on abortion access in the United States'. *Obstetrics & Gynecology 114* (3): 623–30.

Fox, Dov, I. Glenn Cohen, and Eli Adashi. 2020. '*June Medical Services v Russo*—the future of abortion access in the US'. *JAMA Health Forum 1* (9): e201107.

Fox, Marie, and Horgan, Goretti. 2020. 'The effects of decriminalisation in Northern Ireland'. In *Decriminalisation of Abortion in the UK: What Would it Mean?*, edited by Sally Sheldon and Kaye Wellings, pp. 1–16. Bristol: Policy Press.

Fox, Marie, and Sheelagh McGuinness. 2018. 'In the matter of an application for judicial review by the Northern Ireland Human Rights Commission *(2015)*'. In *Women's Legal Landmarks: Celebrating the history of women and law in the UK and Ireland*, edited by Erika Rackley and Rosemary Auchmuty, pp. 619–27. Oxford: Hart Publishing.

Freudenberg, Nicholas, and Peter M. Yellowlees. 2014. 'Telepsychiatry as part of a comprehensive care plan'. *American Medical Association Journal of Ethics 16* (12): 964–8.

Fried, Marlene G. 1997. 'Abortion in the US: barriers to access'. *Reproductive Health Matters 5* (9): 37–45.

Gambir, Katherine, Camille Garnsey, Kelly Ann Necastro, and Thoai D. Ngo. 2020. 'Effectiveness, safety and acceptability of medical abortion at home versus in the clinic: a systematic review and meta-analysis in response to COVID-19'. *BMJ Global Health 5*: e003934.

Gatter, Mary, Katrina Kimport, Diana Greene Foster, Tracy A. Weitz, and Ushma Upadhyay. 2014. 'Relationship between ultrasound viewing and proceeding to abortion'. *Obstetrics & Gynecology 123* (1): 81–7.

General Medical Council a. 'Remote consultations'. Available at: https://www.gmc-uk.org/ethical-guidance/ethical-hub/remote-consultations.

General Medical Council. 2013. 'Personal beliefs and medical practice'. Available at: https://www.gmc-uk.org/ethical-guidance/ethical-guidance-for-doctors/personal-beliefs-and-medical-practice.

Gerdts, Caitlin, Loren Dobkin, Diana Greene Foster, and Eleanor Bimla Schwarz. 2016. 'Side effects, physical health consequences, and mortality associated with abortion and birth after an unwanted pregnancy'. *Women's Health Issues 26* (1): 55–9.

Gillett, M. Tyler. 2020. 'Virginia governor signs bill rolling back abortion restrictions'. Available at: https://www.jurist.org/news/2020/04/virginia-governor-signs-bill-rolling-back-abortion-restrictions/.

Gomperts, R.J., K. Jelinska, S. Davies, K. Gemzell-Danielsson, and G. Kleiverda. 2008. 'Using telemedicine for termination of pregnancy with mifepristone and misoprostol in settings where there is no access to safe services'. *British Journal of Obstetrics and Gynaecology 115* (9): 1171–8.

Gomperts, Rebecca, Sabine A.M. Petow, Kinga Jelinska, Louis Steen, Kristina Gemzell-Danielsson, and Gunilla Kleiverda. 2012. 'Regional differences in surgical intervention following medical termination of pregnancy provided by telemedicine'. *Acta Obstetricia et Gynecologica Scandinavica 91* (2): 226–31.

Gomperts, Rebecca, Kirsten van der Vleuten, Kinga Jelinska, Cecilia Veiera da Costa, Kristina Gemzell-Danielsson, and Gunilla Kleiverda. 2014. 'Provision of medical abortion using telemedicine in Brazil'. *Contraception 89* (2): 129–33.

Goodwin, Michele. 2017. '*Whole Women's Health v. Hellerstedt*: the empirical case against trap laws'. *Medical Law Review 25* (2): 340–51.

Goodwin, Michele. 2020. *Policing the Womb: Invisible Women and the Criminalization of Motherhood.* Cambridge: Cambridge University Press.

Government Equalities Office. 2017. 'Letter from Justine Greening on abortion in England'. Available at: https://assets.publishing.service.gov.uk/government/uploads/system/uploads/attachment_data/file/623669/Letter_from_Justine_Greening_on_Abortion_in_England.pdf.

Grimes, David A., M. Susan Smith, and Angela D. Witham. 2004. 'Mifepristone and misoprostol *versus* dilation and evacuation for midtrimester abortion: a pilot randomised controlled trial'. *British Journal of Obstetrics and Gynaecology 111* (2): 148–53.

Grossman, Daniel, Kate Grindlay, Todd Buchacker, Kathleen Lane, and Kelly Blanchard. 2011. 'Effectiveness and acceptability of medical abortion provided through telemedicine'. *Obstetrics & Gynecology 118* (2): 296–303.

Grossman, Daniel A., Kate Grindlay, Todd Buchacker, Joseph E. Potter, and Carl P. Schmertmann. 2013. 'Changes in service delivery patterns after introduction of telemedicine provision of medical abortion in Iowa'. *American Journal of Public Health 103* (1): 73–8.

Grossman, Daniel, and Philip Goldstone. 2015. 'Mifepristone by prescription: a dream in the United States but reality in Australia'. *Contraception 92* (3): 186–9.

Grossman, Daniel, Sarah Raifman, Tshegofatso Bessenaar, Lan Dung Duong, Anand Tamang, and Monica V. Dragoman. 2019. 'Experiences with pain of early medical abortion: qualitative results from Nepal, South Africa, and Vietnam'. *BMC Women's Health 19*: 118.

Grubb, Andrew. 1990. 'Abortion law in England: the medicalization of a crime'. *Law, Medicine and Health Care 18* (1–2): 146–61.

Grubb, Andrew. 1991. 'The new law of abortion: clarification or ambiguity?' *Criminal Law Review Sept.*: 659–70.

Guttmacher Institute. 2020. 'Unintended pregnancy and abortion worldwide'. Available at: https://www.guttmacher.org/fact-sheet/induced-abortion-worldwide.

Guttmacher Institute. 2021. 'Refusing to provide health services'. Available at: https://www.guttmacher.org/state-policy/explore/refusing-provide-health-services.

Halfmann, Drew. 2011. *Doctors and Demonstrators: How Political Institutions Shape Abortion Law in the United States, Britain, and Canada.* Chicago: University of Chicago Press.

Hall, Kelli Stidham, Goleen Samari, Samantha Garbers, Sara E. Casey, Dazon Dixon Diallo, Miriam Orcutt, Rachel T. Moresky, Micaela Elvira Martinez, and Terry McGovern. 2020. 'Centring sexual and reproductive health and justice in the global COVID-19 response'. *Lancet 395* (10231): 1175–7.

Halliday, Samantha. 2016. 'Protecting human dignity: reframing the abortion debate to respect the dignity of choice and life'. *Contemporary Issues in Law 13* (4): 287–322.

Hanks, Angela, Danyelle Solomon, and Christian E. Weller. 2018. 'Systematic inequality: how America's structural racism helped create the black-white wealth gap'. *Centre for American Progress.* Available at: https://www.americanprogress.org/issues/race/reports/2018/02/21/447051/systematic-inequality/.

Harpwood, Vivienne. 1996. *Legal Issues in Obstetrics.* London: Dartmouth Publishing Company.

Hasstedt, Kinsey. 2015. 'Abortion coverage under the Affordable Care Act: advancing transparency, ensuring choice and facilitating access'. *Guttmacher Policy Review 18* (1): 14–20.

Hawkins, James, Anna Glasier, Stephen Hall, and Lesley Regan, on behalf of the RCOG Telemedicine Cost-Effectiveness Working Group. 2021. 'Early medical abortion by telemedicine in the United Kingdom: a cost-effectiveness analysis'. *medRxiv* [online first]: 10.1101/2021.02.26.21252518.

Health Professions Council of South Africa. 2014. 'General ethical guidelines for good practice in telemedicine'. Available at: https://www.hpcsa.co.za/Uploads/Professional_Practice/Conduct%20%26%20Ethics/Booklet%2010%20Telemedicine%20September%20%202016.pdf.

Health Professions Council of South Africa. 2020a. 'Guidance on the application of telemedicine guidelines during the COVID-19 pandemic'. Available at: https://www.hpcsa.co.za/Uploads/Events/Announcements/APPLICATION_OF_TELEMEDICINE_GUIDELINES.pdf.

Health Professions Council of South Africa. 2020b. 'Notice to amend telemedicine guidelines during COVID-19—dated 3 April 2020'. Available at: https://www.hpcsa-blogs.co.za/notice-to-amend-telemedicine-guidelines-during-covid-19/.

Henney, Jane E., and Helene D. Gayle. 2019. 'Time to reevaluate U.S. mifepristone restrictions'. *New England Journal of Medicine 381* (7): 597–8.

Hervey, Tamara, and Sally Sheldon. 2019. 'Abortion by telemedicine in the European Union'. *International Journal of Gynecology & Obstetrics 145* (1): 125–8.

Hill, B. Jessie. 2020. 'Essentially elective: the law and ideology of restricting abortion during the COVID-19 pandemic'. *Virginia Law Review 106*: 99–123.

Holt, Kelsey, Elizabeth Janiak, Marie C. McCormick, Ellica Lieberman, Christine Dehlendorf, Sandhya Kajeepeta, Jacquelyn M. Caglia, and Ana Langer. 2017. 'Pregnancy options counseling and abortion referrals among US primary care physicians: results from a national survey'. *Family Medicine 49* (7): 527–36.

Honkanen, Helena, Gilda Piaggio, Helena von Hertzen, Gyorgy Bártfai, Radnaabazar Erdenetungalag, Kristina Gemzell-Danielsson, Sarala Gopalan, Mihai Horga, Fridtjof Jerve, Suneeta Mittal, Nguyen Thi Nhu Ngoc, Alexandre Peregoudov, R.N.V. Prasad, Alenka Pretnar-Darovec, Rashmi S. Shah, Si Song, Oi Shan Tang, and Shang Chun Wu, for the WHO Research Group on Post-Ovulatory Methods for Fertility Regulation. 2004. 'WHO multinational study of three misoprostol regimens after mifepristone for early medical abortion. II: side effects and women's perceptions'. *British Journal of Obstetrics and Gynaecology 111* (7): 715–25.

House of Commons Science and Technology Committee. 2007. 'Scientific developments relating to the Abortion Act 1967'. Available at: https://publications.parliament.uk/pa/cm200607/cmselect/cmsctech/1045/1045i.pdf.

Humanists UK. 2018. 'Home use of abortion medication comes into force in Wales'. Available at: https://humanism.org.uk/2018/07/02/home-use-of-abortion-medication-comes-into-force-in-wales/.

Humbyrd, Casey Jo. 2019. 'Virtue ethics in a value-driven world: ethical telemedicine'. *Clinical Orthopaedics and Related Research 477* (12): 2639–41.

Hyland, Paul, Elizabeth G. Raymond, and Erica Chong. 2018. 'A direct-to-patient telemedicine abortion service in Australia: Retrospective analysis of the first 18 months'. *Australian and New Zealand Journal of Obstetrics and Gynaecology 58* (3): 335–40.

Information Services Division Scotland. 2019. 'Termination of pregnancy report: year ending December 2018'. Available at: https://www.isdscotland.org/Health-Topics/Sexual-Health/Publications/2019-05-28/2019-05-28-Terminations-2018-Report.pdf.

Jackson, Emily. 2000. 'Abortion, autonomy and prenatal diagnosis'. *Social & Legal Studies 9* (4): 467–94.

Jackson, Emily. 2001. *Regulating Reproduction: Law, Technology and Autonomy*. Oxford: Hart Publishing.

Janiak, Elizabeth, and Alisa B. Goldberg. 2016. 'Eliminating the phrase "elective abortion": why language matters'. *Contraception 93* (2): 89–92.

Jerman, Jenna, and Rachel K. Jones. 2014. 'Secondary measures of access to abortion services in the United States, 2011 and 2012: gestational age limits, cost, and harassment'. *Women's Health Issues 24* (4): e419–e424.

Jones, Rachel K., and Jenna Jerman. 2014. 'Abortion incidence and service availability in the United States, 2011'. *Perspectives on Sexual and Reproductive Health 46* (1): 3–14.

Jones, Rachel K., Meghan Ingerick, and Jenna Jerman. 2018. 'Differences in abortion service delivery in hostile, middle-ground, and supportive states in 2014'. *Women's Health Issues 28* (3): 212–18.

Jones, Rachel K., Elizabeth Witwer, and Jenna Jerman. 2019. 'Abortion incidence and service availability in the United States, 2017'. Available at: https://www.guttmacher.org/sites/default/files/report_pdf/abortion-incidence-service-availability-us-2017.pdf.

Joyce, Theodore. 2011. 'The supply-side economics of abortion'. *New England Journal of Medicine 365* (16): 1466–9.

Kaller, Shelly, Sara Daniel, Sarah Raifman, M. Antonia Biggs, and Daniel Grossman. 2021. 'Pre-abortion informed consent through telemedicine vs. in person: differences in patient demographics and visit satisfaction'. *Women's Health Issues 31* (3): 227–235.

Kapp, Nathalie, and Patricia A. Lohr. 2020. 'Modern methods to induce abortion: safety, efficacy and choice'. *Best Practice & Research Clinical Obstetrics & Gynaecology 63*: 37–44.

Karki, Chanda, Hanoon Pokharel, Anu Kushwaha, Durga Manandhar, Hillary Bracken, and Beverly Winikoff. 2009. 'Acceptability and feasibility of medical abortion in Nepal'. *International Journal of Gynecology & Obstetrics 106* (1): 39–42.

Kaye, Julia, Rachel Reeves, and Lorie Chaiten. 2021. 'The mifepristone REMS: a needless and unlawful barrier to care'. *Contraception 104* (1): 12–15. https://doi.org/10.1016/j.contraception.2021.04.025

Keown, John. 1988. *Abortion, Doctors and the Law: Some Aspects of the Legal Regulation of Abortion in England from 1803 to 1982*. Cambridge: Cambridge University Press.

Kerestes, Courtney, Rebecca Delafield, Jennifer Elia, Erica Chong, Bliss Kaneshiro, and Reni Soon. 2021. '"It was close enough, but it wasn't close enough": a qualitative exploration of the impact of direct-to-patient telemedicine abortion on access to abortion care'. *Contraception 104* (1): 67–72. https://doi.org/10.1016/j.contraception.2021.04.028

Kerns, Jennifer L., Alexis Light, Vanessa Dalton, Blair McNamara, Jody Steinauer, and Miriam Kuppermann. 2018. 'Decision satisfaction among women choosing a method of pregnancy termination in the setting of fetal anomalies and other pregnancy complications: a qualitative study'. *Patient Education and Counseling 101* (10): 1859–64.

Khader, Serene J. 2020. 'The feminist case against relational autonomy'. *Journal of Moral Philosophy 17* (5): 499–526.

Killinger, Kristina, Sophie Günther, Rebecca Gomperts, Hazal Atay, and Margit Endler. 2020. 'Why women choose abortion through telemedicine outside the formal health sector in Germany: a mixed-methods study'. *BMJ Sexual & Reproductive Health* [online first]: 10.1136/bmjsrh-2020-200789.

Kimport, Katrina, Kate Cockrill, and Tracy A. Weitz. 2012. 'Analyzing the impacts of abortion clinic structures and processes: a qualitative analysis of women's negative experience of abortion clinics'. *Contraception 85* (2): 204–10.

Kirk, Siobhan, Leanne Morgan, Sandra McDermott, Laura McLaughlin, Caroline Hunter, and Tara Farrington. 2021. 'Introduction of the National Health Service early medical abortion service in Northern Ireland – an emergency response to the COVID-19 pandemic'. *BMJ Sexual & Reproductive Health* [online first]: 10.1136/bmjsrh-2020-200920.

Knowles, Hannah. 2020. 'Ohio clinics ordered to halt abortions deemed 'nonessential' amid coronavirus response'. *Washington Post*. Available at: https://www.washingtonpost.com/health/2020/03/21/ohio-abortion-clinics-coronavirus/.

Kong, Camillia. 2017. *Mental Capacity in Relationship: Decision-Making, Dialogue, and Autonomy*. Cambridge: Cambridge University Press.

Kortsmit, Katherine, Tara C. Jatlaoui, Michele G. Mandel, Jennifer A. Reeves, Titilope Oduyebo, Emily Petersen, and Maura K. Whiteman. 2020. 'Abortion surveillance – United States, 2018'. *Centre for Disease Control and Prevention Morbidity and Mortality Weekly Report Surveillance Summaries 69* (7): 1–29.

Kulier, Regina, Linan Cheng, Anis Fekih, G. Justus Hofmeyr, and Aldo Campana. 2001 [2009 update]. 'Surgical methods for first trimester termination of pregnancy'. *Cochrane Database of Systematic Reviews 4*: CD002900.

Kumar, Manisha, Maura Daly, Eva De Plecker, Christine Jamet, Melissa McRae, Aine Markham, and Carolina Batista. 2020. 'Now is the time: a call for increased access to contraception and safe abortion care during the COVID-19 pandemic'. *BMJ Global Health 5* (7): e003175.

LaRoche, Kathryn J., and Angel M. Foster. 2020. '"It gives you autonomy over your own choices": a qualitative study of Canadian abortion patients' experiences with mifepristone and misoprostol'. *Contraception 102* (1): 61–5.

LaRoche, Kathryn J., Kristen N. Jozkowski, Brandon L. Crawford, and Katherine R. Haus. 2021. 'Attitudes of US adults toward using telemedicine to prescribe medication abortion during COVID-19: a mixed methods study'. *Contraception 104* (1): 104–110. https://doi.org/10.1016/j.contraception.2021.04.001

Larrea, Sara, Laia Palència, and Glòria Perez. 2015. '[Medical abortion provided by telemedicine to women in Latin America: complications and their treatment]'. *Gaceta Sanitaria 29* (3): 198–204.

Lee, Ellie. 2003. 'Tensions in the Regulation of Abortion in Britain'. *Journal of Law and Society 30* (4): 532–53.

Lemmers, M., M.A.C. Verschoor, A.B. Hooker, B.C. Opmeer, J. Limpens, J.A.F. Huirne, W.M. Ankum, and B.W.M. Mol. 2016. 'Dilatation and curettage increases the risk of subsequent preterm birth: a systematic review and meta-analysis'. *Human Reproduction 31* (1): 34–45.

Les, Krisztina, Rebecca Gomperts, and Kristina Gemzell-Danielsson. 2017. 'Experiences of women living in Hungary seeking a medical abortion online'. *European Journal of Contraception & Reproductive Health Care 22* (5): 360–2.

Lindberg, Laura D., David L. Bell, and Leslie M. Kantor. 2020a. 'The sexual and reproductive health of adolescents and young adults during the COVID-19 pandemic'. *Perspectives on Sexual and Reproductive Health 52* (2): 75–9.

Lindberg, Laura D., Alicia VandeVusse, Jennifer Mueller, and Marielle Kirstein. 2020b. 'Early impacts of the COVID-19 pandemic: findings from the 2020 Guttmacher Survey of Reproductive Health Experiences'. Available at: https://www.guttmacher.org/sites/default/files/report_pdf/early-impacts-covid-19-pandemic-findings-2020-guttmacher-survey-reproductive-health.pdf.

Lindblom, Charles E. 1959. 'The science of "muddling through"'. *Public Administration Review 19* (2): 79–88.

Littlefield, Amy. 2021. 'As the pandemic raged, abortion access nearly flickered out'. *The Nation*. Available at: https://www.thenation.com/article/society/abortion-access-covid-pandemic/.

Lohr, Patricia A., Jonathan Lord, and Sam Rowlands. 2020. 'How would decriminalisation affect women's health?'. In *Decriminalising Abortion in the UK*, edited by Sally Sheldon and Kaye Wellings, pp. 37–56. Bristol: Policy Press.

Lord, Jonathan, Lesley Regan, Asha Kasliwal, Louise Massey, and Sharon Cameron. 2018. 'Early medical abortion: best practice now lawful in Scotland and Wales but not available to women in England'. *BMJ Sexual & Reproductive Health 44* (3): 155–8.

Love, Gillian. 2021. 'Abortion stigma, class and embodiment in neoliberal England'. *Culture, Health & Sexuality 23* (3): 317–22.

Madgavkar, Anu, Olivia White, Mekala Krishnan, Deepa Mahajan, and Xavier Azcue. 2020. 'COVID-19 and gender equality: countering the regressive effects'. *McKinsey Global Institute*. Available at: https://www.mckinsey.com/featured-insights/future-of-work/covid-19-and-gender-equality-countering-the-regressive-effects#.

Major, Brenda, Mark Appelbaum, Linda Beckman, Mary Ann Dutton, Nancy Felipe Russo, and Carolyn West. 2009. 'Abortion and mental health: evaluating the evidence'. *American Psychologist 64* (9): 863–90.

Malosso, Elena, Rita Magro, Gabriele Saccone, Biagio Simonetti, Massimo Squillante, and Vincenzo Berghella. 2018. 'US trends in abortion and preterm birth'. *The Journal of Maternal-Fetal & Neonatal Medicine 31* (18): 2463–7.

McGuinness, Sheelagh, and Jane Rooney. 2020. 'A legal landmark in reproductive rights: the Abortion (Northern Ireland) Regulations 2020'. *University of Bristol Law School Blog*. Available at: https://legalresearch.blogs.bris.ac.uk/2020/04/a-legal-landmark-in-reproductive-rights-the-abortion-northern-ireland-regulations-2020/.

Meurice, Marielle E., Katherine C. Whitehouse, Rebecca Blaylock, Jenny J. Chang, and Patricia A. Lohr. 2021. 'Client satisfaction and experience of telemedicine and home use of mifepristone and misoprostol for abortion up to 10 weeks' gestation at British Pregnancy Advisory Service: a cross-sectional evaluation'. *Contraception 104* (1): 61–66. https://doi.org/10.1016/j.contraception.2021.04.027

Mifeprex REMS Study Group. 2017. 'Sixteen years of overregulation: Time to unburden mifeprex'. *New England Journal of Medicine 376* (8): 790–4.

Mill, John Stuart. 1845. 'The claims of labour'. *Edinburgh Review 81*: 498–525. Reprinted in *The Collected Works of John Stuart Mill, Volume IV – Essays on Economics and Society*, edited by J.M. Robson, pp. 363–389. Toronto: University of Toronto Press.

Milne, Emma. 2019. 'Concealment of birth: time to repeal a 200-year-old "convenient stop-gap"?'. *Feminist Legal Studies 27*: 139–62.

Milne, Emma. 2020. 'Putting the fetus first – legal regulation, motherhood, and pregnancy'. *Michigan Journal of Gender & Law 27* (1): 149–211.

Milne, Emma. 2021a. 'Banning safe home-use abortion pills will leave more women in crisis'. *The Conversation*. Available at: https://theconversation.com/banning-safe-home-use-abortion-pills-will-leave-more-women-in-crisis-154594.

Milne, Emma. 2021b. *Criminal Justice Responses to Maternal Filicide: Judging the Failed Mother*. West Yorkshire: Emerald Publishing.

Moreau, Caroline, Mridula Shankar, Anna Glasier, Sharon Cameron, and Kristina Gemzell-Danielsson. 2020. 'Abortion regulation in Europe in the era of COVID-19: a spectrum of policy responses'. *BMJ Sexual & Reproductive Health* [online first]: 10.1136/bmjsrh-2020-200724.

MSI Reproductive Choices. 2020. 'More than a third of UK women unsure how to access contraception during COVID-19'. Available at: https://www.msichoices.org.uk/news/press-release-more-than-a-third-of-uk-women-unsure-how-to-access-contraception-during-covid-19/#_edn1.

Nandagiri, Rishita, Ernestina Coast, and Joe Strong. 2020. 'COVID-19 and abortion: making structural violence visible'. *International Perspectives on Sexual and Reproductive Health 46* (S1): 83–9.

National Health Service. 2019. 'The NHS long term plan'. Available at: https://www.longtermplan.nhs.uk/wp-content/uploads/2019/08/nhs-long-term-plan-version-1.2.pdf.

National Health Service. 2020. 'Integrating care: next steps to building strong and effective integrated care systems across England'. Available at: https://www.england.nhs.uk/wp-content/uploads/2021/01/integrating-care-next-steps-to-building-strong-and-effective-integrated-care-systems.pdf.

National Institute for Health and Care Excellence. 2019. 'Abortion care [NG140]'. Available at: https://www.nice.org.uk/guidance/ng140/.

National Network of Abortion Funds. 2021. 'National Network of Abortion Funds'. Available at: https://abortionfunds.org/about/.

Ngo, Thoai D., Min Hae Park, Haleema Shakur, and Caroline Free. 2011. 'Comparative effectiveness, safety and acceptability of medical abortion at home and in a clinic: a systematic review'. *Bulletin of the World Health Organization 89*: 360–70.

NHS National Services Scotland. 2019. 'Termination of pregnancy: year ending December 2018'. Available at: https://www.isdscotland.org/Health-Topics/Sexual-Health/Publications/2019-05-28/2019-05-28-Terminations-2018-Report.pdf.

Northern Ireland Department of Health. 2020. 'Public consultation document on the introduction of a statutory opt-out system for organ donation for Northern Ireland'. Available at: https://www.health-ni.gov.uk/consultations/organ-donation.

Office for National Statistics. 2020. 'Updating ethnic contrasts in deaths involving the coronavirus (COVID-19), England and Wales: deaths occurring 2 March to 28 July 2020'. Available

at: https://www.ons.gov.uk/peoplepopulationandcommunity/birthsdeathsandmarriages/
deaths/articles/updatingethniccontrastsindeathsinvolvingthecoronaviruscovid19englandan
dwales/deathsoccurring2marchto28july2020.

Open letter. 2020. 'Open letter to: Rt Hon Matt Hancock MP, Secretary of State for Health'.
Available at: https://drive.google.com/file/d/1TujbubXHjaN7H6FD2U5CvZvtFTmqjCXD/
view.

Oppenheim, Maya. 2020. 'Northern Ireland women turning to backstreet abortions and some
'have even attempted suicide' over lack of services'. *The Independent*. Available at: https://
www.independent.co.uk/news/uk/home-news/abortion-northern-ireland-women-health-
minister-b1374876.html.

Oppenheim, Maya. 2021. 'Pandemic triggered 1.4 million unintended pregnancies due to almost 12 million women losing access to contraception, UN study finds'. *The Independent*.
Available at: https://www.independent.co.uk/news/world/unintended-pregnancies-
contraception-women-b1815321.html.

Oshana, Marina A.L. 1998. 'Personal autonomy and society'. *Journal of Social Philosophy 29*
(1): 81–102.

Parish, T.N. 1935. 'A thousand cases of abortion'. *British Journal of Obstetrics and Gynaecology
42* (6): 1107–21.

Parsons, Jordan A. 2020. '2017-19 governmental decisions to allow home use of misoprostol for
early medical abortion in the UK'. *Health Policy 124* (7): 679–83.

Parsons, Jordan A., and Elizabeth Chloe Romanis. 2020. '2020 developments in the provision of
early medical abortion by telemedicine in the UK'. *Health Policy 125* (1): 17–21.

Parsons, Jordan A. 2021a. 'The telemedical imperative'. *Bioethics 35* (4): 298–306.

Parsons, Jordan A. 2021b. 'Deemed consent for organ donation: a comparison of the English
and Scottish approaches'. *Journal of Law and the Biosciences 8* (1): lsab003.

Peterman, Amber, Aliana Potts, Megan O'Donnell, Kelly Thompson, Niyati Shah, Sabine
Oertelt-Prigione, and Nicole van Gelder. 2020. 'Pandemics and Violence Against Women
and Children'. Available at: https://www.un.org/sexualviolenceinconflict/wp-content/up-
loads/2020/05/press/pandemics-and-violence-against-women-and-children/pandemics-
and-vawg-april2.pdf

Pizzarossa, Lucia Berro. 2019. '"Women are not in the best position to make these decisions by
themselves": gender stereotypes in the Uruguayan abortion law'. *University of Oxford Human
Rights Hub Journal 1*: 25–54.

Priaulx, Nicky, and Natalie L. Jones. 2018. 'Abortion Act 1967'. In *Women's Legal
Landmarks: Celebrating the History of Women and Law in the UK and Ireland*, edited by Erika
Rackley and Rosemary Auchmuty, pp. 275–81. Oxford: Hart Publishing.

Public Health Scotland. 2020. 'Termination of pregnancy: year ending December 2019'.
Available at: https://beta.isdscotland.org/find-publications-and-data/population-health/
sexual-health/termination-of-pregnancy-statistics/.

Public Health Wales. 2018. 'Sexual health Review 2017/2018 Final Report'. Available at: http://
www.wales.nhs.uk/sitesplus/documents/888/A%20Review%20of%20Sexual%20Health%20
in%20Wales%20-%20Final%20Report.pdf.

Radaelli, Claudio M. 1995. 'The role of knowledge in the policy process'. *Journal of European
Public Policy 2* (2): 159–83.

Raymond, Elizabeth, and David A. Grimes. 2012. 'The comparative safety of legal induced
abortion and childbirth in the United States'. *Obstetrics & Gynecology 119* (2): 215–9.

Raymond, Elizabeth G., Caitlin Shannon, Mark A. Weaver, and Beverly Winikoff. 2013. 'First-
trimester medical abortion with mifepristone 200 mg and misoprostol: a systematic review'.
Contraception 87 (1): 26–37.

Raymond, Elizabeth, Erica Chong, Beverly Winikoff, Ingrida Platais, Meighan Mary, Tatyana Lotarevich, Philicia W. Castillo, Bliss Kaneshiro, Mary Tschann, Tiana Fontanilla, Maureen Baldwin, Ariela Schnyer, Leah Coplon, Nicole Mathieu, Paula Bednarek, Meghan Keady, and Esther Priegue. 2019. 'TelAbortion: evaluation of a direct to patient telemedicine abortion service in the United States'. *Contraception 100* (3): 173–7.

Raymond, Elizabeth G., Daniel Grossman, Alice Mark, Ushma D. Upadhyay, Gillian Dean, Mitchell D. Creinin, Leah Coplon, Jamila Perritt, Jessica M. Atrio, DeShawn Taylor, and Marji Gold. 2020. 'Commentary: no-test medication abortion: a sample protocol for increasing access during a pandemic and beyond'. Contraception *101* (6): 361–66.

Rebouché, Rachel. 'Abortion opportunism'. *Journal of Law and the Biosciences 7* (1): lsaa029.

Reynolds-Wright, John Joseph, Anne Johnstone, Karen McCabe, Emily Evans, and Sharon Cameron. 2021. 'Telemedicine medical abortion at home under 12 weeks' gestation: a prospective observational cohort study during the COVID-19 pandemic'. *BMJ Sexual & Reproductive Health*[online first]: 10.1136/bmjsrh-2020-200976.

Richards, Tessa, Angela Coulter, and Paul Wicks. 2015. 'Time to deliver patient centred care'. *British Medical Journal 350*: h530.

Roberts, Sarah C.M., David K. Turok, Elise Belusa, Sarah Combellick, and Ushma D. Upadhyay. 2016. 'Utah's 72-hour waiting period for abortion: experiences among a clinic-based sample of women'. *Perspectives on Sexual and Reproductive Health 48* (4): 179–87.

Romanis, Elizabeth Chloe. 2020a. 'Is 'viability' viable? Abortion, conceptual confusion and the law in England and Wales and the United States'. *Journal of Law and the Biosciences 7* (1): lsaa059.

Romanis, Elizabeth Chloe. 2020b. 'Artificial womb technology and the choice to gestate *ex utero*: is partial ectogenesis the business of the criminal law?'. *Medical Law Review 28* (2): 342–74.

Romanis, Elizabeth Chloe. 2020c. 'Sally Sheldon and Kaye Wellings (eds), *Decriminalising Abortion in the UK: What Would It Mean?*'. *Medical Law Review* [online first]: 10.1093/medlaw/fwaa033.

Romanis, Elizabeth Chloe. 2020d. 'Challenging the 'born alive' threshold: fetal surgery, artificial wombs, and the English approach to legal personhood'. *Medical Law Review 28* (1): 93–123.

Romanis, Elizabeth Chloe, and Anna Nelson. 2020. 'Homebirthing in the United Kingdom during COVID-19'. *Medical Law International 20* (3): 183–200.

Romanis, Elizabeth Chloe, and Jordan A. Parsons. 2020a. 'Legal and policy responses to the delivery of abortion care during COVID-19'. *International Journal of Gynecology & Obstetrics 151* (3): 479–86.

Romanis, Elizabeth Chloe, and Jordan A. Parsons. 2020b. 'COVID-19 and abortion care: why we need remote access to reproductive health services'. *BMJ Sexual & Reproductive Health Blog*. Available at: https://blogs.bmj.com/bmjsrh/2020/03/21/covid-19-abortion/.

Romanis, Elizabeth Chloe, Jordan A. Parsons, and Nathan A. Hodson. 2020a. 'COVID-19 and reproductive justice in Great Britain and the United States: ensuring access to abortion care during a pandemic'. *Journal of Law and the Biosciences 7* (1): lsaa027.

Romanis, Elizabeth Chloe, Jordan A. Parsons, and Nathan Hodson. 2020b. 'COVID-19 and abortion care update: Department of Health and Social Care "error"'. *BMJ Sexual and Reproductive Health Blog*. Available at: https://blogs.bmj.com/bmjsrh/2020/03/24/covid-19-abortion-3/.

Romanis, Elizabeth Chloe, Jordan A. Parsons, and Nathan Hodson. 2020c. 'COVID'19 and remote access to abortion care: an update'. *BMJ Sexual and Reproductive Health Blog*. Available at: https://blogs.bmj.com/bmjsrh/2020/03/23/covid-19-abortion-update/.

Rosenbloom, Cara. 2020. 'Another routine the pandemic has disrupted: your period'. *Washington Post*. Available at: https://www.washingtonpost.com/lifestyle/wellness/coronavirus-period-menstruation-disruption/2020/08/21/0966b79a-e332-11ea-b69b-64f7b0477ed4_story. html.

Ross, Loretta, and Rickie Solinger. 2017. *Reproductive Justice: An Introduction*. Oakland: University of California Press.

Rouland, Rebecca S., Gretchen E. Ely, and Amelia Caron. 2019. 'Abortion-patient experiences of the forty-eight-hour waiting period policy in Tennessee'. *Journal of Appalachian Studies 25* (1): 87–104.

Rowlands, Sam. 2008. 'The decision to opt for abortion'. *BMJ Sexual & Reproductive Health 34* (3): 175–80.

Rowlands, Sam, and Kevin Thomas. 2020. 'Mandatory Waiting Periods Before Abortion and Sterilization: Theory and Practice'. *International Journal of Women's Health 12*: 577–86.

Royal College of Obstetricians and Gynaecologists. 2018. 'RCOG/FSRH statement on taking misoprostol at home'. Available at: https://www.rcog.org.uk/en/news/rcogfsrh-statement-on-taking-misoprostol-at-home/.

Royal College of Obstetricians and Gynaecologists. 2019. 'Clinical guidelines for early medical abortion at home—England'. Available at: https://www.rcog.org.uk/en/guidelines-research-services/guidelines/early-medical-abortion-home-england/.

Royal College of Obstetricians and Gynaecologists. 2020. 'Coronavirus (COVID-19) infection and abortion care'. Available at: https://www.rcog.org.uk/globalassets/documents/guide-lines/2020-07-31-coronavirus-covid-19-infection-and-abortion-care.pdf.

Schonberg, Dana, Lin-Fan Wang, Ariana H. Bennett, Marji Gold, and Emily Jackson. 2014. 'The accuracy of using last menstrual period to determine gestational age for first trimester medication abortion: a systematic review'. *Contraception 90* (5): 480–7.

Scott, Rosamund. 2016. 'Risks, reasons and rights: the European Convention on Human Rights and English Abortion Law'. *Medical Law Review 24* (1): 1–33.

Scottish Government Chief Medical Officer Directorate. 2017. 'Abortion—improvement to existing services—approval for misoprostol to be taken at home'. Available at: https://www.sehd.scot.nhs.uk/cmo/CMO(2017)14.pdf.

Scottish Government Chief Medical Officer Directorate. 2020. 'Abortion—Covid-19—approval for mifepristone to be taken at home and other contingency measures'. Available at: https://www.sehd.scot.nhs.uk/cmo/CMO%282020%2909.pdf.

Scottish Government. 2020. 'Consultation on future arrangements for early medical abortion at home'. Available at: https://www.gov.scot/binaries/content/documents/govscot/publications/consultation-paper/2020/09/consultation-future-arrangements-early-medical-abortion-home/documents/consultation-future-arrangements-early-medical-abortion-home/consultation-future-arrangements-early-medical-abortion-home/govscot%3Adocument/consultation-future-arrangements-early-medical-abortion-home.pdf.

Senderowicz, Leigh, and Jenny A. Higgins. 2020. 'Reproductive autonomy is nonnegotiable, even in the time of COVID-19. *International Perspectives on Sexual and Reproductive Health 46*: 147–51.

Shah, Khushbu. 2019. 'The 'escorts' who ward off anti-abortion protestors at Mississippi's lone clinic'. *The Guardian*. Available at: https://www.theguardian.com/world/2019/aug/13/mississippi-lone-abortion-clinic.

Shaw, Kate, Nicole J. Topp, Jonathan G. Shaw, and Paul D. Blumenthal. 2013. 'Mifepristone-misoprostol dosing interval and effect on induction abortion times'. *Obstetrics & Gynecology 121* (6): 1335–47.

Sheldon, Sally. 1997. *Beyond Control: Medical Power and Abortion Law*. London: Pluto.

Sheldon, Sally. 2014. 'The medical framework and early abortion in the U.K.: how can a state control swallowing?'. In *Abortion Law in Transnational Perspective: Cases and Controversies*, edited by Rebecca J. Cook, Joanna N. Erdman, and Bernard M. Dickens, pp. 189–209. Philadelphia: University of Pennsylvania Press.

Sheldon, Sally. 2016a. 'British abortion law: speaking from the past to govern the future'. *Modern Law Review 79* (2): 283–316.

Sheldon, Sally. 2016b. 'The decriminalisation of abortion: an argument for modernisation'. *Oxford Journal of Legal Studies 36* (2): 334–65.

Sheldon, Sally, Gayle Davis, Jane O'Neill, and Clare Parker. 2019. 'The Abortion Act (1967): a biography'. *Legal Studies 39* (1): 18–35.

Sheldon, Sally, and Wellings, Kaye. 2020. 'Introduction'. In *Decriminalising Abortion in the UK: What Would It Mean?*, edited by Sally Sheldon and Kaye Wellings, pp. 1–16. Bristol: Bristol Policy Press.

Sjöström S, M. Dragoman, M.S. Fønhus, B. Ganatra, and K. Gemzell-Danielsson. 2017. 'Effectiveness, safety, and acceptability of first-trimester medical termination of pregnancy performed by non-doctor providers: a systematic review'. *British Journal of Obstetrics and Gynaecology 124* (13): 1928–40.

Soares, Jeanette M. 2006. 'Abortion'. *Georgetown Journal of Gender and the Law 7* (3): 1099–128.

Society for the Protection of Unborn Children. 2017. 'SPUC Scotland gives Scottish Govt three weeks to drop home abortion policy'. Available at: https://www.spuc.org.uk/News/ID/379527/SPUC-Scotland-gives-Scottish-Govt-three-weeks-to-drop-home-abortion-policy.

Stack, Liam. 2015. 'A brief history of deadly attacks on abortion providers'. *New York Times*. Available at: https://www.nytimes.com/interactive/2015/11/29/us/30abortion-clinic-violence.html?mtrref=www.google.com&assetType=REGIWALL.

State of California Office of the Attorney General. 2020. Available at: https://ag.ny.gov/sites/default/files/final_ag_letter_hhs_medication_abortion_2020.pdf.

Tan, Yi-Ling, Kuldip Singh, Kok Hian Tan, Arundhati Gosavi, Daniel Koh, Dina Abbas, and Beverly Winikoff. 2018. 'Acceptability and feasibility of outpatient medical abortion with mifepristone and misoprostol up to 70 days gestation in Singapore'. *European Journal of Obstetrics & Gynecology and Reproductive Biology 229*: 144–7.

Thomson-Philbrook, Julia. 2014. 'Doctor knows best: the illusion of reproductive freedom in Canada'. In *Fertile Ground: Exploring Reproduction in Canada*, edited by Stephanie Paterson, Francesca Scala, and Marlene K. Sokolon, pp. 230–49. Montreal: McGill-Queen's University Press.

Todd-Gher, Jaime, and Payal K. Shah. 2020. 'Abortion in the context of COVID-19: a human rights imperative'. *Sexual and Reproductive Health Matters 28* (1): 28–30.

Tousaw, Ellen, Sweet Naw Hser Gay Moo, Grady Arnott, and Angel M. Foster. 2018. ' "It is just like having a period with back pain": exploring women's experiences with community-based distribution of misoprostol for early abortion on the Thailand-Burma border'. *Contraception 97* (2): 122–9.

Tschann, Mary, Elizabeth S. Ly, Sara Hilliard, and Hannah L.H. Lange. 2021. 'Changes to medication abortion clinical practices in response to the COVID-19 pandemic'. *Contraception 104* (1): 77–81. https://doi.org/10.1016/j.contraception.2021.04.010

Turkewitz, Julie, and Jack Healy. 2015. '3 are dead in Colorado Springs shootout at planned parenthood center'. *New York Times*. Available at: https://www.nytimes.com/2015/11/28/us/colorado-planned-parenthood-shooting.html.

United Nations. 2020. 'Policy brief: the impact of COVID-19 on women'. Available at: https://www.unwomen.org/-/media/headquarters/attachments/sections/library/publications/2020/policy-brief-the-impact-of-covid-19-on-women-en.pdf?la=en&vs=1406.

United Nations Committee on the Elimination of Discrimination against Women. 2018. 'Report of the inquiry concerning the United Kingdom of Great Britain and Northern Ireland under article 8 of the Optional Protocol to the Convention on the Elimination of All Forms of Discrimination against Women'. Available at: https://tbinternet.ohchr.org/Treaties/CEDAW/Shared%20Documents/GBR/INT_CEDAW_ITB_GBR_8637_E.pdf.

United States Food and Drug Administration. a. 'Approved Risk Evaluation and Mitigation Strategies (REMS)'. Available at: https://www.accessdata.fda.gov/scripts/cder/rems/index.cfm?event=RemsData.page.

United States Food and Drug Administration. 2016. 'MIFEPREX® (mifepristone) tablets, for oral use'. Available at: https://www.accessdata.fda.gov/drugsatfda_docs/label/2016/020687s020lbl.pdf.

United States Food and Drug Administration. 2019. 'Risk evaluation and mitigation strategy (REMS) single shared system for mifepristone 200mg'. Available at: https://www.accessdata.fda.gov/drugsatfda_docs/rems/Mifepristone_2019_04_11_REMS_Full.pdf.

United States Food and Drug Administration. 2020a [updated January 2021]. 'Conduct of clinical trials of medical products during the COVID-19 public health emergency: guidance for industry, investigators, and institutional review boards'. Available at: https://www.fda.gov/media/136238/download.

United States Food and Drug Administration. 2020b. 'Policy for certain REMS requirements during the COVID-19 public health emergency: guidance for industry and health care professionals'. Available at: https://www.fda.gov/media/136317/download.

Upadhyay, Ushma D. 2017. 'Innovative models are needed for equitable abortion access in the USA'. *Lancet Public Health 2* (11): e484–5.

Wedisinghe, Lilantha, and Deya Elsandabesee. 2010. 'Flexible mifepristone and misoprostol administration interval for first-trimester medical termination'. *Contraception 81* (4): 269–74.

Welsh Government. 2018a. 'The Abortion Act 1967 (approval of place for treatment for the termination of pregnancy) (Wales) 2018'. Available at: https://gov.wales/sites/default/files/publications/2019-07/the-abortion-act-1967-approval-of-place-for-treatment-for-the-termination-of-pregnancy-wales-2018-2018-no-56.pdf.

Welsh Government. 2018b. 'Welsh health circular [WHC/2018/027]'. Available at: https://bsacp.org.uk/wp-content/uploads/2019/03/Home-Use-of-Misoprostol-Welsh-Health-Circular-WHC-2018-027-English-compressed.pdf.

Welsh Government. 2020. 'The Abortion Act 1967—approval of a class of place for treatment for the termination of pregnancy (Wales) 2020'. Available at: https://gov.wales/sites/default/files/publications/2020-04/approval-of-a-class-of-place-for-treatment-for-the-termination-of-pregnancy-wales-2020.pdf.

Wenham, Clare, Julia Smith, and Rosemary Morgan, on behalf of the Gender and COVID-19 Working Group. 2020. 'COVID-19: the gendered impacts of the outbreak'. *Lancet 395* (10227): 846–8.

White, Kari, Janet M. Turan, and Daniel Grossman. 2017. 'Travel for abortion services in Alabama and delays obtaining care'. *Women's Health Issues 27* (5): 523–9.

White, Kari, Bhavik Kumar, Vinita Goyal, Robin Wallace, Sarah C.M. Roberts, and Daniel Grossman. 2021. 'Changes in abortion in Texas following an executive order ban during the coronavirus pandemic'. *Journal of the American Medical Association 325* (7): 691–3.

Williams, Glanville. 1983. *Textbook on Criminal Law*. 2nd edition. London: Stevens & Sons Ltd.

Winkler, Bridger. 2020. 'What about the rule of law? Deviation from the principles of stare decisis in abortion jurisprudence, and an analysis of *June Medical L.L.C. v. Russo* oral arguments'. *UCLA Law Review Discourse 68*: 14–38.

Women on Web. a. 'I need an abortion'. Available at: https://www.womenonweb.org/en/i-need-an-abortion.

Women's Equality Party. 2018. 'Home use'. Available at: https://www.womensequality.org.uk/homeuse.

Woodcock, Janet. *Letter to the American College of Obstetricians and Gynecologists.* Available at: https://www.aclu.org/sites/default/files/field_document/fda_acting_commissioner_letter_to_acog_april_12_2021.pdf

World Health Organization. 2012. 'Safe abortion: technical and policy guidance for health systems'. 2nd edition. Available at: https://www.who.int/reproductivehealth/publications/unsafe_abortion/9789241548434/en/

World Health Organization. 2018. 'Medical management of abortion'. Available at: https://www.who.int/reproductivehealth/publications/medical-management-abortion/en/.

World Health Organization. 2019. 'World Health Organization model list of essential medicines—21st list'. Available at: https://www.who.int/publications/i/item/WHOMVPEMPIAU2019.06.

Yang, T.Y., and Katy B. Kozhimannil. 2016. 'Medication abortion through telemedicine: implications of a ruling by the Iowa Supreme Court'. *Obstetrics & Gynecology 127* (2): 313–16.

Zhou, J., R. Blaylock, and M. Harris. 2020. 'Systematic review of early abortion services in low- and middle-income country primary care: potential for reverse innovation and application in the UK context'. *Globalization and Health 16*: 91.

Index